THE TOFU TOLLBOOTH

by Elizabeth Zipern and Dar Williams,
with help from Heather Horak
and a lot of friends....

Published by Ceres Press/Ardwork Press

Compiled by (in order of revision) Dar Williams, Heather
Horak, Elizabeth Zipern

Book Design: David Caputo and Dar Williams (first edition) -
David Caputo at 1(800)4RA-DSOL, Stacey Hood and Elizabeth
Zipern (second edition)
Graphic Design & Typesetting: Stacey Hood at Big Eyedea Visual
Design, Waitsfield, VT (802)496-5288

Cover Art: Normandie Hyatt
Cover Design: Stacey Hood & Elizabeth Zipern
Back Cover Photo: Doug Plavin
Icons: Annie Moonsong, Amy Fincke, Katryna Nields, Dar
Williams
Map Preparation: Elizabeth Zipern, Stacey Hood, Soraya Rizek &
Ellen Peal
Images: Elizabeth Zipern

Ceres Press in collaboration with Ardwork Press
P.O. Box 87
Woodstock, NY   12498

See order form in back to order copies.

Printed on Recycled Paper using soy based ink.

Welcome to the Second Edition of

THE TOFU TOLLBOOTH

I still have my original copy of this book, though now it is faded purple, torn, tattered and coffee splattered. I ordered it from Dar in 1994 and over the years it has been indispensable. Along each journey I embarked upon, so was the *Tofu Tollbooth* - there to guide me to everything I needed, from soy milk to produce to organic chocolate (and other absolute necessities).

As the *Tollbooth* blossomed into an underground sensation, I discovered I wasn't alone in my reverent use of this directory. Travelers, families, musicians, hippies, business people, hikers and the transient among us used this essential compilation to find stores.

Well, four years have since passed and the natural food industry is flourishing. With a greater awareness of what natural and organic truly means, consumers are learning there is an alternative to what's offered in America's mainstream supermarkets, McDonald's and their junk food brethren. Hooray!

In this updated edition, we have differentiated stores based on their approach to business. We believe there is a voice behind the dollar, a decision that goes along with where our money is spent. We wanted to enable you to make an informed decision in choosing where to shop. Whether you go to a cooperative, independent or chain store, you'll find that natural food stores in general do what most mainstream supermarkets can't; provide the glue that a neighborhood needs to stick together.

Also in this edition, we've included tips to various cities and towns across the nation. We asked store workers and travelers what they found quirky, yummy, enlightening, fantastic and friendly in their travels and at home. These opinions are subjective, but the result is a mosaic of alternative destinations throughout America. Mileage may vary, so if you find something different, let us know!

Some parting notes from the first edition to send you on your way... Join an auto club (membership pays for itself in one towing), keep a flashlight in the car and USE THIS BOOK! It's your best resource to healthier, more delicious food choices wherever you go.

May every road be an adventure.

Elizabeth Zipern

Elizabeth's Thanks:
The Organic Trade Association, Chris Olson at Co-op Directory
Services, Lige Weill with the Vegetarian Awareness Group, The
National Green Pages, Vegetarian Internet Resources, Nikki &
David Goldbeck, Kris Bergbom, David Caputo & friends, Heather
Horak, Talia Rotblum, Matt Wild, Dana Sacks, Ethan Jackson,
Matt Koch at Vermont's Mac & ChReese (Road's End Organics),
Jim Pittman, Josh Billings, Jen McCall, Soraya Rizek, Dan
Gardoqui, Normandie Hyatt, Nancy, Michael & Ben Nordstrom-
Miller, Bubba Duke Freeman, Kevin White, Candace Gyure,
Raquel Heiny, Lori Strazdas, Andrew Zipern, Ed Pepe, Cara
Chinchar, Andy Vota (mucho thanks), Jen (a.k.a. Tofu Jen) Anson,
Alec Bauer, Sheela Peace (thank you bunches!), Martin Zipern,
Ellen Peal, Donna Surhoff, Stacey Hood and a cast of hundreds ...

Dar's Thanks:
Heather Horak, Heidi Creamer, Chris LaClair, Claudia Sperber,
Karen Howery, Charlie Hunter, Kate Bennis, Judy Minor, Lisa
Wittner, Clurie Bennis, Dar's Family, Kris Bergbom, Tom Neff,
David & Nikki Goldbeck, Doug Plavin, Billy Masters, Sianna &
Jya Plavin, Stephanie Winters, Brett Perkins, Sarah Davis, David
Caputo, Dena Marger, Jaimé Morton, Lyndon Haviland, Catherine
Ann, Anne Weiss

Major Contributors:
Jennifer Anson
Stacey Hood
Heather Horak
Andrew Vota
Matt Wild

*If we've missed an awesome store, restaurant, cafe, hiking spot or scenic
vista (or if we've truly glitched something), please let us know. Also, if
you're a new store, congratulations! Give us a call or send us a
postcard of regional splendor!*

Organic facts adapted from information provided by the Organic
Trade Association.

For help organizing a natural food buying club in your community,
contact Kris Olsen, Co-op Directory Services, 919 21st Ave.,
Minneapolis, MN 55404

A percentage of profits from the Tofu Tollbooth will be donated to
NOFA, the Northeastern Organic Farmer's Association. Visit them
on the web at http://www.nofa.org

Visit our web site at http://www.tofutollbooth.com

Table of Contents

Alabama 1
Arizona 4
Arkansas.........................9
California (Northern)....12
California (Southern) 27
Colorado.......................37
Connecticut...................44
Delaware.......................51
Florida..........................53
Georgia.........................68
Idaho 72
Illinois...........................75
Indiana 81
Iowa..............................85
Kansas 88
Kentucky.......................90
Louisiana.......................92
Maine 95
Maryland/D.C. 100
Massachusetts..............106
Michigan 114
Minnesota 119
Mississippi...................129
Missouri 131
Montana......................134

Nebraska.....................137
Nevada 139
New Hampshire 141
New Jersey...................146
New Mexico 152
New York.....................155
North Carolina 172
North Dakota 176
Ohio.............................178
Oklahoma....................183
Oregon 185
Pennsylvania 192
Rhode Island...............200
South Carolina.............203
South Dakota...............206
Tennessee 208
Texas............................211
Utah.............................217
Vermont.......................220
Virginia........................226
Washington 232
West Virginia 240
Wisconsin 243
Wyoming.....................249

The definition of the word organic is in danger.

In an effort to streamline their practices and boost consumer confidence, the organics industry recently asked the USDA to help develop a clear, national criteria for organics. While the proposed regulations do tackle some important issues, they don't address controversial ones like the use of genetically engineered crops, irradiation and municipal wastes.

To learn what you can do, ask your local natural food store for information or check out the proposed rules (along with public comments) on the internet at http://www.ams.usda.gov/nop or see The Pure Food Campaign's "Save Organic Standards" at http://www.purefood.org/organlink.html or write them at:

Pure Food Campaign
860 Highway 61
Little Marais, MN 55614

Key

DELI

BAKERY

CAFE

JUICE BAR

SALAD BAR

COFFEE-TO-GO

BEER/WINE

FILTERED WATER
MACHINE

NUTRITIONIST/
HERBALIST

WHEELCHAIR
ACCESS

BATHROOM

WHEELCHAIR
ACCESSIBLE
BATHROOM

INDEPENDENT
RETAIL

CORPORATE

CO-OP

HOT TIPS

COLLECTIVE

All stores have organic produce
unless otherwise indicated

Alabama

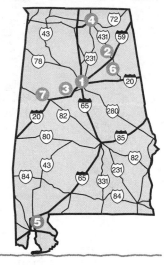

1. BIRMINGHAM
2. GADSDEN
3. HOOVER
4. HUNTSVILLE
5. MOBILE
6. RAINBOW CITY
7. TUSCALOOSA

BIRMINGHAM

Check out 11th Avenue in the 5 Point South district. This 5 way intersection hosts an array of restaurants, cafes, hotels, nightclubs and... it stays open late! "The 5 Point South area is very alternative lifestyle friendly," says one Golden Temple Natural Grocery staffer. Also in the Birmingham vicinity is the Civil Rights Museum. Worth a visit!

GOLDEN TEMPLE NATURAL GROCERY
1901 11th Avenue South, 35205 • (205)933-6333
Organic carrots & some produce.
M-F 8:30-7:00, Sat. 9:30-5:30, Sun. 12-5:30
Restaurant hours: M-F 11:30-6:30, Sat. 11:30-2:30

    From I-65 north: Get off at University Blvd. south exit. Turn right on 8th Ave. and right on 19th St. Store's at 11th Ave. on left. From I-65 south: Take 4th Ave. South exit. Turn left onto 4th Ave and right on 19th St. Same as above.

THE GREEN DOOR
2843 Culver Road, 35223 • (205)871-2651
Organic carrots only.
M-F 9:30-5:30, Sat. 10-5

 From I-280, take Hollywood Blvd. exit. Take a right off exit and go into the village to light. Take a right at light, then a left onto Culver. Store's on south side of street.

GADSDEN

APPLE-A-DAY
280 North 3rd, in Mid-town Gregerson's, 35901 • (205)546-8458
Apple-a-Day is a natural food store in Gregerson's, a 24 hour supermarket (they also sell some organic produce in their Aniston store). When you swing through Gregerson's, by all means ENCOURAGE them to keep it up!
M-Sat. 8:30-8, Sun. 12:30-6

  From I-59, take I-759 (spur), then drive to 411 north. Store's in Midtown Plaza on left.

HOOVER

B & C NUTRITION
1615 Montgomery Highway, 35216 • (205)979-8307
M-F 10-5:30, Sat. 10-5

 From I-459, exit Montgomery Hwy. (Hwy. 31) and drive 1 mile north. Store's on right. From I-65, get on Hwy. 31 south and travel 1 mile. Store's on left.

GOLDEN TEMPLE NATURAL GROCERY
3309 Lorna Road, 35216 • (205)823-7002
No produce. This store is smaller than the Golden Temple in Birmingham.
M-F 10-6:30, Sat. 10-6

 From I-65, take Montgomery Hwy. (Hwy. 31) exit. From north: Go straight off exit ramp onto Lorna Rd. Store's 2-3 miles down on left. From south: Turn left on Hwy. 31, then left on Lorna. Same as above.

HUNTSVILLE

Folks at the Garden Cove Produce Center call Huntsville a "pretty, southern town with a cosmopolitan feel." Discover the area's hipper restaurants, coffee shops and bookstores around the University of Alabama at Huntsville campus.

GARDEN COVE PRODUCE CENTER
628 Meridian Street North, 35801 • (205)534-2683
M-T 10-7, W 9-6, Th. 9-7, F 9-3, Sun. 12-5

 From Memorial Parkway (Hwy. 231), head east on Pratt St. Store's on right at corner of Pratt and Meridian.

PEARLY GATES NATURAL FOODS, INC.
2308 Memorial Parkway South West, 35801 • (205)534-6233
Seasonal produce.
M-Sat. 10-6:30

 On Memorial Parkway (Hwy. 231), store's on west side of street.

MOBILE

ORGANIC FOODS INC.
444B Azalea Road, 36609 • (334)342-9554
No produce.
M-F 10-6, Sat. 10-2

 From I-65, take Airport Blvd. west. Turn left on Azalea Rd. Store's one mile up on right.

RAINBOW CITY

APPLE-A-DAY
115 West Grand Avenue, Suite 63, 35906 • (205)413-1300
M-Sat. 9:30-6

 From I-59, take Rainbow City exit and travel 77 south for 4.1 miles. Store's on corner of Hwy. 411 south and 77 north.

TUSCALOOSA

The University of Alabama brings a nice diversity into this town and University Boulevard heads through it all. Go there to find laundromats, restaurants, bookstores and cafes.

MANNA GROCERY NATURAL GOURMET & ETHNIC FOODS
2300 McFarland Boulevard #12, 35405 • (205)752-9955
M-Sat. 9-7, Deli 11-3

From I-20/59, take McFarland Blvd. exit. From north: Exit right. From south: Exit right and bear left on McFarland. Store's in Meadowbrook Shopping Center.

Organic Fact Nº1

SUPPORT A TRUE ECONOMY

Although organic foods might seem more expensive than conventional, conventional food prices do not reflect hidden costs borne by tax payers (as in federal farming subsidies). Other hidden costs include pesticide regulation and testing, hazardous waste disposal and clean up, and environmental damage. Consumers can pay now or pay later. Organic foods are priced for paying now for a more sustainable environment.

Arizona

1. APACHE JCT.
2. BISBEE
3. CHANDLER
4. COTTONWOOD
5. FLAGSTAFF
6. MESA
7. PHOENIX
8. PRESCOTT
9. SCOTTSDALE
10. SEDONA
11. TEMPE
12. TUCSON
13. YUMA

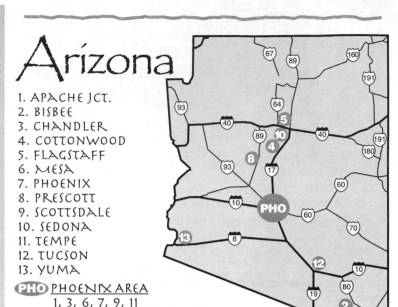

PHO PHOENIX AREA
1, 3, 6, 7, 9, 11

APACHE JUNCTION

GOOD EARTH NATURAL MARKET
100 North Plaza Drive, 85220 • (602)982-2239
M-Sat. 8-8, Sun. 9-6

 From Superstition Hwy. (US 60), get off on Idaho. Take that to Apache Trail/Main St. and turn left onto Apache Trail/Main St. At first light, turn right (will be Basha's Plaza parking lot). Store's on northwest corner of street in Basha's Plaza.

BISBEE

"Bisbee is a quaint, charming little town," says Alex at the Bisbee Food Co-op. "It's also an artist's community. When the mine that ran the town closed in 1975, land became cheap so lots of hippies came out from California and New Mexico and bought property. Now there's always something going on. It's great for a town of 6,000."

BISBEE FOOD CO-OP
72 Erie Street, 85603 • (520)432-4011
M-Sat. 9-6, Sun. 11-5

 Now located in the Lowell area, take Rte. 80 and go past Old Bisbee and around the Lavender pit. Take a right into store parking lot.

CHANDLER

NATURE'S HEALTH
973 West Elliot Street, Suite #2, 85224 • (602)821-1986
M-F 9-9, Sat. 9-6, Sun. 10-5

From I-10, take Superstition Freeway (60) east toward Mesa. Exit on Alma School Rd. and head south. The third light is Elliot. Look for store in southeast corner of street in Fry's strip mall (store is left of Fry's).

COTTONWOOD

MOUNT HOPE NATURAL FOODS
1123 North Main Street, 86326 • (520)634-8251
Staff loves to take out a map and help travelers find what they need.
M-Sat. 9-7, Sun. 10-5

 From I-17, take Camp Verde/Cottonwood exit. Follow signs to Cottonwood. Turn left on Main St. and store's 3 miles up on right.

FLAGSTAFF

 Dubbed "Flag" by locals, this funky, mountainous, college town has lots of places to stay, eat and do laundry. Surrounding areas have excellent hiking and various snow sport activities. Check out Cafe Express on N. San Francisco (mostly vegetarian) and Morning Glory Cafe.

NEW FRONTIERS NATURAL FOODS
1000 South Milton Road, 86001 • (520)774-5747
New Frontiers is big, clean and easy to find. Their mantra: "We're the most complete natural food store in Northern Arizona."
M-Sat. 9-8, Sun. 10-7

 From I-40, take I-17 exit.
I-17 north turns into Milton Rd. Go through town and find store on right.

MESA

NATURE'S HEALTH
2665 East Broadway, 85204 • (602)649-6145
M-F 9-7, Sat. 9-6

 From Rte. 60, get off at Gilbert Rd. and travel north. At fifth light, make a right onto Broadway. Travel 1 mile and go over a canal. Make a right turn into parking lot (which is on southwest corner of Lindsey & Broadway). Store is in middle of a strip mall.

PHOENIX

Mark at Wild Oats recommends exploring South Mountain Park. Take the Pima Canyon entrance to find biking and hiking trails. At night, enter on Central Avenue and drive in for an elevated, panoramic view of the city lights. Need relief from the desert heat? Rent a tube and float down the Salt River.

Recommended restaurants: The Farm at South Mountain on South 32nd Street offers vegetarian and organic fare served outside in their pecan grove (ingredients are taken from their garden whenever possible). Green Leaf Cafe on N. 19th Avenue also comes recommended.

WILD OATS MARKET
4730 E. Warner Road, Phoenix, 85044 • (602)598-5227
(One month this store featured belly dancing and Middle Eastern specialties in the deli).
Sun.-Sun. 7-10

From I-10 heading south (toward Tucson), take Warner St. exit. Go west (or make a right) and drive 1/4 mile. Store's behind a McDonalds's at northwest corner of 48th and Warner. Additional locating info: Store's in the Ahwatukee region.

WILD OATS MARKET
3933 E. Camelback Road, 85018 • (602)954-0584
Sun.-Sun. 7-10

From I-17, take Camelback Rd. exit. Head east about 10 miles.
Store's before light on right at southwest corner of Camelback and 40th.

PRESCOTT
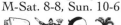

Check out Maya, a great down home Mexican restaurant. Also visit
Groom Creek and Spruce Mountain, Wolf Creek and Thumb Butte.

NEW FRONTIERS NATURAL FOODS
1112 Iron Springs Road, 86301 • (520)445-7370
M-Sat. 8-8, Sun. 10-6

From Hwy. 69, get
onto Gurley then
turn right onto
Montezuma. Montezuma wraps around and becomes Iron Springs. Store's on right.

PRESCOTT NATURAL FOODS
330 West Gurley Street, 86301 • (520)778-5875
M-Sat. 8-8, Sun. 10-6

Hwy. 69 becomes Gurley. Store's on east side
of street, one block past town square.

SCOTTSDALE

Check out Jewel of the Crown on N. Scottsdale Road for Indian fare.

WILD OATS MARKET
7129 East Shea Boulevard, 85245 • (602)905-1441
Sun.-Sun. 7-10

From I-10, take Squaw Peak Freeway (51) all the way to Shea Blvd. (As of 11/97,
the freeway ends there). Take a right onto Shea. Drive down to corner of Scottsdale
Rd. and Shea. Look for Wild Oats Plaza sign and turn into store's parking lot.

SEDONA

"It's beautiful here," says one New Frontier staffer about Sedona.
"I think there's something in the rocks. It's just a different feeling."

NEW FRONTIERS NATURAL FOODS
2055 West Highway 89A, 86336 • (520)282-6311
M-Sat. 8-8. Sun. 10-8

On east side of Hwy. 89A
in west Sedona. (Not in
the tourist section). P.S. The drive in from Flagstaff is spectacular!

TEMPE

In Tempe (pronounced tem-pee), stop by Mill Avenue, a hip college district that has a more progressive attitude than the rest of the Phoenix area. "Tempe is really an open minded, liberal town," says one Phoenix Wild Oats staffer. For good eats, head over to Pita Jungle and Haji Babas (both on Apache) and Tico Tica Tacos, a Colombian restaurant on Camelback Road.

GENTLE STRENGTH COOPERATIVE
234 West University, 85281 • (602)968-4831
Their pancakes are out of this world! We highly recommend dining outside on the patio. mmm....
M-F 9-9, Sat. & Sun. 9-8

 From I-10/I-17 west: Turn left off University exit. You'll curve with road and then see the store just past railroad tracks. From I-10/I-17 east: Turn right off Broadway exit, go left on Mill Ave., and left on University. Store's on right.

TUCSON

Tucson offers absolutely luscious dining options from around the globe. Pick up the city's arts and entertainment guide, The Tucson Weekly, for more restaurant listings and area happenings.

Inexpensive, authentic Mexican food can be found at Rosa's on Campbell and Ft. Lowell (their salsa is excellent!). Zachary's has excellent pizza and over 20 beers on tap. India House on Campbell features a yummy (and cheap) Indian buffet. Order the samosas!

The Loft on Speedway is an alternative movie theater while Pink Motel Video & Casa Video both rent great, obscure videos (Casa offers free popcorn as you browse). 4th Avenue is a casual, crunchy, alternative spot, and Value Village thrift store on 4th should not be missed.

Head over to Gates Pass for incredible sunset, sunrise and moonrise views of the Tucson Mountains. Just over the pass, explore the cacti and other succulents in Saguaro National Park. But do soak in the desert. Disastrously uncomfortable to some, it's a heaven on earth for the dry heat lovin' lizards among us.

FOOD CONSPIRACY CO-OP
412 North 4th Avenue, 85705 • (520)624-4821
A deliciously airy, bright store in the middle of 4th Avenue. Quite aesthetically pleasing! (Ok, and Elizabeth also used to work there). The store's name emerged from their history as a buying club. The members' motto was "food for people, not for profit." They then began saying, "what we have here is a food conspiracy." And so it goes...
M-Sat. 9-8, Sun. 9-7

 From I-10, take St. Mary's exit east (becomes 6th St.). Turn right on 4th Ave. Store's on left in middle of block.

REAY'S RANCH MARKET
3360 East Speedway, 85716 • (520)795-9844
Sun.-Sun. 7-10

From I-10, take Speedway exit east about 6 miles. Store's in a strip mall on right, a block or so past Tucson Blvd.

REAY'S RANCH MARKET
4751 East Sunrise, 85718 • (520)299-8858
Sun.-Sun. 7-10

From I-10, take Ina Rd. exit north/east (becomes Sunrise). Store's on right.

REAY'S RANCH MARKET
7133 N. Oracle, 85704 • (520)297-5394
Sun.-Sun. 7-10

From I-10, take Ina exit to Oracle Rd. Make a right onto Oracle. The store will be at the intersection on west side of street.

YUMA

YUMA HEALTH FOOD STORE
2099 South 4th Avenue, 85364 • (602)783-5158
No produce.
M-F 9-6, Sat. 9-5

  Get off I-10 on 16th St. and drive to 4th Ave. Store's 3/4 mile down on corner of 24th St. and 4th Ave.

Organic Fact №2

PROTECT TOP SOIL

The Soil Conservation Service estimates that over 3 billion tons of top soil is eroded from US croplands annually. The cause? Intensive mono-cropping and chemically-intensive practices. The results? The worst topsoil erosion in history.

Arkansas

1. FAYETTEVILLE
2. FORTSMITH
3. HARRISON
4. JONESBORO
5. LESLIE
6. LITTLEROCK
7. HOT SPRINGS
8. PINE BLUFF
9. SHERWOOD
10. SPRINGDALE
11. VANBUREN

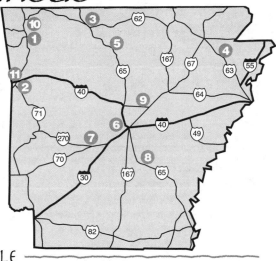

FAYETTEVILLE

 Ozark Food Co-op produce manager, Rod, recommends University of Arkansas thoroughfare Dixon Street where you can find bars, restaurants and on most weekends, live music.

"Fayetteville is in the most beautiful part of the Ozarks. Within 20 minutes we have 3 rivers and 5 lakes," claims Rod. "Also, we were the first home of the newly married Bill & Hillary Clinton, And if you like Bill Clinton, we have lots of ex-Governors that we'd be glad to send you."

OZARK NATURAL FOODS CO-OP
205 West Dixon, 72701 • (501)521-7558
The only Co-op in Arkansas. All their produce is organic!
M-Sat. 9-8, Sun. 12-5

 From Rte. 71, turn west on Dixon. Store's on left.

FORT SMITH

OLDE FASHIONED FOODS
123 North 18th Street, 72901 • (501)782-6183
M-Sat. 9-6

From I-40, take Rogers Ave. exit and go south/west on Rogers Ave. Turn right on 18th St. Store's in a yellow house on left.

OLDE FASHIONED FOODS MARKET
4900 Towson Avenue, 72901 • (501)649-8200
M-Sat. 9-6, Cafe: 11-5

 From I-40, take Phoenix St. exit. Travel west on Phoenix, then make a right onto Towson Ave. Store's on corner of the Phoenix Village Square.

HARRISON

ALMOND TREE, INC.
126 North Willow Street, 72601 • (501)741-8980
Small, mostly seasonal produce section.
M-F 9-5:30, Sat. 9:30-3

 Take Business 65 exit and travel 1.5 blocks west of Hwy. 65 into Harrison's downtown square.

HOT SPRINGS

Situated inside Hot Springs National Park, you'll find area campgrounds, restaurants, a wax museum and just plain weirdness readily available.

With a name like Hot Springs, you'd expect to find free, open pool bathing readily available... but don't look too hard. Though the front of the Visitor's Center does feature a warm, spring fed, bubbling fountain, taking a dip into this pool could bring you a ticket or jailtime (We checked into this). Consider yourself warned.

THE OLD COUNTRY STORE
455 Broadway, 71901 • (501)624-1172
Store has "Roma" to go (Roma is a caffeine-free brew made from chicory & barley). Store's nutritionist is also a Doctor. He sees patients in-store.
M-F 9-5:30

From Hwy. 70, drive one block east onto Broadway. Store's on right.

JONESBORO

JONESBORO HEALTH FOODS
1321A Stone Street, 72401 • (501)932-5301
Carrots only.
M-Th. 10-5, F 10-6, Sat. 10-4

From I-55, take 76 Hwy. to Caraway St. Go north to Nettleton St. and take a right. Go 1 block and take a left onto Stone. Store's on left.

LESLIE

Visit the Ozark Heritage Art Center.

COVE CREEK EXCHANGE
P.O. Box 434, Main Street, 72645 • (870)447-2724
Limited seasonal produce. Store features a large selection of pottery and local craft items as well as a line of natural snacks for travelers. Stop by the organic bakery next door!
M-F 9-5, Sat. 10-2

 From Hwy. 65, go east on Oak. Turn left on Main St. Store's on left.

LITTLE ROCK

Beans & Grains & Things staffers recommend The Community Bakery for yummy baked goods, coffee and the occasional round of Scrabble. Also try Vino's, a microbrewery and restaurant (their calzones are reportedly amazing), El Porton for Mexican cuisine and Star Of India, an Indian Cafe.

BEANS & GRAINS & THINGS
10700 North Rodney Parham, 72212 • (501)221-2331
This store offers automatic shopping carts for wheelchairs.
Sun.- Sun. 8-9

Off I-630, take Mississippi/Rodney Parham exit. Head north on Rodney Parham Rd.
Go 1 1/4 miles and make a right into Village Shopping Center. Store's behind Chili's.

PINE BLUFF

SWEET CLOVER HEALTH FOODS
2624 West 28th Street, 71603 • (501)536-0107
No produce.
M-F 10-5, Sat., 10-4

From Little Rock, get to Blake St. (Hwy. 79) and drive into Pine Bluff.
Once in Pine Bluff, bear left at fork onto Bay St. Continue to 28th St.
Turn left onto 28th. Store's on right, behind a bank in Old Village
Shopping Center.

SHERWOOD

ANN'S HEALTH FOOD STORE
9800 Highway 107, 72120 • (501)835-6415
Store carries organic carrots and a small selection of assorted produce.
M-F 8:30-6

From I-630, take Kiehl exit. At second stop light on Kiehl, make
a right onto Hwy. 107. Store's 6 blocks north on right.

SPRINGDALE

MARY'S NATURAL FOODS
220 South Thompson, 72764 • (501)751-4224
Organic carrots only.
M-Sat. 9-6

From I-71, take Rte. 412 east. Turn north onto Business 71 (Business
71 becomes Thompson). Store's on left.

VAN BUREN

Folks at Squash Blossom report their town has a restored downtown
district and beautiful mountains nearby. "It's quite a unique place," says
one staffer.

SQUASH BLOSSOM
5005 Dora Road, 72956 • (501) 474-1147
*Squash Blossom is housed in a 100 year old restored general store. Located
directly off I-40, the store still retains a country atmosphere.*
M-Sat. 9-6

From I-40 west: Take exit 1 (Dora/Fortsmith exit.).
Go 8/10 of a mile and store's on left. From I-40 east:
Take Dora/Fortsmith exit. Make a left onto Dora
Rd., cross interstate and store's on right.

Northern California

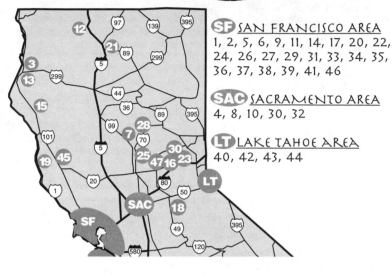

SF SAN FRANCISCO AREA
1, 2, 5, 6, 9, 11, 14, 17, 20, 22, 24, 26, 27, 29, 31, 33, 34, 35, 36, 37, 38, 39, 41, 46

SAC SACRAMENTO AREA
4, 8, 10, 30, 32

LT LAKE TAHOE AREA
40, 42, 43, 44

1. ALAMO
2. ANGWIN
3. ARCATA
4. AUBURN
5. BERKELEY
6. BURLINGAME
7. CHICO
8. CITRUS HEIGHTS
9. CORTE MADERA
10. DAVIS
11. EL CERRITO
12. ETNA
13. EUREKA
14. FAIRFAX
15. GARBERVILLE
16. GRASS VALLEY
17. HALF MOON BAY
18. JACKSON
19. MENDOCINO
20. MILL VALLEY
21. MOUNT SHASTA
22. NAPA
23. NEVADA CITY
24. OAKLAND

25. OROVILLE
26. PALO ALTO
27. PACIFICA
28. PARADISE
29. PETALUMA
30. QUINCY
31. RICHMOND
32. SACRAMENTO
33. SAN ANSELMO
34. SAN FRANCISCO
35. SAN RAFAEL
36. SANTA ROSA
37. SAUSALITO
38. SEBASTAPOL
39. SONOMA
40. SOUTH LAKE TAHOE
41. SUNNYVALE
42. TAHOE CITY
43. TAHOE VISTA
44. TRUCKEE
45. UKIAH
46. VACAVILLE
47. YUBA CITY

ALAMO

NATURAL TEMPTATIONS
190 A Alma Plaza, 94507 • (510)820-0606
Whole Grain Natural Bread Company is next door. They have a deli, bakery and juice bar.
M-F 9:30-6, Sat. 9:30-5:30, Sun. 11-3

From 680, take Stone Valley Rd. west. Turn right at Danville Blvd., then left into Natural Temptations parking lot. Store's next to Safeway.

ANGWIN

ANGWIN COMMUNITY MARKET
15 Angwin Plaza, 94508 • (707)965-6321
Sun.-Th. 7:30-7:30, F 7:30-3:30 (closes at 5 in summer)

From Hwy. 29 north, go right on Deer Park (toward Pacific Union College - 8 miles out of St. Helena). Go to top of hill and store's on Pacific Union College campus.

ARCATA

Suggested Arcata stops: May through November, check out the Farmer's Market in the town square for fresh organic produce and local crafts. Also stop by the Humboldt Brewery, the Wildflower Cafe, the Daybreak Cafe and the Arcata Marsh (a wheelchair accessible wildlife sanctuary).

ARCATA FOOD CO-OP
811 "I" Street, 95521 • (707)822-5947
Eureka and Arcata Co-ops are affiliated as the Northcoast Cooperative.
Sun.-Sun. 7-9 (bakery closes at 8:30)

From 101, take Samoa Blvd. exit west. Turn right on "I" St. Store's on left.

AUBURN

Latitudes (downtown) serves vegetarian fare.

SUNSHINE NATURAL FOODS
2160 Grass Valley Highway, 95603 • (916)888-8973
M-F 9:30-6, Sat. 9:30-5, Sun. 12-5

From 80, take Hwy. 49 exit and make a left. Head toward Nevada City and Grass Valley. Store's 1 mile up on right.

BERKELEY

"Diversity! That's the greatest thing about Berkeley," exclaims one Whole Foods staffer. "There's a really good mix of lots of cultures, young and old. It just meshes really well."

Berkeley recommendations...

Check out UC Berkeley and the Shattuck area in the heart of downtown Berkeley. There you'll find movie theaters galore and Long Life Veggie House, a completely vegetarian Chinese restaurant. There's also Taste of Africa and Michael's All American Diner where everything is prepared vegan, from milkshakes to cheese fries.

"The most beautiful spot in Berkeley is the Marina at sunset," says Roxanne at Wild Oats. "There's a panoramic view of the entire bay and you can see all 3 bridges." Roxanne also recommends Telegraph Avenue for cheap, funky thrift shop shopping.

Oliver at Whole Foods also suggests the Telegraph area. "Telegraph Avenue is like the old crazy hippie life," he says. "Dogs running around, the smell of incense, people selling stuff. It's cool."

BERKELEY NATURAL GROCERY
1336 Gilman Street, 94706 • (510)548-7008
Store has a "tofu bar!"
Sun.-Sun. 9-8

 From I-80, take Gilman St. exit. Store's on right.

ELMWOOD NATURAL FOODS
2944 College Avenue, 94705 • (510)841-3871
M-Sat. 10-7, Sun. 11-5

 From I-80, take Rte. 13 exit (Ashby Ave.). Turn left on College. Store's right there.

MACROBIOTIC GROCERY & ORGANIC CAFE
1050 40th Street, 94608 • (510)653-6510
Customers can purchase pre-paid meal cards for convenient dining. Staff says the cafe functions as a community center.
Sun.-Sun. 8-9, Cafe: M-F 11:30-2, 5:30-8, Sat. & Sun. 11-2, 5:30-8

 From I-80, take 27th St. exit north. Turn left on Telegraph, left on 40th. Store's on right.

WHOLE FOODS MARKET
3000 Telegraph Avenue, 94705 • (510)649-1333
Sun.-Sun. 9-10 (bakery opens at 8)

From I-80, take Ashby exit (Hwy. 13). Store's on corner of Ashby and Telegraph.

WILD OATS MARKET
1581 University Avenue, 94703 • (510)549-1714
Sun.-Sun. 8-10

From I-80, take University exit. Drive 2 miles east on University. Store's on left in a purple building.

BURLINGAME

EARTHBEAM
1399 Broadway, 94010 • (650)347-2058
Next to Earthbeam, check out Cafe Cappuccino.
M-Sat. 9-7, Sun. 10-6

 From 101, take Broadway exit west. Store's on left corner of Broadway and Cappuccino (3 miles south of San Francisco International Airport).

CHICO

Recommended stops: Bidwell Park starts in town, works its way into the foothills and features a collection of bike trails. Head down to Butte creek in Butte Creek Canyon to swim, sun and hang out with the locals. Also, the Sacramento River is a good bet for tubing.

Chico Natural Foods General Manager, Jason, recommends strolling Chico's historic downtown area and Madison Bear Garden, a decades old local drinking establishment which he calls "funky, old, weird and neat." Also visit the Sierra Nevada Brewery (they call Chico home) and Cafe Sandino, an all vegetarian cafe.

CHICO NATURAL FOODS
818 Main Street, 95928 • (916)891-1713
M-Sat. 8-9, Sun. 10-6

From Hwy. 99, take Hwy. 32 exit and head west on Hwy. 32 (8th St.). Store's on left at corner of 8th and Main St.

CITRUS HEIGHTS

ELLIOTT'S NATURAL FOODS NO. 2
8063 Greenback Lane, 95610 • (916)726-3033
Store manager has a degree in Oriental Medicine.
M-Sat. 9:30-6 (Th. 'til 8), Sun. 11-5

From I-80, take Greenback Lane and drive five miles. Store's on left in Greenback Square Shopping Center.

CORTE MADERA

SUPERNATURAL FOODS
147 Town Center, 94925 • (415)924-7777
M-Sat. 9-8, Sun. 10-6

From 101 south: Exit at Paradise Dr. Go left over the overpass and store's on right in Town Center Shopping Center (next to Safeway). From 101 north: Exit at Madera Blvd. and store's on right.

DAVIS

Davis is very bicycle friendly! This town has 5 bike shops and most streets feature bike lanes. Check out the path that goes through the University of California at Davis campus and adjacent sanctuary.

DAVIS FOOD CO-OP
620 G Street, 95616 • (916)758-2667
Big, clean and not exclusively stocked with good-for-you products.
Sun.-Sun. 8:30-10

From I-80, take Davis exit north (you'll be on E Street). Turn right on 6th. Store's on right, corner of 6th and G.

EL CERRITO

EL CERRITO NATURAL GROCERY
10367 San Pablo Avenue, 94530 • (510)526-1155
Sun.-Sun. 9-8

From I-80, take Central Ave. exit. Turn left on San Pablo, then left on Stockton. Store's right there.

ETNA

GREAT SCOTT NATURAL FOODS
423 Main, 96027 • (916)467-3350
M-F 10-5, Sat. 10-4

 From Hwy. 5 (past Mt. Shasta) take the Yreka exit and go west on Hwy. 3 (for about 45 minutes) straight into Etna. Once in downtown, go right on Main St. Store's on right between autoparts store and hardware store.

EUREKA

 Eureka Co-op staffers recommend old town Eureka and the Lost Coast Brewery. Head over to Arcata for more area attractions.

EUREKA CO-OP
1036 Fifth Street, 95501 • (707)443-6027
Eureka and Arcata Co-ops are affiliated as the Northcoast Cooperative.
M-Sat. 7-8, Sun. 10-8

     Store's at 5th (Hwy. 101 north) and L (1 block south of county courthouse & jail). Store has a huge fruit and veggie mural on building's south face and a cow on the roof.

EUREKA NATURAL FOODS
1626 Broadway Street, 95501 • (707)442-6325
M-F 8-8, Sat. 9-6, Sun. 10-6

  Store's in front of Costco on Hwy. 101 (101 becomes Broadway in Eureka).

FAIRFAX

GOOD EARTH NATURAL FOODS
123 Bolinas Road, 94930 • (415)454-0123
M-Sat. 10-8, Sun. 10-7

  From 101: Take Central San Rafael exit. Go right onto 4th St. and drive about 2 miles through San Rafael. Stay to right throughout as road merges several times. Pass a Jack-in-the-Box on right, then go left by the IGS gas station. Make a right onto Center, left on to Bolinas and store will be on left across from the park.

GARBERVILLE

 Calico Cafe serves vegetarian fare.

CHAUTAUQUA NATURAL FOODS
436 Church Street, 95542 • (707)923-2452
M-Sat. 10-6

  From 101, take Garberville exit. Drive down Redwood Rd. and go right onto Church. Store's 1/2 block down on right.

GRASS VALLEY

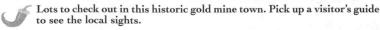 Lots to check out in this historic gold mine town. Pick up a visitor's guide to see the local sights.

BRIAR PATCH COMMUNITY MARKET
10061 Joerschke Drive, 95945 • (916)272-5333
M-F 8:30-8, Sat. 9-7, Sun. 10-6

 From I-80, take Rte. 49 north to Grass Valley. Take Brunswick exit and turn left, then left on Maltman and right on Joerschke Dr. Store's on left.

NATURAL VALLEY HEALTH FOODS
11562 Sutton Way, 95945 • (916)273-6525
This store is 25 years old!
M-Sat. 9:30-5:30

 From I-80, take Hwy. 49 exit to Grass Valley and take Brunswick exit. Store's at corner of Brunswick and Sutton.

HALF MOON BAY
 Though Main Street has tourist shops with kitschy beach memorabilia... the beach is spectacular!

HEALING MOON
523 Main Street, 94019 • (415)726-7881
Store offers prepared soup, salad and cookies.
M-Sat. 10-6, Sun. 11-5

From Hwy. 1, turn east on Kelley. Store's on left at corner of Kelley & Main.

JACKSON
 In the center of the Sierra Nevada foothills, Jackson is an outdoor mecca with lakes, ski areas and mountains close by.

GOLD TRAIL NATURAL FOODS
625 South Highway 49, 95642 • (209)223-1896
They roast their own organic coffee! Store also has a chiropractor.
M-F 10-6, Sat. 10-5

    Store's on east side of Hwy. 49 in the Mother Lode Plaza.

LOMA LINDA
LOMA LINDA MARKET
11161 Anderson Street, 92354 • (909)824-4565
A full vegetarian grocery store. Great if you're driving toward LA on I-10!
M-Th. 7-7, F 7-3, Sun. 8-6

From I-10, take Anderson exit and stay in left lane. Make a left onto Prospect and store's behind Bank of America and post office.

MENDOCINO
 What a beautiful area! Check out Lu's Kitchen (in the same parking lot as Corners of the Mouth). They serve vegetarian and organic fare exclusively.

CORNERS OF THE MOUTH
45015 Ukiah Street (P.O. Box 367), 95460 • (707)937-5345
Sun.- Sun. 9-7

 From Hwy. 1, take Main St. exit. Go west on Main, right on Lansing, left on Ukiah. Store's on left in a red church.

MILL VALLEY

When in Mill Valley, head over to Muir woods and Mount Tamalpais for hiking and mountain biking, local beach access and various water activities.

WHOLE FOODS MARKET
414 Miller Avenue, 94941 • (415)381-1200
M-F 9-8, Sat. & Sun. 8-8

From 101, take Tiburon Belvedere exit. Go west on East Blithedale, left on Camino Alto and right on Miller Ave. Store's on left.

MOUNT SHASTA

BERRYVALE GROCERY
305 S. Mount Shasta Boulevard, 96067 • (916)926-1576
Sun.-Sun. 8:30-7:30 (summer closes 1 hour later)

 From I-5 north, get off at Central exit in Mt. Shasta. Drive east and make a right at stoplight onto Mount Shasta Blvd. Store's 2 blocks on right.

NAPA

Wine tasting galore! Napa valley is home to grapes and more grapes! Check out PJ's Cafe downtown... it's excellent!

THE GOLDEN CARROT
1621 West Imola Avenue, 94559 • (707)224-3117
M-F 10-6, Sat. 10-5, Sun. 12-5

 From Hwy. 29, take Imola exit east. Store's on right in River Park Shopping Center.

NEVADA CITY

EARTH SONG NATURAL FOOD MARKET & CAFE
135 Argall Way, 95959 • (530)265-9392
Sun.-Sun. 8-9, Cafe: 11:30-8 (Cafe open 'til 9 in summer)

From Hwy. 49, exit at Goldflat Rd. Go right on Searls Ave., left on Argall. Store's on left.

OAKLAND

Check out the farmer's market at Jack London Square. Also, Golden Lotus serves Vietnamese fast food.

FOOD MILL
3033 MacArthur Boulevard, 94602 • (510)482-3848
M-Sat. 8:30-6:30, Sun. 11-4

 From 580 east, take 35th Ave. exit. Go left on 35th, left on MacArthur. Store's 2.5 blocks down on left.

MACROBIOTIC CENTER
1050 40th Street, 94608 • (510)653-6510
In business since 1983... great community atmosphere in their full sized macrobiotic restaurant!
Sun.-Sun. 8-9

From 580 (coming from San Fran), take the San Pablo Ave. west exit. Turn right onto San Pablo, then right onto 40th. Store's on left on corner of Linden and 40th.

OROVILLE

NATURAL HEALTH FOOD
2071 Robinson Street, 95965 • (916)533-5089
Seasonal organic produce.
M-F 9:30-5:30, Sat. 9:30-5

From I-70, take Oro Dam exit. Go through town and turn north on Myers, then right on Robinson. Store's right there.

PALO ALTO

 Check out Bangkok Cuisine, Thai City and Homma's Brown Rice Sushi on Birch.

CONSUMERS COOPERATIVE SOCIETY OF PALO ALTO
2605 Middlefield Road, 94306 • (415)327-8474
In business for over 60 years!
Sun.-Sun. 8-9

From I-280: Take Page Mill Rd. exit and drive 3 miles to Middlefield Rd. Go right onto Middlefield. Store's two blocks on left. From 101: Take Oregon Expressway to Middlefield Rd. and go left. Store's 1.5 blocks on left.

COUNTRY SUN
440 California Avenue, 94306 • (415)324-9190
Their sweet logo looks like a cross between Jerry Garcia and a muppet.
Sun.-Sun. 8-9

From 101, take Oregon Expressway west, turn right on El Camino Real and right on California. Store's on left.

WHOLE FOODS MARKET
774 Emerson Street, 94301 • (415)326-8676
Sun.-Sun. 8-10

From 101, take University exit west and turn left on Emerson. Store's on right.

PACIFICA

Known as the Fog Capital (they host a FogFest each year), Pacifica has lots of hiking, parks... and the beach is gorgeous!

GOOD HEALTH NATURAL FOODS
80 West Manor Drive, 94044 • (650)355-5936
M-Th. 9:30-8, F 9:30-7, Sat. 9:30-6, Sun. 12-6

 From Hwy. 1, take Manor Drive exit and head toward ocean. Store's on left.

PARADISE

PARADISE NATURAL FOODS
5729 Almond Street, 95969 • (916)877-5164
Limited organic produce in winter.
M-Th. 9-6, F 9-4, Sun. 10-3 (Friday closes at 6 in Summer)

 From Chico, take Hwy. 99 Skyway to Paradise. Go right onto Pearson Rd., drive 2 blocks and turn left onto Almond. Store's on left. From Hwy. 70, take Clark Rd. (Hwy. 191) to Paradise. Take a left onto Pearson Rd., go through 2 stops and turn right onto Almond. Store's on left.

PETALUMA

Petaluma's downtown area is filled with cafes, restaurants, antique shops and the occasional sushi bar. "It's quite a unique little town," says one Food for Thought staffer. In the mood for a hike? Check out the Helen Putnum Park on the outskirts of town.

FOOD FOR THOUGHT NATURAL FOOD MARKET
621 E. Washington Street, 94952 • (707)762-9352
Store has a full service post office and utility pay station inside!
M-Sat. 8-9, Sun. 10-8

From Hwy. 101, take E. Washington St. exit. Go west 1/2 mile and store's on right.

PETALUMA NATURAL FOODS
137 Kentucky Street, 94952 • (707)762-8522
Small store, good selection.
M-F 9-7, Sat. 9-6, Sun. 10-5

 From 101 north or south: Take Petaluma Blvd. exit. Follow into old downtown area, go left on Western, right on Kentucky. Store will be mid-block on left.

QUINCY

 In the middle of the Sierras.

QUINCY NATURAL FOODS
30 Harbinson Street, 95971 • (916)283-3528
Open since 1978, this small 500 member co-op services the entire county. Store sells organic wines.
M-F 10-6:30, Sat. 11-5, Sun. 11-4

 From Oroville or Chico: Take Hwy. 70 into Quincy on the one way street. Store's on corner by loft, across from library. From Reno or Trukee: Take Hwy. 89 into Quincy. Make a loop and come back around past court house onto Harbinson. Store's on corner.

RICHMOND

WILLIAMS NATURAL FOODS
12249 San Pablo Avenue, 94805 • (510)232-1911
M-F 9:30-7, Sat. 9:30-6, Sun. 11-6

 Store's between Barrett Ave. and McDonald on San Pablo.

SACRAMENTO

Wild Oats staffers recommend Mum's (on Freeport). They feature backyard organic herb gardens, fountains and excellent vegetarian fare. Hiking and biking trails can be found at the American River.

CARMICHAEL NATURAL FOODS
7630 Fair Oaks Boulevard, 95608 • (916)944-7000
M-F 10-6 (Th. til 7), Sat. & Sun. 10-5

 From I-80, take Madison East exit and turn right (south) on Manzanita, then left on Fair Oaks. Store's 1.5 blocks on right.

ELLIOTT'S NATURAL FOODS
3347 El Camino Avenue, 95821 • (916)481-3173
Friendly customer service.
M-F 9-6, Sat. 9-5, Sun. 11-4

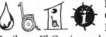 From Business 80, take El Camino exit and go right onto El Camino. Store's 5 miles down on left between Fulton and Watt. From I-80, take Watt Ave. exit and turn right onto Watt. Drive 3 miles to El Camino and store's 1 block on right. From Hwy. 50, take Watt Ave. exit, go left onto Watt, then left onto El Camino. Store's at next block on right.

SACRAMENTO NATURAL FOODS CO-OP
1900 Alhambra Boulevard, 95816 • (916)455-2667
Sun.-Sun. 9-10

 Directions can be complicated, so from any highway, take any exit with the closest letter to "S." Find S Street and 30th St. Alhambra is next to 30th St.

WILD OATS MARKET
5104 Arden Way, 95608 • (916)481-1955
Sun.-Sun. 8-10

 From Hwy. 50, take Watt Ave. north to Fair Oaks Blvd. and turn right. Drive about a mile and store's at corner of Arden and Fair Oaks.

SAN ANSELMO

WILD OATS MARKET
222 Greenfield Avenue, 94960 • (415)258-0660
Store has a Chinese herbalist on staff.
Sun.-Sun. 8-10

From 101, take Central San Rafael exit. From south: Turn left on 3rd St. (becomes Red Hill Ave.), turn left on Sequoia and right on Greenfield Ave. Store's on left. From north: Take Central San Rafael exit and turn right on 3rd St. Same as above.

SAN FRANCISCO

Any guide can help you around San Fran, but here are suggestions we collected. Check out Golden Gate Park, the Golden Gate Bridge (lotsa folks recommended walking across it), Chinatown, North Beach, Muir Woods, Stinson Beach, Point Rays (a birder's paradise) and Bernal Heights Hill which overlooks the city.

10,000 Buddha's is an excellent Asian style vegetarian restaurant that comes highly recommend, as does Raw Living Foods, Ananda Fuara and Herbavore.

Amelia at Good Life Grocery suggests Martunies (south of Market). They serve martini's alongside live show tunes. For Greek food, try Asimakopolis, a small, friendly and yummy Greek restaurant. Amelia recommends the Wild Side West... a funky, eclectic dive (Amelia says it's a dyke bar with a beautiful garden, fun drinks and a pool table).

BUFFALO WHOLE FOOD & GRAIN CO.
598 Castro Street, 94114 • (415)626-7038
M-Sat. 9-8, Sun. 10-8

 From 101 south: Follow signs to Golden Gate Bridge and take Fell St. exit. Turn left on Divisadero (becomes Castro). Store's on right. From north: Take Lombard St. exit to Van Ness. Turn right on Fell, left on Divisadero. Store's on right.

GOOD LIFE GROCERY
448 Cortland Avenue, 94110 • (415)648-3221
M-Sat. 9-8, Sun. 10-6

 From 101 north: Take Army exit to Bayshore Blvd. Turn right on Cortland. Store's on left. From 101 south: Take Silver Ave. exit and turn left off exit, then left on Cortland. Store's on left.

GOOD LIFE GROCERY
1524 20th Street 94107 • (415)282-9204
"A full service natural food store, without the attitude!"
M-Sat. 9-8, Sun. 10-6

 From 101 south: Take Vermont St. exit. Turn right on Vermont, left on 20th St. Store's on left. From north: Head south on Van Ness, turn left on 17th St., right on Connecticut St., left on 20th St. Store's on left.

OTHER AVENUES COMMUNITY FOOD STORE
3930 Judah Street, 94122 • (415)661-7475
Sun.-Sun. 10-8

Located in the Outer Sunset between 44th & 45th Ave.

THE NATURE STOP
1336 Grant Avenue, 94133 • (415)398-3810
M-F 9-10, Sat. & Sun. 10-9

 From 101 north: Take Fremont exit west, turn right on 3rd (becomes Kerny, then Columbia) and right on Grant. Store's on right. From south: Take last San Francisco exit before Bay Bridge. Turn left on 3rd. Same as above.

RAINBOW GROCERY - A WORKER OWNED COLLECTIVE
1745 Folsom Street, 94103 • (415)863-0620
This collective has 170 worker-members. Store is VERY wheelchair accessible.
M-Sat. 9-9, Sun. 10-9

 From 101, exit at Mission and Fell St. At end of ramp, make a right onto Mission. Go right onto Plum (it's a small alleyway). Make a right onto South Van Ness and go left at stoplight on 13th. Store's on corner of 13th & Folsom. Parking lot is the first right you can make after Folsom.

REAL FOOD CO.
3939 24th Street, 94116 • (415)282-9500
Sun.-Sun. 9-8

 From 101 south, get off at Main St./Ceasar Chavez and take a right (west). Drive up to Sanchez and take a right. Go left on 24th and store's on left. (Store's in Noe Valley).

REAL FOOD CO.
2140 Polk, 94109 • (415)673-7420
This store has two floors (top floor is not wheelchair accessible). Real Food Deli is two doors down.
Sun.-Sun. 9-9

 Store's between Broadway and Vallejo.

REAL FOOD CO.
1023 Stanyon, 94117 • (415)564-2800
Store's next to Real Food Deli.
Sun.-Sun. 9-8:30

 Store's up the hill from Golden Gate Park, in the Haight/Ashbury area. Cross street is Carl St.

THOM'S NATURAL FOODS
5843 Geary Boulevard, 94121 • (415)387-6367
Juice bar is wheatgrass only!
Sun.-Sun. 9-8

 From downtown, take 38 Geary bus. Store's located in Richmond district.

VALENCIA WHOLE FOODS
999 Valencia, 94110 • (415)285-0231
Sun.-Sun. 9-9

 From I-280 south: Take San José exit (becomes Guerrero St.) and turn right on 21st St. Store's on corner of 21st and Valencia. From I-101 north: Take Lombard St. exit and turn right on Van Ness, right on Mission, right on 21st. Same as above.

WHOLE FOODS MARKET
1765 California Street, 94109 • (415)674-0500
M-F 9-10, Sat. & Sun. 8-10

Go over Golden Gate Bridge. Turn right on South and left onto California. Store's parking lot is immediately on right.

SAN RAFAEL

WHOLE FOODS MARKET
340 3rd Street, 94901 • (415)451-6333
Sun.-Sun. 9-9, (Deli opens at 8)

From Hwy. 101 (coming from San Francisco): Get off at Central San Rafael exit. Take first right. This will be 2nd St. (merges with 3rd. St.). Store's one mile down on left.

SANTA ROSA

 Stop by Eastwest Cafe.

FOOD FOR THOUGHT NATURAL FOOD MARKET
1181 Yulupa Avenue, 95405 • (707)575-7915
M-Sat. 8-9, Sun. 10-8

From 101, exit at Hwy. 12 east. (Hwy. 12 ends and turns into Hoen). Drive 1 mile and turn left on Yulupa. Store's on left.

SANTA ROSA COMMUNITY MARKET
1899 Mendocino Avenue, 95401 • (707)546-1806
A non-profit, worker-owned and operated store.
M-Sat. 9-9, Sun. 10-8

 From Hwy. 101: Take Steele Lane/ Guerneville Rd. exit. Go east (right if heading north, left if heading south) to Mendocino Ave. and take a right. Store's on left.

SAUSALITO

REAL FOOD CO.
200 Calendonia, 94965 • (415)332-9640
Sun.-Sun. 9-9

 From I-101 south; Take Sausalito exit. Go south on Bridgeway until it forks to right into Caledonia. Store's on left at Turney and Caledonia.

SEBASTAPOL

Check out Slice of Life (next to Food for Thought) and Eastwest Cafe. Both come highly recommended!

FOOD FOR THOUGHT NATURAL FOOD MARKET
6910 McKinley Street, 95472 • (707)829-9801
M-Sat. 8-9, Sun. 10-8

From 101 or Hwy. 12, get to Hwy 116 and drive west toward Sebastapol (Hwy. 116 turns into McKinley in town). Store's on right.

SONOMA

DOWN TO EARTH NATURAL MARKET
201 West Napa - Suite 25, 95476 • (707)996-9898
Sun.-Sun. 9-7

 From Rte. 12 (West Napa St.), drive to 2nd St. west. Enter the Marketplace Shopping Center at corner of West Napa and 2nd St. Store's at rear corner.

SOUTH LAKE TAHOE

GRASSROOTS
2040 Dunlap Drive, 96150 • (916)541-7788
M-Sat. 10-7, Summer: M-Sat. 9:30-7:30, Sun. 11-6

 Store's at intersection of Hwy. 50 and 89.

SQUAW VALLEY

Next to Lake Tahoe and Nevada, Squaw Valley offers skiing and a plethora of outdoor activities.

SQUAW VALLEY COMMUNITY MARKET & VIDEO
1600 Squaw Valley Road, 96146 • (530)581-2014
Located at the foot of Squaw Mountain
M-Sat. 10-8, Sun. 11-6

 From I-80, take Trukee exit for 89 south - Tahoe City/ Squaw Valley. At stop, go left toward Squaw Valley. Drive 10 miles and at Squaw Valley entrance, take a right onto Squaw Valley Rd. Store's two miles up on right (in a strip mall, next to the post office, just before the mountain).

SUNNYVALE

WILD OATS MARKET
1265 S. Mary Street, 94087 • (408)730-1310
M-Sat. 7-10, Sun. 8-9

From I-280, go north on 85. Go to Freemont Rd. and make a right. Drive 1 mile and store's at next intersection on left corner. From 101: Take Freemont and turn left onto Mary. Store's on left at corner.

TAHOE CITY

COMMUNITY WHOLE FOODS MARKET
505 West Lake Boulevard, 96145 • (916)583-3156
Deli open Summer only.
M-Sat. 10-6:30, Sun. 10:30-5:30, (Sun. 11-5 in winter)

 From I-80, take Rte. 89 south to Tahoe City. Turn right on W. Lake Blvd. Store's on right.

TAHOE VISTA

NORTH SHORE COMMUNITY MARKET
North Lake Boulevard, 96148 • (530)546-5770
Sun.-Sun. 10-6

   One half mile west of Safeway.

TRUCKEE

NEW MOON NATURAL FOODS
11357C Donner Pass Road, 96161 • (916)587-7426
M-Sat. 9-7, Sun. 10-6

 From I-80, take Squaw Valley/Hwy. 89 exit. From west: Turn left off ramp. From east: Turn right off ramp. Take first left into Donner Plaza.

UKIAH

Ukiah Natural Foods folks suggest Ukiah's Buddhist Temple which has an all-vegetarian restaurant inside.

UKIAH NATURAL FOODS
721 State Street, 95482 • (707)462-4778
M-F 9-7, Sat. 10-6, Sun. 11-5

 From Hwy. 101, take Gobbi exit and head west on Gobbi. Store's on corner of Main and Gobbi.

VACAVILLE

THE NUTRITION SHOPPE
1005 Alamo Drive, 95687 • (707)447-2306
M-F 9-7, Sat. & Sun. 10-6

 From I-80 east, take Alamo exit and go south on Alamo. Store's on left as soon as you get off freeway in the Food for Less shopping center.

YUBA CITY

SUNFLOWER NATURAL FOODS MARKET
726 Sutter Street, 95991 • (916)671-9511
Store's right next to the Feather River... a great spot for fishing, swimming and boating.
M-Sat. 10-6, Deli: M-Sat. 10-2:30

 From Hwy. 20, take Sutter St. exit and drive 1/4 mile. Store's on right.

Southern California

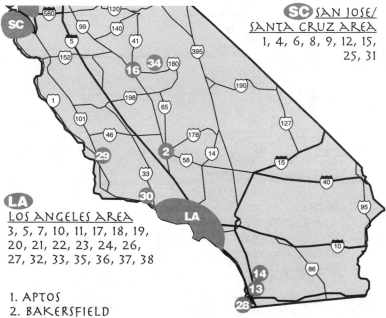

SC SAN JOSE/ SANTA CRUZ AREA
1, 4, 6, 8, 9, 12, 15, 25, 31

LA LOS ANGELES AREA
3, 5, 7, 10, 11, 17, 18, 19, 20, 21, 22, 23, 24, 26, 27, 32, 33, 35, 36, 37, 38

1. APTOS
2. BAKERSFIELD
3. BEVERLY HILLS
4. BOULDER CREEK
5. CAMARILLO
6. CAMPBELL
7. CANOGA PARK
8. CAPITOLA
9. CARMEL
10. COSTA MESA
11. CULVER CITY
12. CUPERTINO
13. DEL MAR
14. ESCONDIDO
15. FELTON
16. FRESNO
17. GLENDALE
18. HUNTINGTON BEACH
19. IRVINE
20. LONG BEACH
21. LOS ANGELES
22. MISSION VIEJO
23. NORTHRIDGE
24. OXNARD
25. PACIFIC GROVE
26. PASADENA
27. REDONDO BEACH
28. SAN DIEGO
29. SAN LUIS OBISPO
30. SANTA BARBARA
31. SANTA CRUZ
32. SANTA MONICA
33. SHERMAN OAKS
34. SQUAW VALLEY
35. THOUSAND OAKS
36. VENICE
37. VENTURA
38. WEST HOLLYWOOD

APTOS

APTOS NATURAL FOODS
7506 Soquel Drive, 95003 • (408)685-3334
Sun.-Sun. 8:30-8

From Rte. 1, take Seacliff Beach exit north. Turn left on Soquel. Store's on left in Aptos Shopping Center.

BAKERSFIELD

 The Garden Spot comes recommended for vegetarian fare.

CONE'S HEALTH FOODS
2701 Ming Avenue #7, 93304 • (805)832-5669
Limited organic produce.
M-F 10-9, Sat. 10-8, Sun. 11-6

From Freeway 99, take Ming Ave. exit. From north: Stay in left lane as you go off ramp. From south: "You'll be dumped right into parking lot."

BEVERLY HILLS

Recommended Bev. Hills stops: The Newsroom Cafe on North Robertson and Beverly Felafel.

WHOLE FOODS MARKET
239 North Crescent Drive, 90210 • (310)274-3360
Sun.-Sun. 8-9

From I-405, take Santa Monica Blvd. exit east. Turn right on Crescent. Store's on right.

BOULDER CREEK

TRUE NATURE FOODS
13070 Highway 9, 95006 • (408)338-2105
M-F 7-9, Sat. & Sun. 7-8

 Store's on east side of Hwy. 9.

CAMARILLO

LASSEN'S HEALTH FOODS
2207 Pickwick Drive, 93010 • (805)482-3287
M-Sat. 9-6:30

From I-101 south: Take Lewis Rd. exit, turn left on Daily Drive, right on Arneill Rd., and left on Pickwick. From north: Take Carmen Rd. exit, turn left on Ventura Blvd., left on Arneill Rd., left on Pickwick. Store's on right.

CAMPBELL

Nearby in San Jose, check out Bode on South 1st Street for Asian natural foods and Vegetarian House on Santa Clara.

WHOLE FOODS MARKET
1690 South Bascom Avenue, 95008 • (408)371-5000
"Best salad bar on the South Bay!"
Sun.-Sun. 7-10

From Hwy. 17, take Hamilton Ave. exit. Turn east at first stoplight onto Bascom.
Store's on left, corner of Hamilton and Bascom.

SUNFLOWER NATURAL FOODS
2230 South Bascom Avenue, 95008 • (408)371-7800
A discount store. Locally owned for over 25 years.
M-F 9:30-7, Sat. 9-6:30, Sun. 11-6

 From Hwy. 17, head east on Hamilton and turn right on
Bascom. Store's on left.

CANOGA PARK

FOLLOW YOUR HEART
21825 Sherman Way, 91303 • (818)348-3240
Sun.-Sun. 8-9

From 101, take
Topanga Canyon north
exit. Drive north on
Topanga, then go right onto Sherman Way. Store's 1 block down on left.

CAPITOLA

 Dharma's on Capitola Road is a recommended natural food restaurant.

NEW LEAF COMMUNITY MARKET
1210 41st Avenue, 95010 • (408)479-7987
Sun.-Sun. 6:30-10, Cafe 7-9

From Hwy. 1, take 41st Ave. exit west. Store's on left in Begonia Plaza.

CARMEL

CORNUCOPIA COMMUNITY MARKET
26135 Carmel Rancho Boulevard, 93923 • (408)625-1454
*A beautiful store designed with a feng shui approach. Won the National
Health Food Industry's store of the year!*
Sun.-Sun. 9-8

 From Hwy. 1, take Carmel Valley Rd. east.
Turn south on Carmel Ranch Blvd. Store's on
left in Carmel Rancho Shopping Center.

COSTA MESA

MOTHER'S MARKET & KITCHEN,
225 East 17th Street, 92627 • (714) 631-4741
Sun.-Sun. 9-10, (Restaurant closes at 9:30)

 From 405, get onto
55 south (ends and
becomes Neort
Blvd.) Drive 2-3 blocks to 17th St. and turn left. Store's one block down on right.

CULVER CITY

Try Chandni on Bagley Avenue for delicious Indian food.

RAINBOW ACRES
13208 Washington Boulevard, 90066 • (310)306-8330
M-F 9-9, Sat. & Sun. 9-8

From 405, take Venice Blvd. exit, drive to Washington and turn west. Store's 1 mile down on north side of street.

CUPERTINO

China House features a full vegetarian menu and Miyake serves an array of inexpensive vegetarian sushi (both are on S. De Anza Blvd). Katmandu West features Nepalese cuisine.

WHOLE FOODS MARKET
20830 Stevens Creek Boulevard, 95014 • (408)257-7000
Sun.-Sun. 8-10

From 280 north, take Wolfe exit south. Store's on corner of Homestead and Wolfe Rd.

DEL MAR

JIMBO'S NATURALLY
12853 El Camino Real, 92130 • (619)793-7755
Sun.-Sun. 9-9

From I-5, take Del Mar Heights exit east. Turn right on Camino Real then left into Del Mar Highlands Town Center.

ESCONDIDO

JIMBO'S NATURALLY
1633 South Centre City Parkway, 92025 • (760)489-7755
Sun.-Sun. 9-9

From I-15, take Felicita exit. Turn left if heading north, right if heading south. Make a right at stop sign. After road winds around, store's on left behind Sav-On.

FELTON

Felton's Pantry on Highway 9 serves vegetarian fare.

NEW LEAF COMMUNITY MARKET
6240 Highway 9, 95018 • (408)335-7322
Sun.-Sun. 9-9

From 17 North, take Big Basin exit. Drive a few miles on Mount Herman Rd. through Scotts Valley. At light, go right on Graham Hill Rd. At next stop light, take a left onto Hwy. 9. Store's on left.

FRESNO

CHRISTINA'S
761 East Barstow, 93710 • (209)224-2222
M-F 9-7, Sat. 9-6

 From Rte. 41, take Shaw Ave. exit two blocks east. Turn left on 1st and left into Headline Shopping Center.

GLENDALE

 Vegetable Delight on Chatsworth St. has great Chinese vegetarian food.

WHOLE FOODS MARKET
826 North Glendale, 91206 • (818)240-9350
Sun.-Sun. 9-9

From Rte. 134, take Glendale Ave. exit north. Store's on right.

HUNTINGTON BEACH

MOTHER'S MARKET & KITCHEN
19770 Beach Boulevard, 92648 • (714)963-6667
Sun.-Sun. 9-10

 From 405 take Beach Blvd. exit and head south. When Utica and Beach cross, make a left into the center.

IRVINE

MOTHER'S MARKET & KITCHEN
2963 Michelson Avenue, 92612 • (714)752-6667
Sun.-Sun. 9-10

 From 405 south, take Jamboree exit and go right (From north, go left). The first street is Michelson - take a left. Store's in Park Place Center.

LONG BEACH

PAPA JON'S NATURAL FOODS
5006 East 2nd Street, 90803 • (562)439-3444
Store has a full service vegetarian-vegan restaurant.
Sun.-Sun. 8-9, Cafe: M-F 9:30-9, Sat. & Sun. 9:30-10

 Follow I-710 to end, turn right on Ocean Blvd., left on Granada, and left on 2nd. Store's on left.

LOS ANGELES

Definitely purchase an L.A. map to avert this city's infamous traffic jams. Area recommendations: La Botre Sante, a natural food restaurant in La Brea (other locations in the area), Inaka (macrobiotic) and for "fake-meat" Asian food, try Alasan in Anaheim.

EREWHON NATURAL FOODS

7660 Beverly Boulevard, 90036 • (213)937-0777
Store has a soup and sushi bar.
M-Sat. 8-10, Sun. 9-9

From I-10 take Fairfax and Washington exit. Go north on Fairfax and turn right on Beverly. Store's on right.

NATURE MART

2080 Hillhurst Avenue, 90027 • (213)660-0052
In the Los Feliz area.
Sun.-Sun. 8-10

From I-5, take Los Feliz exit west, then go south on Hillhurst. Store's 2 blocks down on east side of street.

MISSION VIEJO

WILD OATS MARKET

27142 La Paz Road, 92692 • (714)460-0202
Sun.-Sun. 8-9

From Hwy. 5, take La Paz exit. Cross streets are La Paz and Margurite.

NORTHRIDGE

Check out Canopy in the Sky, a vegetarian restaurant across from Whole Foods.

WHOLE FOODS MARKET

9350 Reseda Boulevard, 91324 • (818)701-5122
Sun.-Sun. 9-9

From 118, exit at Reseda Blvd. and take the exit south. Store's on left.

OXNARD

LASSEN'S HEALTH FOODS

3471 Saviors Road, 93033 • (805)486-8266
M-Sat. 9:30-6:30

From 101 north: Take Oxnard Blvd. exit and head south (Oxnard becomes Saviors). Go south at "Five Points" and head for beach). Store's on right. From south: Take Vineyard exit and turn left on Vineyard, then left on Oxnard. Same as above.

PACIFIC GROVE

GRANARY MARKET
173 Central Avenue, 93950 • (408)647-2150
Granary Market was bought by Whole Foods and is moving to Del Monte Shopping Center in Summer of '98 under its new name. Call for more info.
M-F 8-8, Sat.-Sun. 8-7

 From Hwy. 1, take Del Monte Ave. west (becomes Central in Pacific Grove). Store's on left.

PASADENA

WILD OATS MARKET
603 South Lake Street, 91106 • (626)792-1778
Sun.-Sun. 8-10

From 210, exit at Lake St. From east: Make a right. From west: Go left. Store's at corner of California and South Lake.

REDONDO BEACH

 Check out Greens at the Beach, an all vegetarian cafe with great food and live music on weekends. The Spot features a similar menu but has less atmosphere. Both are excellent!

WHOLE FOODS MARKET
405 North Pacific Coast Highway, 90277 • (310)376-6931
Sun.-Sun. 9-9

 From I-405 north: Turn right off Redondo
Beach Blvd. exit, right on Artesia, left on Aviation Blvd. and left on Pacific Coast Hwy. Store's on right. From south: Exit at Artesia Blvd. Same as above.

SAN DIEGO

San Deigo area recommendations: Frequent traveler Melinda suggests the Krishna Temple on Grand Ave. in Pacific Beach. On Friday nights, pay $3 for all-you-can-eat vegetarian food.

OCEAN BEACH PEOPLE'S NATURAL FOODS MARKET
4765 Voltaire Street, 92107 • (619)224-1387
Sun.-Sun. 9-9

 Follow Hwy. 8W as far as it goes. Turn left on Sunset Cliffs Blvd. and
follow into Ocean Beach. Turn left on Voltaire St. Store's on right.

SUNSHINE ORGANIC FOODS
3918 30th Street, 92104 • (619)294-8055
Store's deli features Maple-glazed seitan and grilled veggie subs.
M-Sat. 9-8, Sun. 10-7

 From I-805, take University Ave. exit west and turn right on 30th St. Store's on left.

SOUTHERN CALIFORNIA

SAN LUIS OBISPO

QUESTA CO-OP
745 Francis Street, 93401 • (805)544-7928
A small, friendly store about 5 miles from the highway. Worth the trip!
Sun.-Sun. 9-9

From Hwy. 101, take Marsh St. exit and go around the bend. Turn right on Broad St. (Follow signs to airport). Turn left on Francis. Store's just behind Circle K Market, at corner of Broad and Francis.

SANTA BARBARA

Recommended Santa Barbara stops: Sojourner Coffeehouse (they feature natural and ethnic foods... Lazy Acre workers characterize the place as "really granola"). Also stop by The Bakery, The Main Squeeze and on State St., The Natural Cafe.

LAZY ACRES
302 Meigs Road, 93109 • (805)564-4410
Store has a pizza oven.
Sun.-Sun. 7-10

From 101, take Carrillo exit and drive west. Store's 2.5 miles down on left.

SANTA CRUZ

Hooray... Santa Cruz is a vegetarian heaven! Visit the worker owned Saturn Cafe (our spies report their "Chocolate Madness" rocks). Also stop by Jahva House on Union St. and Jalapenos Taqueria (Mexican) on Laurel St. Head to Zachary's for breakfast and check out the Bagelry on Center St. for great vegan fare (they have outdoor seating). Check out the hostel on Main for a place to stay and for more local information, go to the message boards at the Saturn Café and the Food Bin.

FOOD BIN-HERB ROOM
1130 Mission Street, 95060 • (408)423-5526
The Food Bin and Herb Room are two separate buildings but both function as the local community food store. The Food Bin has great produce, the Herb Room is one of the biggest in the country. They had at least twelve ideas for detoxing my liver.
Sun.-Sun. 9-midnight

In Santa Cruz, Hwy. 1 becomes Mission St. Store's on north side, at corner of Mission and Laurel.

NEW LEAF COMMUNITY MARKET
2351 Mission Street, 95060 • (408)426-1299
Sun.-Sun. 8-9

From Hwy. 1 south (or from 17), get on Hwy. 1 north and drive 2 miles (becomes Mission St.). Go left at light onto Swift St., then take first left onto Macpherson St. Store's second driveway on left (entrance is off MacPherson).

NEW LEAF COMMUNITY MARKET
1134 Pacific Avenue, 95060• (408)425-1793
Sun.-Sun. 9-9

 From Hwy. 1 drive into town about 4 miles (will be on Mission). Take a right on Front St. Go through 2 lights and store's back parking lot is at corner of second traffic light.

STAFF OF LIFE NATURAL FOODS MARKET
1305 Water Street, 95062 • (408)423-8632
"We've got it all!"
Sun.-Sun. 9-9

From Hwy. 1, take Morrissey exit south. Turn right on Water. Store's on right.

STAPLETON'S
415 River Street, 95060 • (408)425-5888
Sun.-Sun. 9-9

 From Hwy. 1 south, take a left at light onto River St. From north, go right on River St. Store's 3 blocks down on right.

SANTA MONICA

 Check out Love and Serve in Westwood Village (by the UCLA campus). Organarchy on the Third Street Promenade serves 100% organic food and Real Food Daily serves local and organic vegetarian fare.

CO-OPPORTUNITY CONSUMER CO-OP
1525 Broadway, 90404 • (310)451-8902
Sun.-Sun. 8-10

 From I-10 west: Exit right onto Lincoln, pass two lights and take a right onto Broadway. Drive six blocks to 16th St. Store's at 16th and Broadway. From I-10 east: Exit right onto Lincoln. Take a left at stoplight, then go two lights down to Broadway. Take a right on Brodway and store's at corner of 16th.

ONE LIFE NATURAL FOODS
3001 Main Street, 90404 • (310)392-4501
Sun.-Sun. 9-9

 From I-10, take 4th St. exit and go left onto 4th St., right on Pekoe, and left on Main. Store's 1/4 mile down on left at corner of Pier and Main.

SHERMAN OAKS

 Check out Genmai for Japanese food!

WHOLE FOODS MARKET
12905 Riverside Drive, 91423 • (818)762-5548
Sun.-Sun. 9-9

From 101, go north one block off Coldwater Canyon exit. Store's on left.

THOUSAND OAKS

LASSEN'S HEALTH FOODS
2857 E. Thousand Oaks Boulevard, 91361 • (805)495-2609
M-Sat. 9-8

 From 101, take Hampshire St. exit. Go north on Hampshire, left on Thousand Oaks Blvd., right on Skyline Dr. and left into Skyline Plaza.

WHOLE FOODS MARKET
451 Avenida de los Arboles, 91360 • (805)492-5340
Sun.-Sun. 9-9, Cafe opens at 7

From Hwy. 101, take Filmore (Hwy. 23) exit north. Turn left on Avenida de los Arboles. Store's on right.

VENICE

Check out Venus Of Venice on Westminster and A Votre Sante ... both serve vegetarian fare.

VENICE OCEAN PARK FOOD CO-OP
839 Lincoln Boulevard, 90291 • (310)399-5623
Sun.-Sun. 9-9

 From I-10, take Lincoln Blvd. exit and head south. Turn right on Brooks Ave. Store's on right.

VENTURA

LASSEN'S HEALTH FOODS
4013 East Main Street, 93003 • (805)644-6990
M-Sat. 9-8

 From Hwy. 101 south: Take Telephone Rd. exit. Turn left on Telephone, right on Main, and right in PepBoys Plaza. From 101 north: Take Telephone Rd. exit onto Main. Store's 3 blocks down on right.

WEST HOLLYWOOD

WILD OATS MARKET
8611 Santa Monica Boulevard, 90069 • (310)854-6927
Sun.-Sun. 8-10

From I-10, take La Ceinega exit and drive north about 2 miles. Turn left on Santa Monica Blvd. Store's 2 blocks down on right.

Colorado

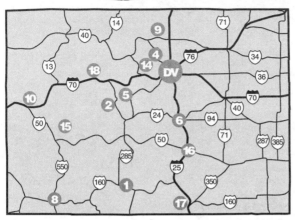

DV
DENVER
AREA
3, 7, 11, 12, 13

1. ALAMOSA
2. ASPEN
3. AURORA
4. BOULDER
5. BRECKENRIDGE
6. COLORADO SPRINGS
7. DENVER
8. DURANGO
9. FORT COLLINS
10. GRAND JUNCTION
11. GREENWOOD VILLAGE
12. LAKEWOOD
13. LITTLETON
14. NEDERLAND
15. PAONIA
16. PUEBLO
17. TRINIDAD
18. VAIL

ALAMOSA

With the Rio Grand National Forest to the west and the Sangre De Christo mountains to the east, the outdoor possibilities around Alamosa are endless. Great Sand Dunes National Monument and the area's geothermal hot springs come especially recommended.

VALLEY FOOD CO-OP
7565 West Highway 160 #5, 81101 • (719)589-5727
M-Sat. 9-6

   Store's on Hwy. 160, just west of Alamosa proper in Villa Mall.

ASPEN

MOUNTAIN NATURAL'S
316B Aspen Airport Business Center, 81611 • (970)925-5502
M-F 8-6, Sat. 10-5

     From Hwy. 82, store's across from airport. (Amoco gas station is next to store and is visible from road).

AURORA

WILD OATS MARKET
12131-F East Iliff Avenue, 80014 • (303)695-8801
Sun.-Sun. 7-11

 From I-225, turn west on
Iliff. Store's two miles down on right at corner of Peoria and Iliff.

BOULDER

In town, check out Settler's Park and Chattauqua Park for great hiking (and climbing boulders!) Ras Kassa's Eithiopian and Creative Vegetarian Cafe come highly recommended.

ALFALFA'S
1651 Broadway, 80302 • (303)442-0082
Store just added a chic hangar-like addition with large juice bar. If you're looking for a nutritionist, the two Wild Oats Markets and Alfalfa's share services of one who makes rounds between all 3. Call ahead for an appointment.
M-Sat. 8-10, Sun 9-10

Take Hwy. 36 north (becomes 28th St.) to Arapahoe. Turn left on Arapahoe. Store's on left.

IDEAL MARKET
1275 Alpine Avenue, 80304 • (303)443-3730
Ideal Market is the only privately owned health food store in Boulder! They're dedicated to "preserving the independently owned and operated neighborhood market as an alternative to large national chains."
M-Sat. 7-10, Sun. 8-10 (8-9 in winter months)

 From Denver,
take I-36 and stay
on as it changes to 28th St. in Boulder. Make a left onto Canyon Blvd., then a right onto Broadway. Store's in plaza on corner of Alpine and Broadway.

WILD OATS VEGETARIAN MARKET
1825 Pearl Street, 80302 • (303)440-9599
Great juice bar and deli. Equally as large as Alfalfa's. No meat in-store!
Sun.-Sun. 8-11

 From I-36, take 28th St. north
and go west on Pearl St. Store's
ten blocks down on right.

WILD OATS MARKET
2584 Baseline Road, 80303 • (303)499-7636
Sun.-Sun. 7-11

From I-36, take Baseline Rd. and exit west. Store's on left in Basemar Shopping Center.

BRECKENRIDGE

AMAZING GRACE NATURAL FOODS
213 Lincoln Avenue, 80424 • (303)453-1445
Store is housed in a historic building circa 1880's.
M-Sat. 11-8, Sun. 12-5

 From I-70, take Hwy. 9 to Breckenridge.
At third light, take a left and go two blocks
down to French St. Store's on corner of Lincoln and French.

COLORADO SPRINGS

Wild Oats staffers say rock formation Garden of the Gods (on the outskirts of
Colorado Springs) should not be missed.

MOUNTAIN MAMA NATURAL FOODS
1625-A West Uintah, 80904 • (719)633-4139
*This 18 year old store is family owned and operated. "We are one of the few
dinosaurs remaining, still wandering around." Staff say they are proud of the
friendly neighborhood feel to their establishment.*
M-Sat. 9-7, Sun. 11-5

 From I-25, take West Uintah exit and head
west about a mile. Store's on left.

THE VITAMIN COTTAGE
5777 North Academy, 80918 • (719)536-9606
They carry organic produce only!
M-F 9-7:30, Sat 9-6, Sun 11-5

 From I-25, take Woodman Dr. exit and go east on
Woodman. Turn south onto Academy and then east onto
Vickers. The store's not very visible, but look for it behind
Lenscrafters, in south-east corner of intersection.

WILD OATS MARKET
5075 North Academy, 80918 • (719)548-1667
Sun.-Sun. 8-10

From I-25 take Academy exit, get onto Academy and turn east. Store's in Union
Square on left.

DENVER

Denver recommendations include: The Mercury Cafe for organic food
and coffee, the Pizza Kitchen on Colfax (open all night for pizza any
time necessary) and the Mayan Theater, an artsy moviehouse that
features short run films.

ALFALFA'S
900 East 11th Avenue, 80218 • (303)832-7701
M-Sat. 7:30-10, Sun. 7:30-9:30

From I-25, take Colfax exit east to Ogden. Store's at Ogden and 11th, on south side of 11th.

ALFALFA'S
201 University Boulevard, 80206 • (303)320-9071
M-Sat. 7:30-10, Sun. 7:30-9

From I-25, go north on University Blvd. Make a left on Second Ave. Second Ave. runs directly into strip mall parking lot where Alfalfa's is located.

WILD OATS MARKET
2260 East Colfax, 80206 • (303)320-1664
Sun.-Sun. 8-9

From I-70, take York St. exit south. Store's on corner of York and Colfax on right.

WILD OATS MARKET
1111 South Washington, 80210 • (303)733-6201
Sun.-Sun. 7-10

From I-25, take Washington St. exit. Store's on corner of I-25 and Buchtel Rd. (which is the road directly in front of I-25). You can't miss it!

DURANGO

DURANGO NATURAL FOODS
575 East 8th Avenue, 81301 • (970)247-8129
M-Sat. 8-8, Sun. 9-7

Get on Hwy. 160. From east: Turn north on Rte. 3 (becomes 8th Ave.) Store's on left at first light. From west: head north on Camino Del Rio and turn right onto 6th St. Store's on right, on corner of 8th and 6th St. (6th St. is College Dr.).

FORT COLLINS

 Check out Avogadro's Number, (a great vegetarian cafe), the Crown Pub for music and also Tony's (where Saturday night is always reggae night).

ALFALFA'S
216 West Horsetooth Road, 80525 • (970)225-1400
Featuring wide aisles and electric carts, this store is particularly handicap accessible (once a roller rink, the building has all hardwood floors). Also, a skylight runs the full length of the building. "Everyone really loves it here," says a staffer. "Everyone who comes from out-of-state says it's the coolest thing they've ever seen and says, 'I want an Alfalfa's in my hometown!'"
Summer: M-Sat. 8-10, Sun 8-9. Winter: M-Sat. 8-9, Sun. 8-8

From I-25, take Harmony Rd. exit and head west (toward mountains). Go about 5 miles and turn right onto College Ave. Turn left on Horsetooth. Store's on right.

FORT COLLIN'S CO-OP

250 East Mountain, 80524 • (970)484-7448

A rustic enclave in a trendy shopping area, this Co-op features a reading room/teaching space, complete with activist magazines and updates.

M-F 8:30-8:30 (11/15 - 3/15 M-F store closes at 7:30), Sat. 8:30-7, Sun. 11-6

From I-25, take Mulberry exit west. Turn right (north) on College Ave. and make another right on Mountain. Store's on left.

WILD OATS MARKET

1611 South College Avenue, 80525 • (970)482-3200

Sun-Sun. 8-9

From I-25, take Prospect Rd. exit and head west on Prospect (toward mountains). Just after College Ave. turn left into the shopping center to find store.

GLENWOOD SPRINGS

GOOD HEALTH GROCERY

730 Cooper Avenue, 81601 • (970)945-0235

M-F 10-7, Sat. 10-6, Sun. 12-5

From I-70, take Glenwood Springs exit, then turn left on 8th Ave. Store's on right at corner of Cooper & 8th.

GRAND JUNCTION

APPLESEED

2830 North Avenue, 81501 • (970)243-5541

M-Sat. 9-6

From I-70, take business loop to North Ave. Store's 3 miles down in East Gate Shopping Center.

SUNDROP GROCERY

321 Rood Avenue, 81501 • (970)243-1175

M-Sat. 9-6

From I-70, take Horizon Dr. exit. Take Horizon Dr. south to 7th St., make a left onto 7th and follow it downtown. Make a right onto Rood Ave. Store's on left in a pale yellow building between 3rd and 4th Streets.

GREENWOOD VILLAGE

WILD OATS MARKET

6000 S. Holly, 80111 • (303)796-0996

Sun.-Sun. 7-9

From I-25, take Orchard exit and go west. Store's about 2 miles down on corner of Orchard and Holly.

LAKEWOOD

VITAMIN COTTAGE

3333 South Wadsworth Boulevard, 80227 • (303)989-4866

The Vitamin Cottage never carries commercial produce and only offers transitional when they can't get it certified. They also have a holistic dietitian on staff who helps customers free-of-charge.

M-F 9-8, Sat. 9-7, Sun. 11-6

From I-285, store's two blocks north of 285 on west side of Wadsworth in Mission Trace Shopping Center.

LITTLETON

 Check out the Highline Canal Trail - excellent for hiking and biking.

ALFALFA'S

5910 South University Boulevard, 80121 • (303)798-9699

Sun.-Sun. 8-9

Take I-25 to Orchard Rd. exit. Go 4 miles west on Orchard Rd. to University Ave. Store's on corner.

NEDERLAND

 Nestled in a beautiful little region of the Rockies, Nederland has a stunning view of the continental divide.

MOUNTAIN PEOPLE'S CO-OP

30 East First Street, 80466 • (303)258-7500

This store has been member owned and operated since 1979. "We are sort of a little oasis here in the mountains for travelers who are into natural foods," say staffers. "We also serve the mountain communities."

Sun.-Sun. 9-8

From Boulder, take Canyon Blvd. 17 miles up the canyon. Make a left at traffic circle in Nederland, then take another left onto First St. Store's on south side of street, halfway down block.

PAONIA

PAONIA WHOLE FOOD MARKET AND SUNNYSIDE CAFE

101 Main Street, 81428 • (970)527-3737

This is the kind of store you don't want to miss. Located on the western slope of a farming community in the Rockies, (known as Fruit Valley), the store grows wheatgrass, buys local organic fruit and even grinds its own flour. Also, Paonia has a large vegan and vegetarian community that they try to cater to. "Our clientele are pretty simple farming folk and bulk is what they want, so that's what we have," says one staffer.

M-Sat. 9-6

Take 133 into Paonia. Go right at first turnoff into Paonia and continue down to the store on corner of 3rd and Main.

PUEBLO

 Check out the downtown area for coffee houses, music and shopping. Head over to some of the local weekend farmer's markets or to the area's many hot springs.

AMBROSIA NATURAL FOODS & BUYERS CO-OP
112 Colorado Avenue, 81001 • (719)545-2958
According to staffers, this two story building (complete with wrap around mural) is "a very funky place." Soon to expand, store will have a juice bar and will also be wheelchair accessible. They carry organic produce only.
M-Sat. 8-8, Sun. 9-5

 From I-25, take Abriendo exit and stay right. Go 3/4 mile, turn left on Colorado Ave. Go 1/2 block. Store's on left.

TRINIDAD

 The Main Street Bakery and Wazubi's coffee house serve vegetarian food. Mission at the Bell offers Mexican fare.

THE NATURAL FOOD STORE
316 Prospect Street, 81082 • (719)846-7577
Small store, but packed!
M-F 10-5:30, Sat. 10-5

 From I-25, take exit 12B and drive west on Hwy. 12 (becomes Prospect Street and zig zags). Store's 1.5 blocks on left.

VAIL

CLARK'S
141 East Meadow Drive, #f-109, 81657 • (970)476-1199
Replacing Vail's now defunct Alfalfa's, Clark's carries a mixture of natural and mainstream supermarket foods. They have some organic produce. Other Clark's are located in Aspen, Norwood and Carbondale.
Sun.-Sun. 7:30-10

 From I-70, take Mainville exit - 176. Head east on South Frontage Rd. and take first right. Halfway down block is a parking booth. Store will validate for 1 hour.

Organic Fact No. 3

PROTECT FUTURE GENERATIONS

The food choices consumers make today will impact their children's health tomorrow.

Connecticut

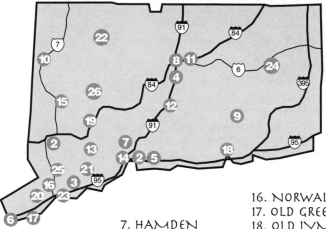

1. BRANFORD
2. DANBURY
3. FAIRFIELD
4. GLASTONBURY
5. GUILFORD
6. GREENWICH
7. HAMDEN
8. HARTFORD
9. HEBRON
10. KENT
11. MANCHESTER
12. MIDDLETOWN
13. MONROE
14. NEW HAVEN
15. NEW MILFORD
16. NORWALK
17. OLD GREENWICH
18. OLD LYME
19. SOUTHBURY
20. STAMFORD
21. STRATFORD
22. TORRINGTON
23. WESTPORT
24. WILLIMANTIC
25. WILTON
26. WOODBURY

BRANFORD

ORCHARD HILL MARKET
875 West Main Street, 06405 • (203)448-2573
This store features outdoor dining in their butterfly gardens. (They also have herb and wildflower gardens!)
M-F 9-7, Sat. 9-6, Sun. 10-5

From 95 north: Take exit 52 to Frontage Rd. (becomes Rte. 1) and stay straight. Store's on right about 2 1/4 miles from highway. From 95 south: Take exit 54 to Cedar St. Make a left off exit, then a right onto Rte. 1. Store's on left 1.5 miles down.

DANBURY

CHAMOMILE NATURAL FOODS
58-60 Newtown Road (Route 6), 06810 • (203)792-8952
M-F 9-7 (Th. 9-8), Sat. 9:30-6

From I-84, take exit 8 and follow road north/east for a half mile. Store's on right in Rte. 6 Plaza.

FAIRFIELD

 Check out Sprouts, a vegetarian restaurant on Black Rock Turnpike.

SWEETWATER NATURAL FOODS
1916 Post Road, 06430 • (203)255-4333
They have a sushi bar!
M-F 8-7 (Th. 8-8), Sun. 9-5

 From I-95, take exit 21. Go east on Mill Plain Rd. to Post Rd. (which is Rte. 1). Make a right onto Post Rd. Store's on right in less that 1/4 mile.

GLASTONBURY

 Garden of Light staffers recommend finding a local farm to go apple and berry picking.

GARDEN OF LIGHT PURE FOODS MARKET
2836 Main Street, 06033 • (860)657-9131
Very clean... lots of great food for travelers. The store won the Hartford Advocate's retail poll for best health food store in the area.
M-F 9:30-8, Sat. 9:30-7, Sun. 11-5

 From I-91, take Putnam Bridge exit (Rte. 3). Cross bridge and take Main St. Glastonbury exit. Turn left on Griswold and right on Main St. The next traffic light is the entrance to Plaza. Make a left there into store's parking lot.

GUILFORD

 Like many coastal Connecticut towns, Guilford features old colonial houses, seasonal fruit picking, easy access to Long Island Sound and miles of beach. At Town Hall or Bishop's Orchards, purchase a 25 cent map and explore Westwood Trails, the extensive trail system that weaves in and around Guilford. Also check out the Shoreline Diner and Vegetarian Enclave.

FOODWORKS
1055 Boston Post Road, 06437 • (203)458-9778
M, Th. 9:30-7:30, T, W, F 9:30-7, Sat. 10-7, Sun. 11-6

 From I-95, take exit 58. Follow signs for Guilford Center and go south on Rte. 77 for 1/2 mile. Store's on corner of Rte. 1 and Rte. 77.

GREENWICH

WHOLE FOODS MARKET
90 East Putnam Avenue, 06830 • (203)661-0631
M-Sat. 8-9, Sun. 8-8

 From I-95, take exit 4 onto Indian Field Rd. (north). Turn left on Putnam Ave. and drive for 2 miles. Store's on left.

HAMDEN

THYME & SEASON
3040 Whitney Avenue, 06518 • (203)407-8128
M-F 9-8, Sat. 9-7, Sun. 11-5

 From I-91, take exit 10 and drive straight to end. Go north on Rte. 10. Store's 1/4 mile on left.

HARTFORD

Head over to the cafe at the Reader's Feast, a cafe and bookstore across from Cheese and Stuff. Also, Pacific Restaurant serves Vietnamese food.

CHEESE AND STUFF
550 Farmington Avenue, 06105 • (860)233-8281
M-Sat. 8-8, Sun. 9-6

From I-84, take Sisson Ave. exit (46) and turn right on Sisson Ave. At second light, turn left onto Farmington Ave., go two blocks and turn right on Kenyon. Store's on left at corner.

HEBRON

HEBRON HEALTH & HARVEST
32 Main, 06248 • (860)228-4101
No produce.
M, T, W, Sat. 9:30-6, Th. & F 9:30-7

From Rte. 2, take exit 13 and go left onto Rte. 66. Store's at second light, across street from Mobil.

KENT

KENKO NATURAL GROCERY
351 Kent Cornwall Road (Route 7), 06757 • (860)927-4079
One of the co-owners, a very friendly 80 year old gentleman named Leonard grows 75% of the produce himself just 16 miles up the road... and it's all organic! The store grinds its own bread flour and they have two herb gardens on-site (customers are encouraged to go out behind the store and cut what they need). Kenko Natural Grocery is locally famous; people wouldn't think of buying their vegetables or bread anywhere else!
M-Sat. 9:30-7, Sun 10-7

From I-84, take Rte. 7 north to Kent. Go 5 miles north of Kent Center. Store's on left.

MANCHESTER

BETTER WAYS MARKETPLACE
1470 Pleasant Valley Road, 06040 • (860)429-4517
M-Sat. 10-9, Sun. 10-6

From I-84 west: Take exit 62. At end of ramp, go straight into Buckland Hills Plaza. Store's in center. From I-84 east: Take exit 62 and go left at end of ramp. Take a left at second stoplight into Plaza.

MIDDLETOWN

IT'S ONLY NATURAL
684 Main Street, 06457 • (860)346-1786
Dar's college town! Restaurant attached, great for holistic student dating. It has a groovy restaurant on one side and a mostly vegan restaurant on the other. Both stores are run with love.
M-Sat. 9-8, Sun. 11-4, Cafe: M-Sat. 11:30-3:00, T-Sun. 5-9, Sun. (brunch) 11:30-3.

From Rte. 9, take exit 16. At light after exit, turn left on Main St. Store's on left.

MONROE

SUNWHEEL HEALTH FOODS
444 Main Street, 06468 • (203)268-2688
M-F 10-6, Sat. 10-5

 Store's on Rte. 25 (Main St.) at intersection of Rte. 59 in back of a big yellow house.

NEW HAVEN

 Check out Edge of the Woods bulletin board to discover New Haven's many cultural and spiritual offerings (there's a Buddhist temple down the street from the store).

EDGE OF THE WOODS
379 Whalley Avenue, 06511 • (203)787-1055
This store sells absolutely no meat products!!
M-F 8:30-7:30, Sat. 8:30-6, Sun. 9-6

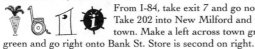 From I-91, take Downtown exit (exit street becomes Frontage St.). Turn right on Ella Grasso Blvd., right on Whalley Ave. Store's on left in Market Square Shopping Center.

NEW MILFORD

BOBBIT'S NATURAL FOODS
10 Bank Street, 06776 • (860)355-1515
M-F. 9:30-6, Sat. 9:30-5:30

 From I-84, take exit 7 and go north 8 miles on Rte. 7/202. Take 202 into New Milford and turn right over bridge into town. Make a left across town green, circle around the green and go right onto Bank St. Store is second on right.

NORWALK

FOOD FOR THOUGHT
596 Westport Avenue, 06851 • (203)847-5233
M-Sat. 8-9, Sun. 9-6

From I-95, take exit 17 in Westport. At end of exit, take a left. Go about 1 mile, then take a left onto Sylvan Rd. Go to light and take another left onto Westport (also US 1). Store's less than a mile down on left.

OLD GREENWICH

ORGANIC GOURMET
177 Sound Beach Avenue, 06870 • (203)637-3035
M-Sat. 9-6

 From I-95, take exit 5. Go east on Post Rd. Take next right onto Sound Beach Ave. and bear right under railroad bridge. Store's in next building on right.

OLD LYME

THE GRIST MILL
Halls Road - P.O. Box 6741, 06371 • (860)434-2990
Store carries a combination of natural food & gourmet items.
M-Sat. 9-6, Sun. 11-5

 From I-95, take exit 70. From south: Go left at end of exit ramp and go under I-95. Take a right onto Halls Rd. Store's 1/2 mile on left. From north: Go straight at exit ramp to light (becomes Halls Rd.). Store's on right about 1/4 mile down in Old Lyme Shopping Center.

OLD SAYBROOK

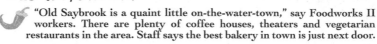 "Old Saybrook is a quaint little on-the-water-town," say Foodworks II workers. There are plenty of coffee houses, theaters and vegetarian restaurants in the area. Staff says the best bakery in town is just next door.

FOODWORKS II
17 Main Street, 06475 • (860)395-0770
M-F 9:30-6, Sat. 10-6, Sun 11-5

  From I-95 south: Take Old Saybrook exit. Go right at stop/yield sign, then go left at first light. Take a left at second light onto Main St. Store's first building on right. From I-95 north: Take Old Saybrook exit and stay right as exit forks. Make a left at third light onto Main St. Store's immediately on right.

SOUTHBURY

THE NATURAL MERCHANT
142 Main Street North, 06488 • (203)264-9954
Small restaurant attached, open 11-3.
M-F 9-7 (Th. 9-8), Sat 8-6, Sun. 9-6

   From I-84, take exit 15 west. Store's less than a half mile down.

STAMFORD

 Check out the Stamford Nature Center, just a half mile from Natural Nutrition.

NATURAL NUTRITION
1055 High Ridge Road, 06905 • (203)329-7400
M-F 9-7, Sat. 9-6, Sun. 11-5

From Merritt Parkway (Rte. 15), take exit 35 and bear right. Store's a half mile down on left.

STRATFORD

NATURE'S WAY NATURAL FOODS
922 Barnum Avenue Cutoff, 06497 • (203)377-3652
M-Sat. 9-9, Sun. 9-5

 From I-95, take West Broad exit (#32). From east: Turn left at first light, left on Main and right on Barnum. Store's on left. From west: Turn left on Main. Same as above.

TORRINGTON

NATURAL LIFE - GABRIELLA'S MARKET
634 Migeon Avenue, 06790 • (860)489-8277
Gabriella's Market & Natural Life are in the same building. Find grocery items in Gabriella's and organic produce in Natural Life.
M-Sat. 9-6:30

 Store's on Rte. 4, west of Rte. 8.

WESTPORT

 Check out the Chef's Table.

FOUNTAIN OF YOUTH
1789 Post Road East, 06880 • (203)259-9378
This store offers free tea in the winter and fall! They're the only store in the area that sells absolutely no meat, chicken, fish or commercial produce... "and that creates such a nice atmosphere," says a staff member.
M-Sat. 9-7, Sun. 10-5

 From I-95, take exit 19. From north: Go straight off ramp and through stop sign. Go right at first light. Store's 1/4 mile up on right. From south: Take a left off ramp and another left at light. Store's 1/4 mile up across from Super Stop & Shop.

ORGANIC MARKET
285 Post Road East, 06880 • (203)227-9007
M-Sat. 9-7, Sun. 11-5

 From I-95, take exit 18. From north, go left at end of ramp. From south, make a right. Take a left at third light onto Post Rd. Store's 3/4 mile on right.

WILLIMANTIC

WILLIMANTIC FOOD CO-OP
27 Meadow Street, 06226 • (860)456-3611
This very cool co-op is the last of its kind in the state. It's located near the popular Everyday Cafe.
M-F 9:30-8, Sat. 9-8, Sun. 10-5 (closed Sun. during July & Aug.)

 From Rte. 44, go south on Rte. 32 (becomes Rte. 66 and turns into Main St. in Willimantic). Turn left on Walnut St. and right on Meadow. Store's on left.

WILTON

WILTON ORGANIC GOURMET
33 Danbury Road, 06897 • (203)762-9711
M-Sat. 9-7, Sun. 11-4

 From either Merritt parkway or I-95, take Rte. 7 Connector north to end. Follow signs to Rte. 7 north. Store's 7/10 mile up on left.

 "I really like it here," says a New Morning Country Store staffer. "It's what most people would call a quaint little town." Check out Kettletown State Park on Lake Zoar and also, the Good News Cafe.

NEW MORNING COUNTRY STORE

P.O. Box 429 or Main Street South, 06798 • (203)263-4868

Free coffee samples!

M-W 8-6, Th.-F 8-8, Sat. 8-6, Sun. 11-5

  From I-84 east: Take exit 15 (Southbury). Go left onto Rte. 67 (turns into Rte. 6 in Woodbury). Store's in strip mall on left. Going west: Take exit 17 and go straight. Take Rte. 64 into Woodbury and go left at junction of Rte. 6. Store's 1/4 mile down on right in strip mall.

Organic Fact №4

SAVE ENERGY

Once family-based small businesses dependent on human energy, farming has turned into large-scale factory farms that are highly dependent on fossil fuels. (Modern farming uses more petroleum than any other single industry). Organic farming is still mainly based on labor intensive practices, green manures and crop covers rather than synthetic fertilizers to build up soil. Organic produce also tends to travel fewer miles from field to table.

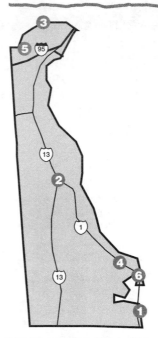

Delaware

1. BETHANY BEACH
2. DOVER
3. HOCKESSIN
4. LEWIS
5. NEWARK
6. REHOBOTH BEACH

BETHANY BEACH

WHOLESOME HABITS
Route 1 Beach Plaza, 19930 • (302)537-0567
Organic carrots only. The Stress Management Center (next door) offers massage, hypnosis and other services.
Sun.-Sun. 9-6

Store's on Rte. 1 in Bethany Beach across from Sea Colony.

DOVER

 El Sombrero has an international vegetarian menu and features vegan options.

KINDRED SPIRITS
200 North New Street, 19904 • (302)678-9692
Limited seasonal organic produce.
M-Sat. 10-6 (Th. 12-8)

From Rte. 13, turn onto Division St./Rte. 8. At fourth light, take a right onto New St. Store's two blocks down on left.

HOCKESSIN

 Capriotti's (in the Lantana Square Shopping Center) features vegetarian "faux meat" sandwiches.

HARVEST MARKET

1252 Old Lancaster Pike, 19707 • (302)234-6779

M-Sat. 10-7

 From I-95, go to Rte. 141 north. Then take Rte. 2 (Kirkwood Hwy.) south. Drive 1 mile to Rte. 41 and travel north for 8 miles into Hockessin. Go to light (the only one in town!) and turn left. The road ends one block ahead, directly in front of store.

LEWIS

GERTIE'S GREEN GROCER

119 2nd Street, 19958 • (302)645-8052

M-Sat. 10-5:30, Sun. 12-4

 From Rte. 1, follow signs to downtown Lewis (not to Ferry), then to downtown historic Lewis and left onto 2nd St. (one way). Store's on right.

NEWARK

 Traveler and former resident, Dana, has recommendations for the Newark area (pronounced new-ark). Check out Main Street restaurants, Sinclairs Cafe (for breakfast and lunch) and Jude's Diner. Capriotti's features vegetarian "faux meat" sandwiches (really good), King's has a vegetarian - vegan selection of Chinese food and Jam' n Java offers coffee, art exhibits and occasional poetry/performances.

Dana also suggests: Stanton Family Thrift shop "a must visit in Newark," and the East End Cafe for beer and music. Carpenter State Park (complete with Frisbee golf course) and White Clay Creek are both excellent escapes from city life.

NEWARK NATURAL FOODS COOPERATIVE

280 East Main Street, 19711 • (302)368-5894

M-Sat. 9-8

 Off I-95, take Rte. 896 exit and go north. Turn right on Delaware Ave., left on Library Lane, then left on Main St. Store's on right.

REHOBOTH BEACH

RAINBOW EARTH FOODS

220 Rehoboth Avenue, 19971 • (302)227-3177

M-Sat. 9:30-7, Sun. 10-6

Off Hwy. 1, take bypass (1A). 1A is or becomes Rehoboth Ave., - depending on how you approach it. Store's across from fire station, 2.5 blocks from ocean.

Florida

Check out Publix statewide
for organic produce.

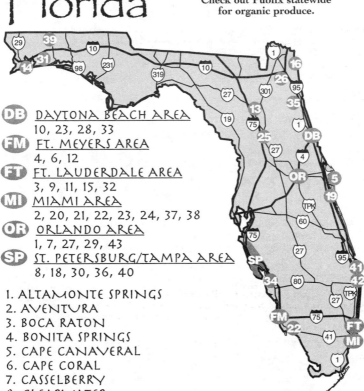

DB DAYTONA BEACH AREA
10, 23, 28, 33

FM FT. MEYERS AREA
4, 6, 12

FT FT. LAUDERDALE AREA
3, 9, 11, 15, 32

MI MIAMI AREA
2, 20, 21, 22, 23, 24, 37, 38

OR ORLANDO AREA
1, 7, 27, 29, 43

SP ST. PETERSBURG/TAMPA AREA
8, 18, 30, 36, 40

1. ALTAMONTE SPRINGS
2. AVENTURA
3. BOCA RATON
4. BONITA SPRINGS
5. CAPE CANAVERAL
6. CAPE CORAL
7. CASSELBERRY
8. CLEARWATER
9. COCONUT GROVE
10. DAYTONA BEACH
11. FORT LAUDERDALE
12. FORT MYERS
13. GAINESVILLE
14. GULF BREEZE
15. HOLLYWOOD
16. JACKSONVILLE
17. KEY WEST
18. LARGO
19. MELBOURNE
20. MIAMI
21. NORTH MIAMI
22. SOUTH MIAMI
23. SOUTH MIAMI BEACH
24. MIAMI LAKES
25. NAPLES
26. NEW SMYRNA BEACH
27. OCALA
28. ORANGE PARK
29. ORLANDO
30. ORMAND BEACH
31. PALM BEACH
32. PALM HARBOR
33. PENSACOLA
34. PLANTATION
35. PORT ORANGE
36. SARASOTA
37. ST. AUGUSTINE
38. ST. PETERSBURG
39. TALLAHASSEE
40. TAMPA
41. TEQUESTA
42. WEST PALM BEACH
43. WINTER PARK

ALTAMONTE SPRINGS

CHAMBERLIN'S MARKET & CAFE

1086 Montgomery Road, 32701 • (407)774-8866

A large natural food store in the middle of residential high-rises, Chamberlin's Market & Cafe is just a short walk from the water.

M-Sat. 9-8:30, Sun. 11-5:30. Cafe: M-Sat. 9-7:30, Sun. 11-4:30

From I-4, take exit 49. Go west to Montgomery Rd. and take a left. Store's on right in Goodings Plaza.

AVENTURA (NORTH MIAMI BEACH)

WHOLE FOODS MARKET

3565 NE 207th Street, 33180 • (305)933-1543

Outside cafe seating.

M-Th. 8-10:30, F & Sat. 8-11, Sun. 10-10:30

From U.S. 1, make a right onto 207th St. Store's one mile down on left at Waterways Shops (just east of Biscayne (US 1) and 207th St.).

BOCA RATON

Check out the Children's Museum at Singing Pines, a non-profit community museum housed in one of the city's oldest wooden buildings. There's also the International Museum of Cartoon Art, a museum devoted to collecting and studying all things cartoon. Folks at the Whole Earth Market recommend Deerfield and Boca Beaches.

ALL AMERICAN NUTRITION, INC.

652 Glades Road, 33431 • (561)395-9599

No produce.

M-F 9-8:30, Sat. 9-6:30, Sun. 11-6

Store's on right in Oaks Plaza, 1 mile east of I-95 on Glades Rd.

ORGANICALLY FRESH

21338 St. Andrews Boulevard, 33433 • (407)362-0770

100% organic store!

M-F 9-7, Sat 10-6

From I-95, exit at Glades Rd. Drive west and go left on St. Andrews. Drive south and store's on right corner in the Town Square Plaza.

WHOLE EARTH MARKET

7110 Beracasa Way, 33433 • (561)394-9438

This store has a kosher and organic cafe & deli. They'll soon be expanding to include a kosher pizza restaurant.

Sun.-Th. 9-9, F 9-8, Sat. 10-8 Cafe: Sun.-Th. 12-4:30, F 12-4, closed Sat.

Take I-95 to Palmetto. Travel 2 miles to intersection of Palmetto and Powerline. Store's in Delmar Shopping Center.

WILD OATS MARKET
2200 W. Glades Road, Bldg. #8, 33431 • (561)392-5100
Sun.-Sun. 8-10

From I-95, take Glades Rd. exit and head west. At bottom of hill after exit, make a
left onto Sheridan Way. Go to light (19th St.) and make a right. Store's third turn on
left. (While address is W. Glades Rd., store is actually in front of 19th St.)

BONITA SPRINGS

MARTHA'S NATURAL FOOD MARKET INC. OF BONITA
9118 Bonita Beach Road, 34135 • (941)992-5838
M-F 9-6, Sat. 9-5, Sun. 1-5

 From I-75, take exit 18 west onto
Bonita Beach Rd. Store's on
right, 1/2 mile before intersection of U.S. 41 in Sunshine Plaza.

CAPE CANAVERAL

Sunseed Food Co-op is 2.5 blocks from the beach, 1 mile from colossal
surf shop, Ron Jon, and just around the corner from the Kennedy Space
Center (they watch shuttles take off from outside their front door!). Staff
says the entire Cape Canaveral/Cocoa Beach area has a plethora of open,
public beaches... so go swimmin'!

SUNSEED FOOD CO-OP INC.
6615 North Atlantic Avenue, 32920 • (407)784-0930
Sunseed Co-op owns the cafe next to the store.
M-Sat. 10-7 (Th. & F 'til 8), Sun 11-6

 From 528, road turns into A1A
(North Atlantic Ave.). From 520,
turn left onto A1A and drive 1.2 miles north. Store's on west side of street.

CAPE CORAL

BACK TO NATURE
1217 SE 47th Terrace, 33904 • (941)549-7667
M-F 9-6, Sat. 9-5

 From I-75, take Daniels Rd. exit (21), turn right
on Hwy. 41 and left on College Parkway. Go
over bridge, turn right on Vincennes and another
right on 47th. Store's on right in a shopping strip.

MOTHER EARTH NATURAL FOODS
1721 Del Prado Boulevard, 33990 • (941)574-6333
Carrots only.
M-F 9-6, Sat. 9-5

From I-75, take exit 26 - Pine Island Rd. (also State Rd. 78).
Head west into Cape Coral. At intersection of Del Prado and
Pine Island, make a left and head south. Store's in Coral Point Shopping Center on left.

CASSELBERRY

CHAMBERLIN'S MARKET & CAFE
1271 Semoran Boulevard, 32707 • (407)678-3100
M-Sat. 9-9, Sun. 11-6 Cafe: M-Sat 9-4, Sun. 11-4

From I-4, take exit 48. Go east about 6 miles. Store's on right in Lake Howell Square Center.

CLEARWATER

NATURE'S FOOD PATCH NATURAL MARKET & DELI CAFE
1225 Cleveland Street 33755 • (813)443-6703
M-Sat. 10-9, Sun. 12-9 Cafe: M-Sat. 11-3

From Hwy. 19, turn west on Gulf-to-Bay, then turn right on Cleveland toward downtown Clearwater. Go 1 mile and find store on left.

COCONUT GROVE

Check out the Groove's Main Street farmer's market on Saturdays. Oak Feed Natural staffers recommend Kolibri Fabulous Natural Foods Restaurant on Red Road and the Last Carrot on Grand Avenue.

OAK FEED NATURAL FOODS
2911 Grand Avenue, 33133 • (305)448-7595
Oak Feed Natural Foods began as a macrobiotic specialty store.
M-Sat. 9-10, Sun. 10-11

From US 1, go left on 27th and right on Oak. Travel to Mary and go left, then take a right on Grand. Look for Planet Hollywood on right. There's validated parking in garage between Planet Hollywood and the store.

DAYTONA BEACH

Check out Main Street in Daytona for shops, restaurants and cafes. Harvest House Natural Food staff recommend Passha's for Middle Eastern treats and Sapporo's for great Japanese food.

HARVEST HOUSE NATURAL FOODS
498 North Nova Road, 32114 • (904)255-0780
Organic carrots and sometimes greens.
M-Sat. 9-6. (W & Th. 'til 7), Sun. 12-5

From I-95, take State Rd. 92 east, then turn left on Nova. Store's 3 blocks down on left.

FORT LAUDERDALE

Birch State park is within walking distance of Wild Oats, (staffers say they love the "non-South Florida" feel to the place). Also check out Secret Woods, one of many great parks around Ft. Lauderdale.

Adam at Wild Oats recommends the Chili Pepper for music and also alternative nightclub, Squeeze. According to Adam, the "best, coolest, blues house in town is The Poor House. It's a hole in the wall, as all good blues bars are."

BREAD OF LIFE NATURAL FOOD MARKET & DELI
2388 North Federal Highway, 33305 • (954)565-7423(RICE)
Sun.-Sun. 8-9

From I-95, take Oakland Park exit east. Turn right on US 1 (Federal Hwy.).
Store's on left in less than 1 mile.

WILD OATS MARKET
2501 East Sunrise Boulevard, 33304 • (954)566-9333
Nutritionist on Mondays & Thursdays.
Sun.-Sun. 8-10

From I-95, take Sunrise Blvd. exit east. Store's across from Galleria Mall.

FORT MYERS

Recommended stops: Sweet Tomatoes, the Garden Green (restaurants) and Fort Myers beach is lovely.

ADA'S NATURAL FOOD MARKET
3418 Fowler Street, 33901 • (941)936-4756
M-Sat. 9-6

 From I-75, take Colonial Blvd. (exit 22). Head west on Colonial and turn right on Fowler. Store's on left.

MOTHER EARTH NATURAL FOODS
15271 McGregor Boulevard, 33908 • (941)489-3377
Carrots only.
M-F 9-6, Sat. 9-5

 From I-75, get off at Daniels Parkway exit (21) and go west. At Summerlin Rd., make a left and head south. Make a right onto Gladiolas St. then make another right on McGregor. Store's in McGregor Point Shopping Center on right.

MOTHER EARTH NATURAL FOODS
4600 Summerlin Road, 33919 • (941)939-0990
Carrots only.
M-F 9-6, Sat. 9-5

From I-75, take exit 22 and drive west to Summerlin Rd. Make a left and store's immediately on right in Colonial Crossing Shopping Center (near Publix).

MOTHER EARTH NATURAL FOODS
16520 S. Tamiami Trail, 33908 • (941)454-8009
Carrots only.
M-F 9-6, Sat. 9-5

From I-75, get off at Daniels Parkway exit (21) and go west. At US 41 (which is Tamiami Trail), make a left and go south. Drive 1.5 miles and make a right onto Island Park Rd., then take an immediate left into Island Park Shopping Center.

MOTHER EARTH NATURAL FOODS

13860 N. Cleveland Avenue C, 33903 • (941)997-6676

Carrots only.

M-F 9-6, Sat. 9-5, Sun. 12-5

From I-75, take exit 26 - Pine Island Rd. (also State Rd. 78) and head west. Drive to North Cleveland Ave. (US 41) and make a left. Head south and store will be just past Pondella Rd. in North Shore Shopping Center on left.

GAINESVILLE

Gainesville stops: Our Place Cafe, Balaji Indian Cuisine, Coney Island Cafe (inexpensive) and Ivey Grill (on W. University). Head inside Books Inc. (next to Mother Earth Market East) for the all-vegetarian, Cafe Books. Check out the University of Florida campus for free cultural events.

MOTHER EARTH MARKET EAST

521 NW 13th Street, 32601 • (352)378-5224

This store features a sushi bar!

M-Sat. 9-9, Sun. 11-7

From I-75, take Newberry Rd. exit and at light, turn right onto Newberry Rd. Drive down to 13th St. and go left. Store's three blocks down on right.

MOTHER EARTH MARKET WEST

1237 NW 76th Boulevard, 32606 • (352)331-5224

M-Sat. 9-9, Sun. 11-7

From I-75, take Newberry Rd. exit and turn left at light onto Newberry Rd. Turn right onto 76th Blvd. and drive to end. Store's in a strip mall on right.

GULF BREEZE

NATURALLY DELICIOUS MARKET

370 Gulf Breeze Parkway, 32561 • (850)934-3400

M-F 9-7, Sat. 10-6

After 3 mile Bridge (Hwy. 98 - Gulf Breeze Parkway) store's in first shopping center (Del Champs Shopping Center) on left.

HOLLYWOOD

Harvest Village Natural Foods has a juice bar and makes smoothies (no produce). Big Herb's farm stand (by the racetrack) has lots of cheap tropical produce.

FOOD AND THOUGHT

4535 Sheridan Street, 33021 • (954)961-1687

M-F 9:30-7, Sat. 9:30-6

From I-95, take Sheridan St. exit and head west for 2 miles. Store's on right at corner of 46th & Sheridan in Post Haste Plaza.

JACKSONVILLE

In Jacksonville, check out Heartworks. They serve vegetarian entrees and feature an art gallery and music on weekend nights. The Natural Food Product Shop (Weise Pharmacy) has homeopathic products, a juice bar and tofu sandwiches. Check 'em out!

GOOD EARTH MARKET
10950 San Jose Boulevard, 32223 • (904)260-9547
M-Sat. 9-7, Sun. 12-5

 From I-295, take San Jose Blvd. exit. Store's 1 block south of I-295, across from small business squasher, the superstore known as Walmart.

HEALTH SOURCE
1011 San Jose Boulevard, 32257 • (904)268-9100
No Produce.
M-F 10-7, Sat. 10-5, Juice Bar: M-F 11-3

   From I-295, get off on San Jose Blvd. and head north. Store's on right.

SOUTHERN NUTRITION CENTER
4345 University Boulevard South, 32216 • (904)737-3312
M-Sat 9-6

 From I-95 north: Take University Blvd./Bowden Rd. exit. Go right onto Bowden and take next left at first stop light onto Spring Park. Take a right at next light (University Blvd.). Store's in a U shaped, pink shopping center 4 blocks down on right (the parking lot follows a Citgo gas station). From I-95 south: Take University Blvd. east exit. Store's 4 blocks down on right.

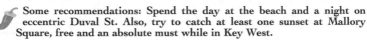

KEY WEST

Some recommendations: Spend the day at the beach and a night on eccentric Duval St. Also, try to catch at least one sunset at Mallory Square, free and an absolute must while in Key West.

Here's a neat comment we heard about Key West. "There's no up-town or down-town in Key West, no dress codes even for the finest of restaurants. Tolerance is the rule and differences are to be celebrated. Daily life in Key West includes a certain off-beat sense of celebration. Each day's setting sun is celebrated and sometimes even applauded at Mallory Square, while artisans, musicians, and street performers pack the city pier with visitors as the famed and often glorious Key West sunsets shimmer over the Gulf of Mexico." Wow.

NATURAL FOOD MARKET
600 Front Street Building A, 33040 • (305)296-3800
M-Sat. 9-9, Sun. 11-8

   Take US 1 down to Duval St. Make a right on Duval and go to end. Make a right onto Front St. then a right again onto Simonton. Store's on left.

LARGO

PIONEER NATURAL FOODS
12788 Indian Rocks Road, 34644 • (813)596-6600
Owner says they have, "the best hummus on the East Coast."
M-F 9-7, Sat. 9-6, Sun. 12-5

 From US 19, take Rte. 688 west. Turn north on Indian Rocks Rd. and drive 1/2 mile. Store's on west side in King's Row Plaza.

MELBOURNE

COMMUNITY HARVEST MARKET AND CAFE
1405 Highland Avenue, 32935 • (407)254-4966
M-F 9-8, Sat. 9-6

From I-95, take exit 72 and drive east 4 miles. Go across US 1 to first traffic light and make a left onto Highland. Store's on east side of street.

NATUREWORKS
461 N. Harbor City Boulevard, 32935 • (407)242-0772
Store may be moving 5/98. Call for new directions.
M-Sat. 9-8, Sun. 10-5

From I-95, take exit 72 and travel east to US 1. Go right on US 1 and travel south (2 traffic lights). Store's on left at corner of Ballard & US 1 (US 1 is N. Harbor City Blvd.)

MIAMI

Traveler and Florida resident, Candace, has recommendations for the Miami area. Check out the Alliance Theater (an excellent film co-op), the Turkish baths on Collins Avenue & 40th (on the beach) and Haulover Park in North Miami Beach for low-key sunbathing in your birthday suit.

The Abbey on Miami Beach brews its own beer and according to Candace, is quite atypical of the "clubish Miami Beach scene." "It's mellow with very small crowds (even on a weekend), plus they have delicious homemade beers and a dart board," she says.

The Thai Orchid has locations in Coral Gables and Kendall (south). They feature a macrobiotic menu and will adjust any dish to a vegan taste. (Incidentally, they brew their own beer with all organic ingredients). Also, there's usually a full moon drum circle on Miami Beach at 26th and Ocean. See south Miami and South Miami Beach for more stores and info.

HALE'S HEALTH FOODS
109 W. Plaza Northside Shopping Center, 33147 • (305)696-2115
M-Sat. 10-6

From I-95, get off on 79th St. Head west to 27th Ave. Store's on north side of street at west side of W. Plaza Northside Shopping Center.

MIAMI LAKES

HALE'S HEALTH FOODS
16427 NW 67th Avenue, 33014 • (305)821-5331
Organic carrots only.
M-F 9:30-6:30, Sat. 10-6

From Palmetto Expressway (826), exit at NW 67th Ave. and head south on 67th for two blocks. Store's on east side of street.

NAPLES

In the mood for a road trip through the Everglades? Alligator Alley, a.k.a. I-75, links Naples on Florida's western edge and Ft. Lauderdale on its eastern coast. Much of the road is fenced, but plenty of alligators resting in the swamp can be spotted.

"Look in the ditches to see eyeballs and backs floating in the Everglade swamp," suggests one traveler.

SUNSPLASH MARKET
850 Neapolitan Way, 33940 • (941)434-7221
M-Sat. 9-8, Sun. 10-6

From I-75, head west off Pine Ridge Rd. exit. Go south for one block on US 41 and turn right on Neapolitan Way. Store's on left in Neapolitan Way Shopping Center.

NEW SMYRNA BEACH

HEATH'S NATURAL FOODS
1323 Saxon Drive, 32169 • (904)423-5126
M-Sat. 9:30-6

From I-95, take Rte. 44 east for 10 miles into New Smyrna Beach. Store's on beach side, 2 blocks from the ocean.

NORTH MIAMI

Check out Sara's Natural Food Restaurant & Pizza on 163rd Street (there's also one in North Miami Beach).

ABUNDANT ENERGY SOURCES, INC.
14248 NW 7th Avenue, 33168 • (305)685-0517
No produce.
M-F 9:30-5:30, F 9:30-6, Sat. 10-5

From I-95, take 441 exit (#18). Follow signs to 441 south (NW 7th) and head south. Store's at corner of 143rd & 7th Ave., on right in Santa Fe Shopping Center.

MAN'S HEALTH IS GOD'S WEALTH
13160 Biscayne Boulevard, 33181 • (305)899-9927
M-Sat. 9-9, Sun. 11-6

Take 135th St. east to US 1 (which is Biscayne Blvd.) Go south on US 1. Store's 3-4 blocks down on west side in Arch Creek Mall.

OCALA

MOTHER EARTH MARKET
1917 E. Silver Springs Boulevard, 34470 • (352)351-5224
Store has a sushi bar.
M-Sat. 9-9, Sun 11-6

From I-75, get on State Rd. 40 (also Silver Springs Blvd.) and go east. Store's about 10 miles down in the Ocala Center on left.

ORANGE PARK

THE GRANARY WHOLE FOODS, INC.
1738 Kingsley Avenue, 32073 • (904)269-7222
M-Sat. 9-6

From I-295, take US 17 exit and travel south for two miles then take a right on Kingsley. Stay in left lane after railroad tracks and store's 2 miles down on left.

ORLANDO

Check out World of Orchids, 2,000 rare and exotic orchids from around the globe. Passage to India on International Drive and Bombay Bistro (downtown) have great Indian cuisine.

Recommendations from Chamberlin's staffers: Looking for a nice deli & cafe? Check out the Nature's Table or visit downtown Orlando for low-key coffee shops and stores. Hiking is limited in Orlando, but there are several parks nearby. Try Turkey Lake State Park on Turkey Lake Road for a little peace of mind.

CHAMBERLIN'S MARKET AND CAFE

7600 Dr. Phillips Boulevard, 32819 • (407)352-2130
M-Sat. 9-8:30, Sun. 11-5:30

From I-4, take exit 29. Go west to Dr. Phillips Blvd. Take a right onto Dr. Phillips Blvd., then go left into Marketplace Center.

CHAMBERLIN'S MARKET AND CAFE

4960 East Colonial Drive, 32803 • (407)894-8452
M-Sat. 9-8:30, Sun. 11-5:30

From I-4, get on Hwy. 50 east to Herndon Village. Store's on right about 3 miles down.

ORMAND BEACH

HARVEST HOUSE NATURAL FOODS

124 S. Nova Road, 32174 • (904)677-7723
M-F 9-7, Sat. 9-6, Sun. 12-5

From I-95, take exit 88 (Rte. 40/Granada Rd) and head east toward beach. Go through a few traffic lights and make a right onto Nova Rd. at the corner of Granada and Nova Rd. Make a right into parking lot of the L shaped Plaza and you can't miss it.

PALM BEACH

SUNRISE HEALTH FOOD STORE

233 Royal Ponnisiana Way, 33480 • (561)655-3557
They've been there for 25 years!
M-F 8:30-6, Sat. 8:30-5

From Breakers Hotel in Palm Beach, make a left onto Royal Ponnisiana Way (one stoplight north of hotel). Store's on right on north side of street.

PALM HARBOR

PALM HARBOR NATURAL FOODS INC.

30657 US 19 North, 34684 • (813)786-1231
M-Sat. 9-7, Sun. 11:30-5

Store's at intersection of US 19 and Curlew in Seabreeze Shopping Center.

PENSACOLA

 Check out museums and turn-of-the-century architecture in historic Pensacola Village. The Pensacola Museum of Art and Quayside, is a large cooperative art gallery that features local and regional artists. Ever'man Natural Foods Co-op folks recommend Pensacola Beach, Fort Pickens National Park and Big Lagoon State Recreation Area for camping.

EVER'MAN NATURAL FOODS CO-OP
1200 North 9th Avenue, 32501 • (904)438-0402
M 8:30-8, Tu.-Sat. 8:30-6:30

 From I-10, take I-110 south. Turn left off Cervantes exit and left on 9th. Store's on right.

PLANTATION

 Plantation is 20 miles west of Ft. Lauderdale. Continue west on I-75 towards Naples and check out Alligator Alley.

BREAD OF LIFE NATURAL FOOD MARKET & DELI
7720 Peters Road, 33324 • (954)236-0600
Sun.-Sun. 8-10

From I-95, look for 595 exit. Take 595 west to University Dr. and head north. About 1 mile down is intersection of Peters Rd. and University. Store's on left corner.

PORT ORANGE

HARVEST HOUSE NATURAL FOODS
4076 S. Ridgewood Avenue, 32127 • (904)756-3800
M-F 9-7, Sat. 9-6, Sun. 12-5

 From US 1, get onto Dunlawton. Store's at corner of Dunlawton and S. Ridgewood in Port Orange Plaza.

SARASOTA

 Monica, a staffer at the Granary, recommends a few vegetarian restaurants: WildFlower, Mim's and La Saison, a French vegetarian restaurant! Also check out Myakka River State Park for birding and hiking.

THE GRANARY (NORTH)
8421 North Tamiami Trail, 34243 • (941)351-4671
M-Sat. 9-8, Sun. 10-6

 From I-75, take exit #40 and head west on University Parkway. Turn right on Tamiami Trail (US 41). Store's on right.

THE GRANARY (SOUTH)
1930 Stickney Point Road, 34231 • (941)924-4754
M-Sat. 8:30-9, Sun. 10-8

From I-75, take Clark Rd. exit (#37) west. (Clark becomes Stickney after US 41). Store's at corner on left.

ST. AUGUSTINE

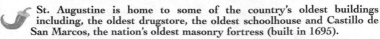

St. Augustine is home to some of the country's oldest buildings including, the oldest drugstore, the oldest schoolhouse and Castillo de San Marcos, the nation's oldest masonry fortress (built in 1695).

For great food, Amy at Diane's Natural Food Market recommends The Manatee Cafe, and the Gypsy Cab Company. "They'll substitute tofu for anything!" she says. Amy also recommends Washington Oaks State Park for hiking and general beach fun.

DIANE'S NATURAL FOOD MARKET

2085 State Road # 3, 32084 • (904)471-3796

Occasional local organic produce, though otherwise highly recommended by regional expert, Steve!

M-Sat. 9:30-6, Sun. 12-5

 From US 1, turn east on Rte. 312, right on State Rd. 3 and right into Portman Plaza.

NEW DAWN

110 Anastasia Boulevard, 32084 • (904)824-1337

M-Sat. 9-5:30, Lunch Bar: M-Sat. 10-3

 From US 1, get onto State Rd. 312. Head east over 312 bridge. Turn left at traffic light (after bridge) onto SR3/Anastasia Blvd. Drive 3 miles and store's on right.

ST. PETERSBURG

Close to Clearwater and Tampa Bay, St. Petersburg has a myriad of attractions. Check out Great Explorations Hands-on Museum for children, the Salvador Dali Museum and the Museum of Science and Industry's small planetarium. There's also The N.K. Cafe on W. Kennedy — they serve natural food and the staff is great!

NATURE'S FINEST FOODS

6651 Central Avenue, 33710 • (813)347-5682

M-Sat. 9-9

From I-275, take exit 11 and go through light. Go 5 blocks on 20th St. and then drive west on Central. Store's 40 blocks down on right.

SOUTH MIAMI

BEEHIVE NATURAL FOODS

5750 Bird Road, 33155 • (305)666-3360

M-Sat. 9-6

From I-95, get onto US 1 and drive to Bird Rd. (which is SW 40th St.). Go west on Bird Rd. for 2.5 miles and store will be on left.

NATURAL FOOD MARKET (KENDALL LOCATION)
9455 South Dixie Highway, 33156 • (305)666-3514
"More organic produce than anyone in the southeast!" Better check it out.
M-Sat. 9-9, Sun. 11-8

 Take Palmetto Expressway (826)
south to Kendall East exit. Stay on
Kendall for 1/2 mile. Turn right onto South Dixie Hwy. Store's in Sadeland Plaza on left.

SOUTH MIAMI BEACH (SOUTH BEACH)

APPLE-A-DAY NATURAL FOOD MARKET
1534 Alton Road, 33139 • (305)538-4569
M-Sat. 9-10, Sun. 9-9

 From I-95 north: Exit at Alton Rd. south. Drive to
15th Terrace and make a right. Store's in a shopping
plaza on left at corner of Alton and 15th Terrace. From I-95 south: Exit onto 395. Take
Alton Rd. north. Turn left on 15th Terrace and store's on left. Store has free parking!

NATURAL FOOD MARKET
1011 5th Street, 33139 • (305)535-9050
M-Sat. 9-10, Sun. 11-9

Take I-95 to 395 (turns into the Causeway). This brings you to Miami Beach-5th St.
Store's on left at corner of Michigan & 5th.

TALLAHASSEE

The **Black Archives Research Center and Museum** (free!) features an extensive collection of African-American artifacts. Check out **The Epitome**, a highly recommended coffeehouse downtown near the FSU campus. Indian fare can be found at Samrat on Apalachee Parkway.

Wakulla Springs, a fresh water spring for swimming and fishing (45 minutes from Tallahassee) was suggested by the folks at New Leaf Market. Incidentally, Tallahassee is a Muskogee word that means "Old Town."

HONEYTREE NATURAL FOODS
1660 N. Monroe Street, 32303 • (850)681-2000
No organic produce, but a great deli menu!
M-F 9:30-7, Sat. 9:30-6

 Corner of Monroe and
Tharp in the old Kmart
Shopping Center.

NEW LEAF MARKET
1235 Apalachee Parkway, 32301 • (850)942-2557
M-Sat. 9-9, Sun. 12-6 Deli: M-Sat. 10:30-4

From I-10, take US 27 - Apalachee Parkway south (it takes a 90 degree turn in front
of the Old Capital). Store's one mile down Apalachee on east end of Parkway
Shopping Center.

TAMPA

Ybor City (a district on 7th Avenue) has bars, vegetarian restaurants and coffee shops. On weekend nights, a section of the street is blocked off and the atmosphere changes dramatically. "It's kind of like Mardi Gras every Friday and Saturday night," says Nature's Harvest Market & Deli staffer Matthew. "It's a free for all."

Also check out Bertha's Natural Cafe on W. Neptune.

ANSLEY'S NATURAL MARKETPLACE
402 East Sligh Avenue, 33604 • (813)239-2700
M-F 9-7, Sat. 9-6, Sun. 11-5

 From I-275, take exit 31 (Sligh Ave.) Store's one block west of I-275.

ANSLEY'S NATURAL MARKETPLACE
3936 W. Kennedy, 33609 • (813)879-6625
No produce.
M-F 9-7, Sat. 9-6

 From I-275, exit at Dale Mavery South. Go west on Kennedy, then take a left onto Grady. Store's on corner of Kennedy and Grady (look for Lindale Honda sign).

NATURE'S HARVEST MARKET & DELI
1021 North MacDill Avenue, 33607 • (813)873-7428
M-F 9-9, Sat. 9-7, Sun. 11-6

 From I-275, take Howard/Armenia exit. Take Armenia south, turn right on Cypress and right on MacDill. Store's on right.

TEQUESTA

MORNING SUN HEALTH FOODS
120 Bridge Road, 33469 • (561)747-0037
M-F 9-6, Sat. 9-5 Deli: M-Sat. 11-3

 From US 1 north: Turn west on Bridge Rd. (Bridge Rd. is one block south of Tequesta Drive). Make a U-turn across US 1, then find the store on left. From US 1 south: Take a left onto alternate A1A, a right onto Old Dixie Hwy., then another right on Bridge Rd. Store's on right.

WEST PALM BEACH

WILD OATS MARKET
7735 S. Dixie Highway, 33405 • (561)585-8800
Sun.-Sun. 8-8, (Closes at 6 on Sun.)

From I-95, get off at exit 45 - Forest Hill Blvd. and drive east toward US 1. Go south on US 1 for 1 mile and store's in a shopping center on right.

CHAMBERLIN'S MARKET & CAFE

430 North Orlando Avenue, 32789 • (407)647-6661
M-Sat. 8-9:30, Sun. 10-7 Cafe: M-Sat. 8-8:30, Sun. 10-6

From I-4, take exit 46 (Lee Rd.) and drive east. Turn right on Orlando Ave. and go through light. Turn left into Winter Park Mall and find the store.

Organic Fact № 5

HELP SMALL FARMERS, KEEP RURAL COMMUNITIES HEALTHY

The USDA predicts that by the year 2000, half of U.S. farm production will come from only 1% of farms. Organic farming may be one of the few survival tactics left for the family farm and rural communities. Most organic farms are independently owned and operated family farms of less than 100 acres.

Georgia

1. ATHENS
2. ATLANTA
3. AUGUSTA
4. BRUNSWICK
5. HINESVILLE
6. MARIETTA
7. SAVANNAH
8. VALDOSTA

ATHENS

Check out Broad Street, the main strip in Athens for cafes, restaurants and bookstores. Recommended restaurants: The Grit on Prince, Guaranteed on Broad, The Grill on College Avenue (a 24 hour "diner" that serves faux meat selections and other vegetarian fare) and the Bluebird Cafe for great breakfasts. For music, check out the Manhattan and the 40 Watt Club.

DAILY GROCERIES FOOD CO-OP
523 Prince Avenue, 30601 • (706)548-1732
They honor other co-op memberships with a 5% discount. In Athens for a few days? Pick up a shift or two and get a full worker's discount.
M-Sat. 10-9, Sun. 12-9

 From I-85, exit at Commerce and 441 south. Take 441 South to loop that goes around Athens. Go south/west on Route 10. Get off at Chase St. exit. Turn left onto Prince. Store's a half mile down on right.

PHOENIX NATURAL FOOD MARKET
296 West Broad Street, 30601 • (706)548-1780
M-Sat. 9:30-6

 From the loop, take Downtown Athens exit. From north, turn right. From south, turn left. This will be Broad St. Store's about a mile down, across the street from University of Georgia campus on corner of Broad and Pulaski.

ZUCCHINI'S
1055 Gaines School Road, 30605 • (706)353-8066
M-Sat. 9-9, Sun. 12-9

 From I-78, get off at Gaines School Rd. Turn right onto Gaines School. Store's 1.5 miles ahead on left.

ATLANTA

The Little Five Points area is a hip, funky, diverse section of Atlanta which is full of cool restaurants, shops and used bookstores. But Little Five Points' claim to fame are the tattoo and body piercing shops where you can get anything pierced. "We are kind of behind the times here," says a Sevananda staffer. "We're still into those things like tattoos and piercing that other cities like Miami and New York got over in the 80's."

Recommended food stops: Cafe Sunflower, Brookhaven Cafe. Soul Vegetarian on Abernathy Blvd. serves African fare.

RAINBOW NATURAL FOODS GROCERY & RESTAURANT
2118 North Decatur Road NE, 30033 • (404)636-5553
People love this store as much as Sevananda. Less patchouli though.
M-Sat. 10-8, Sun. 11-5

 From downtown Atlanta, take I-85 north to Clairmont Rd. exit. Go right and drive 4.5 miles to North Decatur Rd. Store's on left at corner of Clairmont and North Decatur in North Decatur Plaza.

RETURN TO EDEN
2335 Cheshire Bridge Road, 30324 • (404)320-3336
This large vegetarian supermarket sells organic produce only! Check out In the Shade Cafe, the vegetarian restaurant next door owned by the same folks.
M-Sat. 10-8, Sun. 10-6

 From I-85 north: Take exit 30, go left and drive underneath the interstate. Store's 2 blocks down on left. From I-85 south: Take exit 28 (Buford Hwy.). Follow signs for Lenox/Cheshire Bridge Rd. and take a right on Lenox (changes to Cheshire Bridge Rd.). Store's 2 blocks down on left. (Additional locating tips: Return to Eden is situated in mid-town Atlanta near Emory University).

SEVANANDA
1111 Euclid Avenue, 30307 • (404)681-2831
The Southeast's largest and oldest natural foods cooperative, Sevananda is a Sanskrit word which loosely translated means, 'Service is bliss.' Located in the heart of the 5 Point South area, this wonderful store offers prepared vegan food from their cooler.
M-Sat. 9-9, Sun. 11-9

 From north: Take I-75 or I-85 south and exit at North Ave. Turn left on North Ave., go 2 miles and turn right on Moreland, then right on Euclid. Store's on left. From south: Take I-20, exit at Moreland Ave. north and go left on Euclid. Store's on left.

UNITY NATURAL FOODS
2955 Peachtree Road North, 30305 • (404)261-8776
M-Sat. 10-7, Sun. 12-6

 From I-85 north: Take Georgia 400 north and get off at Lenox/Piedmont Rd. exit. Go left at light onto Piedmont Rd. (it will dead end). Go right on Peachtree. Store's on left 2 blocks down (cross street is Pharr Rd.). From I-85 south: Take Lenox Rd/Cheshire Bridge exit. Find Piedmont or Peachtree. Look for Pharr/Peach Rd. and go south. Follow above directions.

AUGUSTA

FOODS FOR BETTER LIVING
2606 McDowell Street, 30904 • (706)738-3215
No organic produce.
M-F 9-6 (Th. to 5:30), Sat. 10-5

 From I-20, take Bobby Jones Expressway (520) and turn left on Wrightsboro Rd. Go left on Highland Ave. and right on McDowell. Store's on right.

BRUNSWICK

HAPPY DAYS
1514 Newcastle Street, 31520 • (912)265-1595
No produce.
M-F 10-6, Sat. 10-5

 Directly off of I-95, take 7A or 7B to Brunswick. Go straight to downtown, store's 5 miles from the interstate between the first two traffic lights.

HINESVILLE

FARMER'S NATURAL FOODS
754 E.G. Miles Parkway, 31313 • (912)368-7803
Carrots only.
M-F 9-7, Sat. 9-6

 From I-95, take Midway/Hinesville/Fort Stewart exit. Head toward Hinesville. Take a right at General Scrivin (fourth light), and a left at second light. Store's one mile down on left.

MARIETTA

 Dana Bazar in the East Marietta Shopping Center (right down from Life Grocery) has a vegetarian deli.

LIFE GROCERY
1453 Roswell Road, 30062 • (770)977-9583
Organic produce only!
M-Sat. 9-8, Sun. 11-6

 From I-75, take exit 112 and turn right onto the 120 loop. Go through two intersections, then exit right to Hwy. 120 (Roswell Rd.). Go left at light onto Roswell Rd. and drive one mile. Store's in Baby Super Store Plaza on right.

SAVANNAH

 Andy at Brighter Day Natural Foods makes the following Savannah recommendations. Check out North Beach Grill, an excellent restaurant that serves Low Country-Jamaican cuisine. For a nice place to relax, go to Tybee island (no golf courses!) Also, check out Savannah's historic district, one of the oldest in country.

"It's a beautiful town, but Savannah is not too vegetarian friendly," says Andy. "Brighter Day is a bastion in the middle of an island of meat consumption and fried foods."

BRIGHTER DAY NATURAL FOODS
1102 Bull Street, 31401 • (912)236-4703
M-Sat. 10-6, Sun. 12:30-5:30

From I-95, take the 1-16 exit, then turn right off Gwinett exit. Go right on Whitaker St. and left on Park Ave. Store's on right (Look for a mural with organic tomatoes wearing sunglasses!)

VALDOSTA

MA PERKINS NATURAL
2110 North Ashley Street, 31602 • (912)244-5440
Carrots only.
M-Sat. 9:30-6

Store's in middle of Valdosta on North Ashley (next to Checkers).

Organic Fact № 6

PROTECT FARM WORKER HEALTH

A National Cancer Institute study found that farmers exposed to herbicides had a six times greater risk than non-farmers of contracting cancer. Organic farms eliminate that risk by eliminating harmful pesticides and other chemical inputs from their practices.

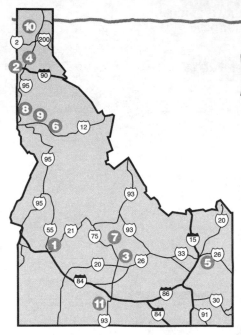

Idaho

1. BOISE
2. COEUR D'ALENE
3. HAILEY
4. HAYDEN LAKE
5. IDAHO FALLS
6. KAMIAH
7. KETCHUM
8. MOSCOW
9. OROFINIO
10. SANDPOINT
11. TWIN FALLS

BOISE

Check out Govinda's Cuisine Of India on W. Main and the ever enduring Koffee Klatsch coffeehouse (at the 8th Street Market), open since 1979.

In Boise during the Summer? Float down the Boise River on a tube... Or play at Sandy Point, a bathing area beneath the Lucky Peak Dam. Also, the wilderness north of Boise is sprinkled with enticing hot springs. Try these free ones: Deer Creek Hot Springs, Pine Flats Hot Springs, Boiling Springs and Trail Creek Hot Springs. Have fun!

BOISE CONSUMER CO-OP
888 W. Fort Street, 83702 • (208)342-6652
M-Sat. 9-9, Sun. 9-8

 From I-84 east: Take City Center exit and head downtown. Make a left onto Capital Blvd., then a right onto 8th St. Store's entrance is on 8th St. From I-84 west: Take Broadway exit, go north on Broadway and turn left onto Fort St. (near hospital). Store's a mile down on right.

COEUR D'ALENE

Check out Java on Sherman.

A TRIP TO BOUNTIFUL
1401 North 4th Street, 83814 • (208)664-4626
M-Sat. 9-5:30, Sun. 12-4

 From I-90, exit on 4th St. and head south 7 blocks. Turn left on Walnut and store is on corner.

HAILEY

ATKINSON'S
Alturas Plaza, 83333 • (208)788-2294
This mainstream supermarket carries organic produce and natural food.
Sun.-Sun. 7:30-9

From Hwy. 75, go east
on Croy St. to Alturas
Plaza.

HAYDEN LAKE

FLOUR MILL NATURAL FOODS
88 W. Commerce Drive, 83835 • (208)772-2911
They mill their own flour!
M-F 9-5:30, Sat. 10-5

From I-95, exit at Hwy. 95 and go north about 5 miles to
Hayden Lake. Take a right on Honeysuckle and a left on
Commerce. Store's 1/2 mile down on right.

IDAHO FALLS

WEALTH OF HEALTH
489 Park Avenue, 83402 • (208)523-7600
No Produce
M-F 9-6, Sat. 9-6:30

From Hwy. 15, go east on Broadway past Falls. Go left onto River Parkway
for 2 blocks. Go right on B St. Store's on right.

KAMIAH

CLEARWATER VALLEY NATURAL FOOD
501 4th Street, 83536 • (208)935-0695
M-F 10-5:30, Sat. 10-2

Turn off of Hwy. 12 onto Main St. Go 1 block and turn left onto 4th
St. Store's in first block on right.

KETCHUM

ATKINSON'S
Giacobbi Square, 83340 • (208)726-5668
This mainstream supermarket carries organic produce and natural food.
Sun.-Sun. 7:30-9
From Hwy. 75, store's one block east on 4th Ave. in Giacobbi Square.

MOSCOW

MOSCOW FOOD CO-OP
310 West Third Street, 83843 • (208)882-8537
Sun.- Sun. 8-8

 From Rte. 95, turn west on
Third St. (also Hwy. 8). Store's less than 3 blocks down on right.

OROFINIO

CLEARWATER VALLEY NATURAL FOOD
300 Michigan Avenue, 83544 • (208)476-4091
M-F 10-5:30, Sat. 10-2

 Store's in the Viesta View building on Michigan, directly across bridge and close to post office.

SANDPOINT

 Amber at Evergreen Market Co-op reports Sandpoint is a beautiful town surrounded by "wilderness forever." She suggests Lake Pend Oreille for various water activities.

EVERGREEN MARKET CO-OP
1201 Michigan Street, 83864 • (208)263-1658
M-F 10-6, Sat. 10-4

 Store's off Hwy. 200 on Michigan St. in Sandpoint (across from Dairy Depot gas station).

TWIN FALLS

THE HEALTH FOOD PLACE
657 Blue Lakes Boulevard North, 83301 • (208)733-1411
Organic produce in summer.
M-F 9:30-7:30, Sat. 10-5, Sun. 12-5

From I-84, take Sun Valley/Wells, Nevada exit (#173). Go into Twin Falls, cross Snake River and road becomes Blue Lakes Blvd. Store's on right in Centennial Square.

Organic Fact №7

PROTECT WATER QUALITY

The EPA estimates pesticides, some cancer causing, contaminate the groundwater in 38 states, polluting the primary source of drinking water for more than half the country's population.

Illinois

1. BLOOMINGTON
2. CARBONDALE
3. CHICAGO
4. DE KALB
5. EVANSTON
6. EDWARDSVILLE
7. MATTESON
8. MT. CARROLL
9. MOUNT PROSPECT
10. MT. VERNON
11. NEW LENOX
12. PALATINE
13. PEORIA
14. RIVER FOREST
15. SPRINGFIELD
16. URBANA
17. WHEATON

CH CHICAGO AREA
3, 5, 7, 9, 11, 12, 14, 17

BLOOMINGTON

COMMON GROUND GROCERY
516 North Main Street, 61701 • (309)829-2621
No produce.
M-Sat. 9:30-5:30

 From Rte. 55, turn left on Market St. (both directions). Go 2 miles and turn north on Main St. Store's on left.

CARBONDALE

 Check out Carbondale's celebrated bagel carts!

NEIGHBORHOOD CO-OP
104 E. Jackson Street, 62901 • (618)529-3533
M-F 9-7, Sat. 9-6, Sun. 11-5

   From Rte. 113 heading west, turn north on Washington St. and west onto Jackson. Store's on north side of street.

CHICAGO

When in Chicago, visit the Heartland Cafe, A Natural Harvest on S. Jeffery Blvd., Lo-Calzone on Rush St. and Andies on N. Clark. In Arlington Heights (Chicago suburb), check out the Chow Patty for cheap veggie eats.

Cafe Voltaire on North Clark serves flavorful, organic, vegetarian food alongside their basement performance theater and art gallery. The Chicago Diner on N. Halsted features 100% vegetarian dishes. Don't miss it!!!

Two suggested museums: The Museum of Holography (one ex-Chicagoan claims there are few better places to go when stoned in Chicago). Visit the Botanical Conservatory, a turn of the century steel structure that houses a rainforest.

HYDE PARK COOPERATIVE SOCIETY

1526 E. 55th Street, 60615 • (773)667-1444
Hyde Park Co-op is 65 years old! After browsing the store, check out the Museum of Science and Industry just down the street
M-Sat. 8-10, Sun. 8-9

From Lakeshore Dr., exit at 53rd St. Drive 2 blocks west to Lake Park Ave., then go 2 blocks south to 55th St. Store's 2 blocks down in Hyde Park Shopping Center at corner of Lake Park Ave. & 55th St. (on Chicago's South side).

MR. G CO-OP

1226 E. 53rd, 60615 • (773)363-2175
Sun.-Sun. 7-11

From I-94, take 55th St. exit and travel east to Woodlawn. Turn left at Woodlawn, drive 2 blocks and store's on northeast corner in Kimbark Plaza.

SHERWYN'S

645 West Diversey Parkway, 60614 • (773)477-1934
All organic produce!
M-F 9-8, Sat. 10-7, Sun. 11-7

From I-90/94 (stay off express lanes to exit in time) take California exit (46a) and head east on Diversey for 3 miles to intersection of Clark, Diversey, and Broadway. Store's on right at southwest corner of Diversey (in the Lakeview neighborhood).

WHOLE FOODS MARKET

1000 West North Avenue, 60622 • (312)587-0648
Store features a sit down restaurant upstairs.
Sun.-Sun. 8-10

From I-90/94, take North Ave. exit. Go east on North and find store on corner of North & Sheffield (turn left on Sheffield). Other locating tips: Store's north of I-290 and there's also a North Ave. exit off I-55.

WHOLE FOODS MARKET
3300 North Ashland, 60657 • (773)244-4200
Sun.-Sun. 8-10

From Lakeshore Dr., exit at Belmont (which is 3200 North). Head west for 1 mile (about 8-10 lights). Make a right onto Ashland (6 way intersection there... be careful). Store's one block from intersection on west side of street. From I-90/94 (Kennedy) exit at Addison (3600 North) and head west 2 miles. Make a right onto Ashland. Store's on west side of street, 3 blocks down.

DE KALB

DUCK SOUP CO-OP
129 East Hillcrest, 60115 • (815)756-7044
M-F 9-8, Sat.-Sun. 9-5

From I-88, take Annie Glidden exit and drive two miles north. Turn right on Hillcrest. Store's 1 mile down on left.

EVANSTON

 **Blind Faith Cafe on Dempster St. features an all-vegetarian menu with an ethnic and organic emphasis!**

J D MILLS FOOD COMPANY INC.
635 Chicago Avenue, 60204 • (847)491-0940
Bulk, bulk and more bulk! Store also carries a large variety of teas, coffees and spices.
M-F 9-8, Sat. 9-6, Sun. 11-5

From Chicago, travel north on Lakeshore Dr. and take Sheridan Blvd. into Evanston. At Chicago Ave. (becomes Chicago Ave. from Clark St.), take a right. Store will be on right.

WHOLE FOODS MARKET
1640 Chicago Avenue, 60201 • (847)733-1600
Sun.-Sun. 8-9

From I-94, take Dempster St. exit east. Drive about 8 miles, then take a left onto Chicago Ave. Store's 4 blocks down on left. Additional locating tips: Store's 3 blocks from the shore of Lake Michigan.

EDWARDSVILLE

GREEN EARTH
219 Hillsboro Street, 62025 • (618)656-3375
M-Th. 9-6:30, F 9-8, Sat 9-5

From 270, get off on 159 and head toward Glen Carbon. Go into Edwardsville and drive past the business district. Come to a stop light (Rte. 143) and turn left. Make the first right onto N. Kansas. Store's on corner of N. Kansas and Hillsboro.

MATTESON

SOUTH SUBURBAN FOOD CO-OP
21750 Main Street, 60443 • (708)747-2256
A great members-only co-op. They honor other memberships and once-thru travelers.
M & Tu. 11-8, Th. 2-8, F 11-8, Sat. 9:30-3:30

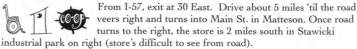

From I-57, exit at 30 East. Drive about 5 miles 'til the road veers right and turns into Main St. in Matteson. Once road turns to the right, the store is 2 miles south in Stawicki industrial park on right (store's difficult to see from road).

MT. CARROLL

STRADDLE CREEK FOOD CO-OP
112 West Market Street, 61053 • (815)244-2667
No produce.
Th. & F 12-4, Sat. 10-4

From I-80, take Rte. 88 to 78 north. Stay on through Mt. Carroll, then go west on Market St. Drive 2-3 blocks and store's on left.

MOUNT PROSPECT

SWEETGRASS VITAMIN & HEALTH MARKET
1742 West Gold Road, 60056 • (847)956-1939
Limited organic produce.
M-F 9-9, Sat. 9-6, Sun. 10-5:30

From Kennedy Expressway, get onto Northwest Tollway and head west out of Chicago. Exit at Elmhurst Rd. and go north to Gold Rd. Go left on Golf. Store's on northwest corner of Golf and Busse.

MT. VERNON

NATURE'S WAY FOOD CENTER
102 South 4th Street, 62864 • (618)244-2327
No organic produce.
M-F 9:30-5, Sat. 9:30-1

From Hwy. 15, drive east and turn north onto Fourth St. Store's on right.

NEW LENOX

NATURAL CHOICES HEALTH FOOD STORE
1340 North Cedar Road, 60451 • (815)485-5572
M-F 10-6, Sat. 10-4

From I-80, take Maple St. - Rte. 30 exit. Drive east on Rte. 30 and turn left (north) at third light onto Cedar Rd. Store's 1 mile down on right in a beige building.

PALATINE

WHOLE FOODS MARKET
1331 North Rand Road, 60067 • (847)776-8080
Store has a stir fry bar!
M-Sat. 8-9, Sun. 8-8

From I-53, take Rand exit west and turn right into Park Place Shopping Center.

PEORIA

 Check out One World Coffee on University.

NATURALLY YOURS GROCERY
4700 N. University Street, 61614 • (309)692-4448
M-Sat. 10-9

 From I-474, take University exit north. Store's 2 miles north on right in Metro Shopping Center.

RIVER FOREST

WHOLE FOODS MARKET
7245 Lake Street, 60305 • (708)366-1045
Sun.-Th. 8-9, F & Sat. 8-10

From I-290, take Harlem exit north. Go 2 miles to intersection of Harlem and Lake. Store's at intersection in River Forest Town Center. (River Forest is a suburb of Chicago next to Oak Park).

SPRINGFIELD

FOOD FANTASIES
1512 West Wabash, 62704 • (217)793-8009
M-F 9-8, Sat. 9-6, Sun. 12-4

 From I-55, take South Grand exit west (goes west only). Turn left on MacArthur (curves into Wabash). Store's on left.

URBANA

 Nearby in Champaign, check out The Fiesta Cafe on S. First Street (Mexican). Also, The Red Herring on the University Of Illinois Campus serves wonderful food (open during spring and fall semesters only).

JERRY'S IGA
2010 South Philo Road, 61801 • (217)367-1166.
Jerry's is a mainstream supermarket with health food store inside.
Organic carrots only.
Sun.-Sun. 24 hrs

 From I-74, take Cunningham exit south. (Cunningham becomes Vine). Turn left on Florida and right on Philo. Store's on left in Southgate Shopping Center.

STRAWBERRY FIELDS

306 W. Springfield Avenue, 61801 • (217)328-1655
Cafe opens at 7:30
M-Sat. 8-8, Sun. 10-6

From I-74, exit at Lincoln Ave. South. Drive to Springfield Ave. and turn left. Store's less than 1 mile on left in Old Main Square shopping Plaza. (One block west of Race St.)

WHEATON

WHOLE FOODS MARKET

151 Rice Lake Square (Butterfield Road), 60187 • (630)588-1500
Sun.-Sun. 8-10

From I-88, take Naperville Rd. and exit north. At end of ramp, turn left and head north to Butterfield Rd. (Rte. 56). Turn right on Butterfield and drive east 1.5 blocks. Store's on left (north) side of street, next to Borders Bookstore.

Organic Fact №8

ORGANIC PURCHASING PERCENTAGES

According to a 1995 Food Marketing Institute's report, The Food Marketing Industry Speaks:

Percentage of mainstream stores carrying organic produce: 42%

Percentage of shoppers who buy natural or organic foods at least once a week from supermarkets: 25%

Percentage of senior management who believe that organic and natural foods are an upcoming trend: 75%

Indiana

1. ANDERSON
2. BERNE
3. BLOOMINGTON
4. FORT WAYNE
5. GOSHEN
6. GREENFIELD
7. INDIANAPOLIS
8. KOKOMO
9. MISHAWAKA
10. RICHMOND
11. WEST LAFAYETTE

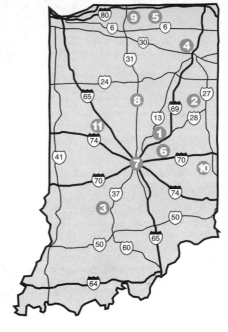

ANDERSON

FRIST HEALTH FOOD CENTER, INC.
1203 East 53rd Street, 46013 • (765)642-8992
Carrots only.
M-Th. 9-6, F 9-5 (Th. open til' 7), Sun. 1-5

 From 109, make a left onto 53rd. Store's a half mile down on left.

BERNE

EARTHEN TREASURES NATURAL FOOD MARKET
906 North US 27, 46711 • (219)589-3675
Body work, massage and reflexology available.
M-F 9-8, Sat. 9-6

 From I-69, take State Rd. 218 exit. Follow into Berne to North US 27 (turn left at the stoplight). Travel 1 mile and store will be on west side of street.

BLOOMINGTON

 Bloomingfood staffers recommend walking through Indiana University's wooded campus. Also, Lakeman Row is close by for hiking.

Check out the Encore Cafe and the Laughing Planet Cafe, both serve vegetarian fare. Norbu Cafe on E. 4th Street serves spicy Tibetan food.

BLOOMINGFOODS
3220 East Third, 47401 • (812)336-5400
Bloomingfoods has two stores. Third Street is bigger, Kirkwood is a bit groovier. Deli uses non-disposable dishware!
Sun.-Sun. 8-10

Off Hwy. 37, take 46 Bypass. Go left on Third St. Store's on right.

BLOOMINGFOODS
419 East Kirkwood Avenue, 47408 • (812)336-5300
Less seating, less parking (store's downtown) and it's on a 2nd floor (no wheelchair access).
M-Sat. 8-8, Sun. 9-7

Off Hwy. 37, take 46 Bypass. Turn right on College Ave., then left on Kirkwood Ave. Store's down an alley on left.

FORT WAYNE

THE HEALTH FOOD SHOPPE OF FORT WAYNE
3515 North Anthony Boulevard, 46805 • (219)483-5211
M-Sat. 9-7

From I-69, take Coldwater Rd. exit south to 930. Turn left onto 930 to Anthony Blvd. (at Indiana Perdue University). Store will be 1.5 blocks down on right.

THREE RIVERS CO-OP NATURAL FOODS & DELI
1126 Broadway, 46802 • (219)424-8812
M-F 9-8, Sat. 9-6, Sun. 12-6

From I-69, take US 24 (becomes Jefferson Blvd.) east into Fort Wayne. Turn right on Broadway and store's on right (7 blocks west of downtown).

GOSHEN

CENTRE-IN CO-OP
314 South Main Street, 46526 • (219)534-2355
M-F 9:30-6:30, Sat. 9:30-5:30

From the I-20 Bypass traveling south/east, exit on US 33 - Goshen. Continue on 33 south to downtown Goshen. Store's on east side of street.

GREENFIELD

THE GOOD THINGS NATURALLY

610 W. Main Street, 46140 • (317)462-2004

No produce.

M-F 10-6, Sat. 10-5

 From I-70, take Greenfield exit (Hwy. 9 south). Turn right on Hwy. 40 (Main St.) and store's on right, 6 blocks from downtown.

INDIANAPOLIS

Check out the Broad Ripple area, a mid-western oasis of music and international restaurants. "Broad ripple is wonderful. It's very ethnic and has lots of sidewalk cafes," says one Good Earth staffer.

Suggested stops: Alice's Greenhouse, Essential Edibles and Cafe Patachou serve vegetarian fare, the Bangkok Restaurant serves Thai, Queen Of Sheba on Indiana Ave. has Ethiopian cuisine and Oriental Health Cuisine on E. 86th Street features Chinese-Japanese fare.

GEORGETOWN MARKET

4375 Georgetown Road, 46254 • (317)293-9525

They've been in business for over 20 years!

M-Sat. 9-8, Sun. 9-5

From I-465, take 38th St. exit and head east. At Lafayette Rd., turn north and go past the mall. Turn right at Georgetown Rd. Store's on right next to an auto part store.

GOOD EARTH NATURAL FOOD STORE

6350 North Guilford Avenue, 46220 • (317)253-3709

This beautiful store can be found in a historic house in the Broad Ripple area. Voted #1 health food store in Central Indiana. Visit the park nearby.

M-Sat. 9-7, Sun. 12-5

 From north side of I-465 loop, go south on US 31 about 3 miles. Turn left on 71st St., right on College Ave., then left on 64th St. Make the third right onto Guilford and store's halfway down on right.

VINTAGE WHOLE FOODS

7391 North Shadeland Avenue, 46250 • (317)842-1032

Large produce section.

M & W F 9-7, Tu. & Th. 9-8, Sat. 9-6, Sun. 12-5:30

 From I-465 south: Take Shadeland Ave. exit north. Store's three stoplights down in Shadeland Station Shopping Center on right. From north: Take Rte. 37 south. Go east on 75th. Store's on left.

KOKOMO

SUNSPOT NATURAL FOODS

314 E. Markland Avenue, 46901 • (765)459-4717

M-Sat. 10-6

 Traveling north on 41, turn west onto Markland Ave. (also Hwy. 22/35). Store's 4 stoplights down on north side of street behind Jack's Pizza (look for dark green awning).

MISHAWAKA

GARDEN PATCH MARKET
228 West Edison Road, 46545 • (219)255-3151
Organic apples and carrots only.
M-Sat. 10-7

From I-80/90 (Indiana Toll Road), take Mishawaka exit. Go west on Rte. 23 to Main St. and go south (left). Turn right on Edison and store's on right.

RICHMOND

CLEAR CREEK FOOD COOP
Box E290, Earlham College, 47374 • (765)983-1547
Earlham is a renowned progressive Quaker College. The co-op was started by students, but is now independent of the college. Deli open during school year.
M-F 11-6, Sat. 11-5, Sun. 11-4

From I-70: Take Williamsburg Pike south (toward Earlham College). Turn right on Hwy. 40, then left on College Ave. Turn right at "Earlham College D St." entrance, and turn left at end. Store's in Physical Plant building with maintenance and security. (Technically, the address is 701 W. National Rd.)

WEST LAFAYETTE

SAS HEALTH FOODS
951 Sagamore Parkway West, 47906 • (765)463-4827
No produce.
M-Sat. 10-7

From I-65, take exit 25 toward Lafayette. Turn right on US 52. Store's one mile down in Osco Shopping Plaza on left.

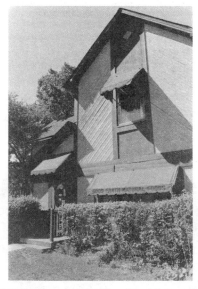

Good Earth Natural Foods, Indianapolis, Indiana

Iowa

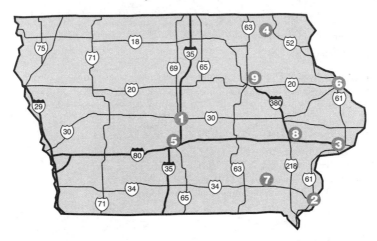

1. AMES
2. BURLINGTON
3. DAVENPORT
4. DECORAH
5. DES MOINES
6. DUBUQUE
7. FAIRFIELD
8. IOWA CITY
9. WATERLOO

AMES

Check out the Ledges State Park for camping and hiking. Staff at the Wheatsfield Grocery Cooperative suggest the blues bar, the Maintenance Shop, ("You'll never see acts that good in a room that small for a ticket price that cheap," they say.)

Recommended stops: Panchero's Mexican Grill on Welch Ave., Cafe Beaudelaire on Lincoln serves Brazilian fare and Lucullan's on Main Street features Italian with a multitude of vegetarian options.

WHEATSFIELD GROCERY COOPERATIVE

413 Douglas Avenue North, 50010 • (515)232-4094
M-Sat. 9-9

From Rte. 35, take 13th St. exit and drive west about 3 miles. Turn left on Duff, right on 6th and left on Douglas. Store's on right.

BURLINGTON

Folks at Nature's Corner recommend checking out the ultra twisty street, Snake Alley, 2 blocks from the store.

NATURE'S CORNER

423 Jefferson Street, 52601 • (319)754-8653
Carrots only.
M-F 9:30-5:30, Sat. 9:30-5

From Hwy. 34, take downtown exit by bridge. Go south on Main for three blocks, then make a right on Jefferson. Store's at bottom of hill on southeast corner of 5th & Jefferson.

DAVENPORT

GREATEST GRAINS
1600 Harrison Street, 52803 • (319)323-7521
M-F 9-8, Sat. 9-6, Sun. 12-5

From I-74, take the Middle Rd. exit. Drive west into Davenport (road turns into Locust). Turn left on Harrison and store's on right corner.

DECORAH

Elizabeth at Oneota Community Food Co-op gives a review of her town.

"Decorah lies in rolling hills, bluffs and river land, unlike anything you'd expect in Iowa. People come here to camp, fish, hike, bike, canoe and are pleased to find that our little town has a coffee shop, bike shop, historic diner, a liberal arts college and tons of other interesting stuff. The highlight, in my opinion, is our thriving food co-op with 1200 member-owners! Can you believe it?"

ONEOTA COMMUNITY FOOD CO-OP
415 West Water Street, 52101 • (319)382-4666
M-Sat. 9-6 (Th. 'til 9), Sun. 12-4

From Hwy. 52 north, take Luther College turn. Follow that down College Dr. (turns into Water St.). Store's on right about 2 blocks down.

DES MOINES

Check out the Des Moines Art Center, Timbuktu on 42nd Street (great vegetarian menu) and Campbell's Nutrition Center on University Avenue has a vegetarian buffet. Also, the Raccoon River Brewing Company is said to pour a great pint of beer!

NEW CITY MARKET
4721 University Avenue, 50311 • (515)255-7380
M & F 9-6:30, Tu.-Th. 9-8, Sat. 9-6, Sun 11-5

From I-235 east: Go north three blocks on 42nd, then left on University. Store's on right. From west: Take 63rd north, right on University. Store's on left.

DUBUQUE

BREITBACH'S FARMERS' MARKET FOOD STORE
1109 Iowa Street, 52001 • (319)557-1777
M-F 10-5:30, Sat. 8-5

In the downtown area near City Hall, store's just off Hwy. 61 at intersection of 61 & 151.

FAIRFIELD

Everybody's Market staffers recommend the Noodle House (organic Thai food) in the Fairfield Square on Court Street.

EVERYBODY'S MARKET
501 N. 2nd Street, 52556 • (515)472-5199
Cafe serves breakfast, lunch and dinner (buffet).
Sun.-Sun. 8:30-9:30

Store's on 2nd Street (also Highway 1 north). Turn north on 2nd and you can't miss it.

IOWA CITY

 Try the Cottage Bakery on Linn St. (vegetarian sandwiches). Also, the Kitchen on Washington St. features a variety of pastas and accompanying sauces.

NEW PIONEER CO-OP
22 South Van Buren Street, 52240 • (319)338-9441
One of Dar & Elizabeth's favorite natural food stores!
Sun.-Sun. 8-10

 From I-80, take University of Iowa exit (#244). Drive down Dubuque St. to end. Turn left on Washington St. Store's on left.

WATERLOO

GREEN FIELDS HEALTH FOOD CENTER
2920 Falls Avenue, 50701 • (319)235-9990
No produce.
M-Sat. 9-5:30

 From I-20, go north on Green Hill Rd. Turn left on University and left on Falls Ave. Store's on left.

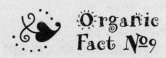

Organic Fact Nº9

KEEP WILDLIFE ALIVE AND WELL ON THE FARM

Organic agriculture respects the balance demanded of a healthy ecosystem. An organic farm is a lively place where birds, small animals and insects live in harmony with a more natural system of farming.

Kansas

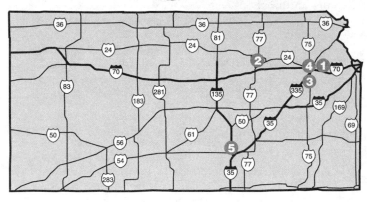

1. LAWRENCE   3. SHAWNEE   5. WICHITA
2. MANHATTAN   4. TOPEKA

LAWRENCE

"Lawrence has rolling hills and lots of trees," says Community Mercantile Co-op staffer, David. "People have conceptions about Kansas, but Lawrence is a little bit different."

Recommended stops: Try the Glass Onion Cafe and the Paradise Cafe.

THE COMMUNITY MERCANTILE CO-OP
901 Mississippi Street, 66044 • (913)843-8544

A big, wonderful co-op... probably the easiest to get to from I-70 heading west to Denver. Another of Dar's favorite stores!

Sun.-Sun. 7-10

From I-70, take East Lawrence exit. At stop sign turn left on N. 2nd St. (2nd St. becomes Vermont after you cross bridge). Turn right on 9th. Store's on left in a big yellow building on corner of 9th and Mississippi.

MANHATTAN

Kate at People's Grocery recommends visiting the Konza Prairie (off I-70). "It's a beautiful, huge prairie... a nice place to go out and hike, and you can see for miles," she says. "There are buffalo, deer and wildflowers... it's amazing."

PEOPLE'S GROCERY CO-OP
811 Colorado Street, 66502 • (913)539-4811

M-F 10-7, Sat. 9-5, Sun. 12-5

 From I-70, take Manhattan/Hwy. 177 exit about eight miles north. Hwy. 177 becomes Pierre. Turn left on Juliette and right on Colorado. Store's on left.

SHAWNEE

FOOD BIN
12268 Shawnee Mission Parkway, 66216 • (913)268-4103
M-W & F 10-7, Th. 10-8, Sat. 10-6, Sun. 12-5

 From I-35, take the Shawnee Mission Parkway exit and travel 3 miles. Stores at corner of Quivira and Shawnee.

TOPEKA

TOPEKA FOOD CO-OP
1195 Southwest Buchanan Street, 66604 • (913)235-2309
"We are the only natural and organic grocery store in Topeka."
M-F 4-7, Sat. 11-5, Sun. 12-2

 From I-70, take Topeka Ave. exit. Go south on Topeka, then west on 12th St. to Buchanan. Go 1/2 block past Buchanan and go right into an alley (follow Topeka Food Co-op signs... very easy). Store's on back side of Buchanan school.

WICHITA

 Wichita Recommendations: Javaleuah Cafe, the Blue Sky Saloon and the Watermark Bookstore, a small, independent bookseller.

FOOD FOR THOUGHT
2929 East Central Avenue, 67214 • (316)683-6078
M-F 9:30-6, Sat. 9:30-5:30

  From I-135 north: Take Central Ave. exit and head east about 11 or 12 blocks. Store's on right between
Hillside and Grove. From I-135 south: Take 1st St. exit and head east. Turn left on Grove St. and right on Central. Store's on right between Hillside and Grove.

NATURE'S MERCANTILE LTD.
2900 East Central Avenue, 67214 • (316)685-3888
M-F 9:30-6, Sat. 9:30-5:30

 From I-235, take Central Ave. exit east to Erie. Store's on corner of Erie and Central.

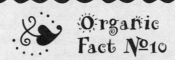

Organic Fact No10

TASTE BETTER FLAVOR

Organic tastes better! Organic farming starts with the nourishment of the soil which eventually leads to the nourishment of the plant, and ultimately, our palates

KANSAS

89

Kentucky

1. LEXINGTON
2. LOUISVILLE

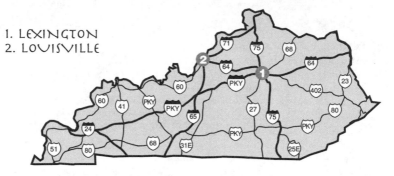

LEXINGTON

 Surrounded by rolling hills and horse farms, Lexington sits in the heart of the bluegrass. Ben at the Good Foods Co-op recommends driving 90 minutes northeast to the Red River Gorge for "some of the finest rock climbing east of the Mississippi".

Ben suggests: Lyna's Tavern - The University of Kentucky's "off campus social Mecca," Alfalfa on Limestone and go to Everybody's Health Foods Deli for vegan and vegetarian entrees, deli stuff and a juice bar.

GOOD FOODS CO-OP
439 Southland Drive, 40503 • (606)278-1813
They're about to expand.
M-Sat. 9-9, Sun. 12-7

 From I-64, take 922 south. Exit, turn right onto Nicholasville Rd. and drive toward and through town. Turn right on Southland. Store's on right.

RAINBOW BLOSSOM NATURAL FOODS
4101 Tate's Creek Center-Suite 122, 40517 • (606)273-0579
M-Sat. 9-9, Sun. 12-6

From I-64, take Man-O-War Blvd. a few miles down to Tate's Creek. Store's at intersection (on right) in Tate's Creek Center.

LOUISVILLE

 Michelle at the Fairfax Rainbow Blossom suggests the Veggie Vault on Frankfurt Ave., Twice Told coffee shop and also, Lynn's Paradise Cafe, an eclectic spot which features cool yard art (look for the purple pigs). "It has a bizarre, funky taste that makes you smile when you're around it," Michelle laughs. For Kentucky's best Bloody Mary's, Michelle recommends The Outlook Inn.

Folks at Apple Annie's suggest Louisville's new riverfront park on River Road and the Theater of the Arts.

AMAZING GRACE
1133 Bardstown Road, 40204 • (502)485-1122
Store serves chai.
M-Sat. 9-9, Sun. 11-6

 From I-64, take Grinstead Dr. exit west and go left on Bardstown Rd. Store's one block down on left.

APPLE ANNIE'S
5120 Dixie Highway, 40216 • (502)447-3353
No organic produce.
M-F 10-7, Sat. 10-6, Sun. 1-5

 From I-264, exit at Fort Knox. Go 1.5 miles and store's on right.

RAINBOW BLOSSOM NATURAL FOODS
106 Fairfax Avenue, 40207 • (502)896-0189
M-Sat. 9-9, Sun. 12-6

 From I-264, take Breckenridge Lane exit and head north. Turn right on Dayton and left on Fairfax. Store's on left.

RAINBOW BLOSSOM NATURAL FOODS
12401 Shelbyville Road, 40243 • (502)244-2022
Store is next to Great Harvest, a natural bakery.
M-Sat. 9-9, Sun. 12-6

 From I-265, take Hwy. 60 exit toward town. Store's on right.

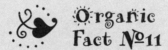

Organic Fact № 11

COOKBOOK OF THE YEAR

The winner in the "Award of Excellence" in the "Chef of the Year" category at the annual International Association for Culinary Professionals 1997 Awards Ceremony was chef Nora Pouillon, of Restaurant Nora in Washington, D.C. Her cookbook, *Cooking with Nora*, also received a nomination for cookbook of the year. Pouillon estimates approximately 95 percent of the ingredients used at Restaurant Nora are organic.

Louisiana

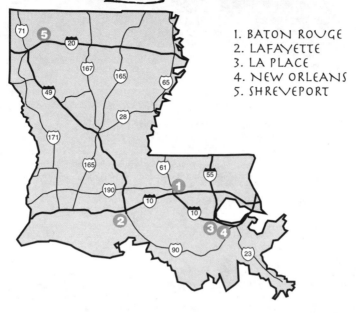

1. BATON ROUGE
2. LAFAYETTE
3. LA PLACE
4. NEW ORLEANS
5. SHREVEPORT

BATON ROUGE

 Maggie at Living Foods recommends: The Spanish Moon Cafe (all vegetarian restaurant & bar) and Tabby's Bluesbox. Also check out India's and Louisiana Pizza Kitchen (both on Essen Lane). A good bet for coffee is at the Perk's coffee houses in and around Baton Rouge.

LIVING FOODS
3033 Perkins Road, 70808 • (504)346-1886
M-Sat. 9-6, Sun. 12-6

 From I-10, take Perkins Rd. exit. Store's 2 blocks east on right.

LIVING FOODS
8875-A Highland Road, 70808 • (504)767-8222
M-Sat. 9-6:30 (Sat. closes at 6), Sun. 12-6:30

 From I-10, take Essen exit and make a right into the shopping center before Highland Rd. (Store's on right at corner of Highland and Staring).

OUR DAILY BREAD MARKET & BAKERY
9414 Florida Boulevard, 70815 • (504)924-9910
M-Sat. 8-6, Sun. 12-5

 From I-12, take Hwy. 61 (Airline Hwy.) east, away from Baton Rouge. Turn right on Florida and store's on right, 2 blocks east of Cortana Mall.

LAFAYETTE

OIL CENTER HEALTH FOODS
326 Travis, 70503 • (318)232-7774
Organic produce when available.
M-F 9:30-5:30, Sat. 9-4

 From I-49 south, continue to Hwy. 90 to Pinhook Rd. Go right onto Pinhook past three lights. Turn right on Travis. Store's two blocks down on right.

LA PLACE

NATURALLY YOURS HEALTH FOODS
421 West Airline Highway, 70068 • (504)652-2975
M-F 10-6, Sat. 10-3

 From I-10 west: Take first exit from Kenner (Hwy. 51). Take a left onto Airline Hwy. (51 ends there). Store's at intersection of Rte. 51 and Airline Hwy. in a cluster of pink buildings. From I-10 east: Take second La Place exit and turn right onto Hwy. 51. If you get lost, look for huge sign that says Health Foods.

NEW ORLEANS

New Orleans offers an eclectic, European ambiance in its streets and attractions. One traveler loved reading Anne Rice novels as she toured the city's notorious graveyards, while another dug the French Quarter's colorful restaurants and live music.

French Quarter recommendations: Siam offers excellent Thai food along with live music, the Funky Butt also has live music, and an excellent out-of-the-way bar is Vaughn's. Old Dog New Trick Cafe and Jack Sprat serve vegetarian fare and check out East African Harvest on Gentilly Blvd.

ALL NATURAL FOODS & DELI
5517 Magazine Street, 70115 • (504)891-2651
M-Th. 9-8, F 9-7, Sat. & Sun. 9-6

 From I-10, take Carrollton exit and head south/west toward river. Turn left on St. Charles Ave., right on Nashville, and left on Magazine. Store's on left.

EVE'S MARKET
7700 Cohn Street, 70118 • (504)861-1626
M-Sat. 10-7

 From I-10, take Carrollton Ave. exit south. Cross Hwy. 90 and turn left on Cohn. Store's on right.

WHOLE FOODS MARKET
3135 Esplanade, 70119 • (504)943-1626
Outside cafe seating.
Sun.-Sun. 8:30-9:30

 From I-10 west: Follow signs to New Orleans business district. Take Metairie Rd./City Park exit and turn left on City Park. Turn left on Carrollton and right on Esplanade. Store's on left. From I-10 east: Go to I-610. Take Paris Ave. exit and turn left at bottom of exit. Turn right on Gentilly Blvd. and stay in middle lane. Turn right on Ponce De Leon and store's at end of road.

SHREVEPORT

Check out **Earthereal** on Line Ave. for natural foods and baked goods.

GOOD LIFE HEALTH FOODS & DELI
6132 Hearne Avenue, 71108 • (318)635-4753
M-F 9-5, Sat. 10-5

From I-20, take Hearne Ave. exit south. Store's on right at the intersection between Hollywood and 70th (store's in a building with a cluster of other stores).

SUNSHINE
2328 Line Avenue, 71104 • (318)425-3042
M-Sat. 9-6

From I-20, take Line Ave. exit and go south. Store's 3/4 mile down on right.

Organic Fact Nº 12

PESTICIDE EXPENDITURES

In 1995, pesticide expenditures reached new highs as Americans spent $104 billion on pesticides. (The Natural Resources Defense Council & U.S. Public Interest Research Group). To compare, Americans spent $8.32 per pound on pesticides. The cost of one pound of organic coffee at a retail store in Massachusetts in 1997 is $7.99.

Maine

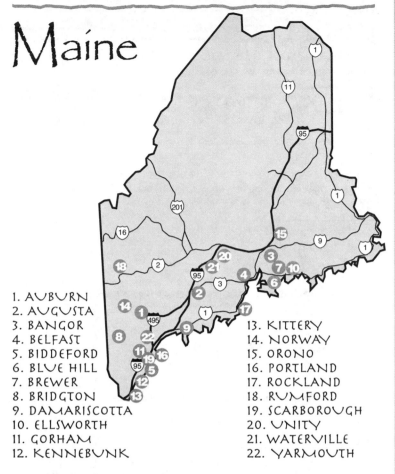

1. AUBURN
2. AUGUSTA
3. BANGOR
4. BELFAST
5. BIDDEFORD
6. BLUE HILL
7. BREWER
8. BRIDGTON
9. DAMARISCOTTA
10. ELLSWORTH
11. GORHAM
12. KENNEBUNK
13. KITTERY
14. NORWAY
15. ORONO
16. PORTLAND
17. ROCKLAND
18. RUMFORD
19. SCARBOROUGH
20. UNITY
21. WATERVILLE
22. YARMOUTH

AUBURN

AXIS NATURAL FOODS LIMITED
250 Center Street, 04210 • (207)782-3348
M-F 9:30-8, Sat. 9:30-6

From Maine Turnpike, exit at Auburn. Drive 5-10 minutes into downtown Auburn. Store's in a strip mall on left (across from Dexter shoes).

AUGUSTA

HARVEST TIME NATURAL FOODS
Capital Shopping Center - Western Avenue, 04330 • (207)623-8700
No produce.
M & T 9-6, W-F 9-8, Sat. 9-6

From I-95, take exit 31-Augusta. Travel straight off exit into Augusta. Store's in second strip mall on right.

BANGOR

 On Center Street in Bangor, check out the Lemon Tree, a restaurant widely admired for its funky vegetarian dishes.

NATURAL LIVING CENTER
570 Stillwater Avenue, 04401 • (207)990-2646
M-Sat. 9:30-7, Sun. 12-5

 From I-95, take Bangor Mall exit. Store's just behind mall at cinema entrance.

BELFAST

 Hosts a large art community of local artisans and crafts people.

Check out "90 Main Street" (on, of course, 90 Main St.) and Darby's on High Street. Both specialize in vegetarian natural food.

BELFAST CO-OP
123 High Street, 04915 • (207)338-2532
M-Sat. 9-7, Sun. 10-5

 From I-95, take Augusta exit onto Rte. 3. Follow Rte. 3 to downtown Belfast and go right onto High St. Store's 100 yards down on left. From Rte. 1 north, take Belfast Business District exit. Store's about one mile down on right.

BIDDEFORD

NEW MORNING NATURAL FOODS
230 Main Street, 04005 • (207)282-1434
M-Sat. 9-5:30 (Th. 'til 7), Cafe: M-Th. 11-2, F - Soup & Salad only.

 From I-95 south: Take Biddeford exit (#4). Go left on Rte. 111 to "5 points in Biddeford." Turn left on Elm St. and right on Main. Store's on left. From I-95 north: Take Exit #5 (Saco) south on Main St. Store's on right.

BLUE HILL

 Recommendations: Left Bank Cafe has yummy baked goods and music, hike Blue Hill mountain, go to the beaches or check out the area's antique shops. Also tune into WERU, a great local public radio station.

BLUE HILL CO-OP
Greene's Hill Place Route 172, 04614 • (207)374-2165
They serve sandwiches, salad & breakfast.
M-F 8-7, Sat. 8-6, Sun. 10-4

 Take Rte. 172 into Blue Hill or from Rte. 1/3, take Rte. 15 south into Blue Hill. Go left on 172. Store's 1/4 mile down on left.

BREWER

NATURAL LIVING CENTER
421 Wilson Street, 04412 • (800)933-4229
Check out Three Sister's Cafe next to the Natural Living Center. It's vegetarian and VERY good!
M-Sat. 9-6 (F 'til 6:30), Sun. 12-2

 From I-95, take North Main St. exit. Turn right on Main. Store's on left in Brewer Shopping Center.

BRIDGTON

MORNING DEW NATURAL FOODS GROCERY
24 Portland Street, 04009 • (207)647-4003
Store carries homebrew supplies.
M-F 9:30-6:30, Sat. 9:30-5:30, Sun. 10-5

Store's on Rte. 302 in Bridgton, south of light.

DAMARISCOTTA

RISING TIDE CO-OP
Business Route 1, Box 38, 04543 • (207)563-5556
M-Sat. 8-7, Sun. 10-4

Take Rte. 1 to Business Rte. 1. Store's 1.5 - 2 miles south of Rte. 1, on west side of street.

ELLSWORTH

 Check out Acadia National Park.

JOHN EDWARD'S WHOLE FOODS MARKET
158 Main Street, 04605 • (207)667-9377
M-Th. 9-5:30, F 9-6, Sat. 9-5, Sun. 1-5

Rte. 1 is Main St. Store's on south/east side.

GORHAM

THE NATURAL GROCER
9 State Street, 04038 • (207)839-6223
Store prepares soup daily.
M-F 9-7, Sat. 9-6, Sun. 10-5

From the Maine Turnpike, take exit 8. Go straight through Westbrook (turns into Rte. 25). Head into Gorham. Store's about 6 miles down on right.

KENNEBUNK

NEW MORNING NATURAL FOODS
1 York Street, 04043 • (207)985-6774
M-Sat. 9:30-6

From I-95, take exit 3. Take two lefts and turn right on Rte. 1 south at lights. Cross a small bridge and store's at top of street on the right in a brick building.

KITTERY

RISING TIDE
165 State Road, 03904 • (207)439-8898
Store has an all vegan deli.
M-Sat. 9-7, Sun. 11-4:30

From I-95, take exit 2 and follow signs to 236/Rte. 1 south to Kittery traffic circle. Store's first building outside circle on Rte. 1 south.

NORWAY

FAIR SHARE MARKET (CO-OP)

18 Tannery Street, 04268 • (207)743-9044
This co-op offers fresh soups and muffins to go.
M-F 9-5, Sat. 10-4

 From Rte. 26, take 117 into Norway. Once at Main St., turn by radio station onto Tannery St. Store's straight ahead.

ORONO

THE STORE & AMPERSAND

22 Mill Street, 04473 • (207)866-4110
No organic produce.
M-Sat. 7-7, Sun. 9-4

  From I-95, take exit 50. Store's two miles down in center of town on left.

PORTLAND

Check out the Portland Museum of Art, The Pepper Club (mostly vegetarian), The Great Lost Bear, Natasha's and Mesa Verde (Mexican fare) on Congress. Also visit the Wine Bar on Wharf Street.

THE WHOLE GROCER

127 Marginal Way, 04101 • (207)774-7711
Store is very accessible and convenient with lots of parking! They also carry an array of international specialties.
M-F 9-8, Sat. 9-7, Sun. 11-6

 From I-295, take Franklin Arterial exit then go right on Marginal Way. Store's 2 blocks down on left.

ROCKLAND

GOOD TERN CO-OP

216 S. Main Street, 04841 • (207)594-9286
M-F 9:30-6, Sat. 9:30-5

 Driving into Rockland on Rte. 1, take a right at third traffic light onto 173 (S. Main St.). Store's two blocks down on right.

RUMFORD

RED HILL NATURAL FOODS

29 Hartford Street, 04276 • (207)369-9141
M-Sat. 9-6, (Th. til 7)

 Take Rte. 4 west to Rumford (turns into 108). Once downtown, take a right onto Canal St. Road ends in front of the store on Hartford St.

SCARBOROUGH

LOIS' NATURAL MARKETPLACE
152 US Route 1, 04074 • (207)885-0602
M-F 9:30-7:30, Sat. 9-6:30, Sun. 11-5

 From I-95, take exit 6A toward Portland. Take the first exit after tollbooth to South Portland. Take second exit to Scarborough and get onto Rte. 1. Store's on left about 1/2 mile up on Rte. 1.

UNITY

UNITY CO-OP
P.O. Box 148 Depot Street, 04988 • (207)948-6161
M-F 9-6, Sat. 10-5

 A stone's throw from intersection of 202 and Rte. 139. Store's across from Unity railroad station.

WATERVILLE

NEW MOON RISING NATURAL FOODS
110 Pleasant Street, 04901 • (207)873-6244
Some organic produce.
M-Sat. 9-6 (F 'til 7), Sun. 10-5

 From I-95, take Main St. exit. Follow signs to Waterville. Store's on right.

YARMOUTH

ROYAL RIVER NATURAL FOODS
881 US Route 1, 04096 • (207)846-1141
M-Sat. 8-8, Sun. 10-6

 From I-95 south: Take exit 16, go right off exit and through one light. Store's in second shopping center on left. From I-95 north: Take exit 17 (Rte. 1 south) and drive a few miles past shopping center. Store's 3/4 mile down on right.

Organic Fact Nº13

1996 PRODUCT SALES

1996 Organic Product Sales:
3.5 billion
1996 Natural Product Sales
$11.5 billion

Maryland/D.C.

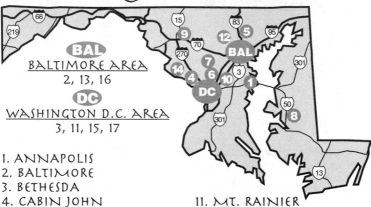

BAL
BALTIMORE AREA
2, 13, 16

DC
WASHINGTON D.C. AREA
3, 11, 15, 17

1. ANNAPOLIS
2. BALTIMORE
3. BETHESDA
4. CABIN JOHN
5. COCKEYSVILLE
6. COLLEGE PARK
7. COLUMBIA
8. EASTON
9. FREDERICK
10. LAUREL

11. MT. RAINIER
12. OWINGS MILLS
13. PIKESVILLE
14. ROCKVILLE
15. SILVER SPRING
16. TOWSON
17. WASHINGTON D.C.

ANNAPOLIS

 Check out the Moon Cafe on Prince George Street.

COUNTRY SUNSHINE MARKET
115 Annapolis Street, 21401 • (410)268-6996
M-F 10-6, Sat. 10-4

  From Hwy. 50, take Rowe Blvd. exit
toward downtown Annapolis. Get in left
lane and turn left on Melvin, then right on Annapolis. Store's on right.

FRESH FIELDS WHOLE FOODS MARKET
2504 Solomon's Island Road, 21401 • (410)573-1802
M-Sat. 9-9, Sun. 9-8

  Heading east on Hwy. 50, take
exit 22 - Aris T. Allen/Riva Rd. and follow signs to Solomon Island Rd./Rte. 2. Turn
left on Solomon Island Rd. Store's on corner in Harbor Place Shopping Center.

SUN & EARTH FOODS
1933 West Street, 21401 • (410)266-6862
M-Sat. 9:30-6:30, Sun. 12-4

 Take Rte. 50 to exit 665 to Chinquapin Round Rd. Go left on
West St., then left on Lee. Store's on corner of West and Lee.

BALTIMORE

Visit Charles Street for the Walters Art Gallery, the Brewer's Art (brewpub) and a diverse selection of cafes and restaurants. Fresh Fields staffers recommend stopping by the Baltimore Museum of Art or the Inner Harbor.

FRESH FIELDS WHOLE FOODS MARKET
1330 Smith Avenue, 21209 • (410)532-6700
M-Sat. 8-9, Sun. 8-8

From I-695 (Baltimore Beltway), get on I-83 and take the first exit off Northern Parkway. Veer toward left off exit ramp. Make a left onto Falls Rd. Once on Falls, go through 2 traffic lights and make a left onto Smith. Follow Smith and store's on right.

GOLDEN TEMPLE
2320 North Charles Street, 21218 • (410)235-1014
Golden Temple is beginning to phase in organic produce.
M-F 9:30-7, Sat. 9:30-6, Sun. 11-5, Cafe: M-F 11-2:30.

From Baltimore Beltway (I-695), get on I-83 exit south. Once on I-83 south, take North Ave. exit and turn left onto North Ave. Go through two lights and make a left on Charles St. Store's between 23rd and 24th Sts.

GREEN EARTH FOOD MARKET
823 N. Charles Street, 21201 • (410)752-1422
This store is 30 years old!
M-Sat. 10-8, Sun. 11-5

Take I-695 toward Harbor. Get off at Russell St. and drive down Russell (very curvy) — stay in far right lane. Turn right onto Pratt, then get in left lane and make a left onto Charles. Drive up Charles (stay in right lane) and find store on right.

OK NATURAL FOOD STORE
11 W. Preston Street, 21201 • (410)837-3911
M-F 9:30-8:30, Sat. 10-8:30, Sun. 10:30-5

Take I-83 to St. Paul St. Make a right onto Preston. Drive 2 blocks to find store.

VILLAGE MARKET NATURAL GROCERY
7006 Reisterstown Road, 21215 • (410)486-0979
M-F 9:30-8, Sat. 9-6, Sun. 9-5

From I-695, get off at Reisterstown Rd. Store two miles down on right.

BETHESDA

Fresh Fields workers suggest Great Falls National Park on the Potomac River for hiking, biking and camping.

NORMAN'S FARM MARKET
4915 Bethesda Avenue, 20815 • (301)215-7533
Specializing in produce from local small farms.
Sun.-Sun. 7:30-9

From 495, take Old Georgetown Rd. toward Bethesda.
Go right onto Arlington, then right onto Bethesda Ave. Store's on right.

FRESH FIELDS WHOLE FOODS MARKET
5269 River Road, 20816 • (301)984-4860
M-Sat. 8-9, Sun. 8-8

 From I-495, take River Rd. south exit toward Wash. DC and drive about 3 miles. Store's on left in Kenwood Station Shopping Center.

CABIN JOHN

BETHESDA CO-OP
6500 Seven Locks Road, 20818 • (301)320-2530
M-Sat. 9-9, Sun. 9-8

 From I-495 take River Rd. exit west (toward Potomac) and go left on Seven Locks Rd. Drive 2 miles and store's on right at corner of MacArthur Blvd. in MacArthur Shopping Center.

COCKEYSVILLE

THE NATURAL
560 Cranbrook Road, 21030 • (410)628-1262
M-F 9-8, Sat. 10-6, Sun. 11-6

 From I-83, take Padonia Rd. exit east, turn left on York and right on Cranbrook. Go 3/4 of a mile and find store in Cranbrook Shopping Center on left.

COLLEGE PARK

Check out Udapi Palace on University Ave and vegetarian coffee house, Planet X.

BEAUTIFUL DAY TRADING CO.
5010 Berwyn Road, 20740 • (301)345-6655
M-Sat. 10-8, Sun. 10-5

 From I-495, take Rte. 1/Baltimore Ave. exit (#25) toward College Park and drive about 1.5 miles. Turn left on Berwyn and store's on left.

MARYLAND FOOD CO-OP
B-0203 Student Union Building, Maryland U, 20742 • (301)314-8089
M 7:30-6, Tu. 7:30-10, W 7:30-11:30, Th. 7:30-10, F 7:30-7, Sat. 11-6, Sun. 12-3

 Take I-95 to College Park exit. Go straight on Rte. 1/Baltimore Ave. Make a right into campus (about 2 miles). Go straight and then up a hill. At third stoplight, go right. Park in the parking garage and co-op is in basement of Hoff Theater Stamp Union.

COLUMBIA

 Stop by The Mango Grove, a recommended restaurant on Dobbin Rd.

DAVID'S NATURAL MARKET
5430-C Lynx Lane, 21044 • (410)730-2304
"One of a kind in Columbia, the only health food store in town."
M-F 9-7, Sat. 9-6, Sun. 11-5

 From Hwy. 29, take
Columbia Town Center
exit west (Rte. 175). Take
Governor Warfield Parkway right as road forks. Turn right on Twin Rivers and left
on Lynx. Store's on right in Village of Wild Lake Shopping Center.

EASTON

RAILRAY MARKET
108 Marlboro Road, 21601 • (410)822-4852
M-F 9-7, Sat. 9-6, Sun. 10-5

 Get on Rte. 50 toward
Ocean City. Take bypass for Easton - Rte. 322. Go left at third light onto Marlboro
Rd. Store's in the Marlboro Shopping Center, the second strip mall down.

FREDERICK

 Check out the natural food cafe, The Orchard, on N. Market St.

COMMON MARKET CO-OP
5813 Buckeystown Pike, 21704 • (301)663-3416
M-Sat. 9-8, Sun. 11-5

 From I-70, take Frederick/Buckeystown exit.
Go south on Rte. 85 (Buckeystown Pike).
Store's on left.

LAUREL

LAUREL HEALTH FOOD
131 Bowie Road, 20707 • (301)498-7191
M-F 10-8, Sat. 10-6

 On US 1, near the intersection of 198 east and Bowie Rd. (near the
Office Depot).

MT. RAINIER

 Check out the Eye-opener coffee shop in this D.C. suburb.

GLUT FOOD CO-OP
4005 34th Street, 20712 • (301)779-1978
Their motto: "Still cheap, still funky."
M-Sat. 10-8 (Th. & F 'til 8), Sun. 10-5

 From Rte. 1, head west on 34th St. Store's on right.

OWINGS MILLS

SPROUTS ALL NATURAL MARKET & CAFE
10027 Reisterstown Road, 21117 • (410)363-4222
Restaurant is vegan (well, except for tuna).
M-Sat. 10-8, Sun. 11-5

 From I-695, exit at Reisterstown
Rd. and drive toward Owings Mills. Store's 2 miles outside Beltway.

PIKESVILLE

VILLAGE MARKET NATURAL GROCER
7006 Reisterstown Road, 21215 • (410)486-0979
Organic produce only!
M-F 9:30-8, Sat. 9:30-6, Sun. 9:30-5

From I-695, take Hwy. 140 (Reisterstown Rd.) exit 20 south. Store's two miles down
in Colonial Village Shopping Center on right.

ROCKVILLE

 **Visit the Vegetable Garden (a highly recommended vegetarian Chinese restaurant) and also, Hard Times Cafe on Nelson St.**

FRESH FIELDS WHOLE FOODS MARKET
1649 Rockville Pike, 20852 • (301)984-4880
M-Sat. 8-9, Sun. 8-8

 From I-495, take North Rockville
Pike exit (Rte. 355). Store's on
left in Congressional Plaza.

MY ORGANIC MARKET (MOM'S)
11711 Parklawn Drive, 20852 • (301)816-4944
M-F 10-8, Sat. 9-7, Sun. 11-6

 From I-495, exit on 355 and go north to Nicholson Lane
(changes to Parklawn). Store's 1/2 mile down on right.

SILVER SPRING

 In Takoma Park, check out the Savory Cafe on Carroll Ave.

TAKOMA PARK SILVER SPRINGS CO-OP
201 Ethan Allen Avenue, 20912 • (301)891-2667
Sun.-Sun. 9-9

 From I-495, get off at New Hampshire Ave. and head
south. Go right on Rte 410. Store's 1/4 mile up on left.

TOWSON

 Check out Live-it-Not-Die-It, a highly recommended Jamaican restaurant.

THE HEALTH CONCERN
28 West Susquehanna Avenue, 21204 • (410)828-4015
M-F 9:30-8, Sat. 9:30-6, Sun. 12-5

 From I-695, take exit 26 south. Turn right on Washington. Go about 4 blocks and down a hill. Turn left on Susquehanna and store's on left.

WASHINGTON D.C.

Head over to Georgetown for a less formal Washington D.C. experience. Check out Wisconsin Avenue for cafes, restaurants and shops. One Fresh Fields staffer recommended The Old Europe for great German food.

FRESH FIELDS WHOLE FOODS MARKET
2323 Wisconsin Avenue NW, 20007 • (202)333-5393
In the Georgetown area.
Sun.-Sun. 8-10

 Take I-95 to 295 (Washington/Baltimore Parkway) and exit at New York Ave. (takes you into D.C.). Continue straight on New York Ave. At Dupont Circle, follow signs for Mass Ave. Follow Mass. and look for Observatory Lane on left, then turn onto it. At light, take a left onto Wisconsin Ave. and store's on left. (Store's in the Georgetown area).

FRESH FIELDS WHOLE FOODS MARKET
4530 40th Street NW, 20016 • (202)237-5800
M-Sat. 8-10, Sun. 8-8

 From 495, take River Rd. exit and turn toward D.C. at exit ramp. At first stop sign (cross road is Wisconsin) look for store. (Across street from intersection of River Rd. and Wisconsin).

GOOD HEALTH NATURAL FOODS
325 Pennsylvania Avenue SE, 20003 • (202)543-2266
No produce.
M-F 10-6 (open 'til 7 in summer), Sat. 11-5

 Store's on Pennsylvania Ave., across from the Library of Congress and the Capital.

HUGO'S NATURAL FOODS MARKET
3813-3817 Livingston Street NW, 20015 • (202)966-6103
M-Sat. 9-8, Sun. 10-6

 From I-495, take Connecticut Ave. exit south. Store's on right, at corner of Connecticut and Livingston.

YES NATURAL GOURMET
1825 Columbia Road NW, 20009 • (202)462-5150
M-Sat. 9-8, Sun. 12-6

 From I-495 loop, take Connecticut Ave. exit south, turn left on Calvert and right on Columbia. Store's on right.

YES NATURAL GOURMET
3425 Connecticut Avenue NW, 20008 • (202)363-1559
M-Sat. 9-9, Sun. 10-8

 From I-495, drive five miles south on Connecticut. Store's on left, a half mile south of Connecticut & Livingston (near the zoo at Cleveland Park metro stop).

Massachusetts

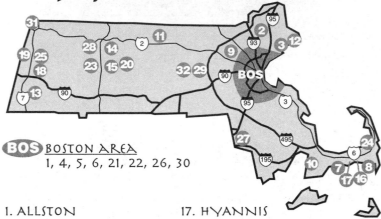

BOS BOSTON AREA
1, 4, 5, 6, 21, 22, 26, 30

1. ALLSTON
2. ANDOVER
3. BEVERLY
4. BOSTON
5. BRIGHTON
6. CAMBRIDGE
7. CENTERVILLE
8. CHATHAM
9. CONCORD
10. FALMOUTH
11. GARDNER
12. GLOUCESTER
13. GREAT BARRINGTON
14. GREENFIELD
15. HADLEY
16. HARWICH PORT

17. HYANNIS
18. LEE
19. LENOX
20. LEVERETT
21. MELROSE
22. NEWTON
23. NORTHAMPTON
24. ORLEANS
25. PITTSFIELD
26. QUINCY
27. SEEKONK
28. SHELBURNE FALLS
29. SHREWSBURY
30. WELLESLEY
31. WILLIAMSTOWN
32. WORCESTER

ALLSTON

HARVEST CO-OP SUPERMARKET

Both Harvest Co-op Supermarkets try to reach out to their communities. This translates into lots of granola and a fair amount of organic produce co-existing with less crunchy name brands. Overall, a noticeable and welcoming involvement with their communities.
449 Cambridge Street, 02134 • (617)787-1416
M-Sat. 9-10, Sun. 9-9

From I-90, take Allston exit (puts you on Cambridge St.). Store's on right.

ANDOVER

THE EARTH FOOD STORE

28 Chestnut Street, 01810 • (978)475-1234

M-Sat. 8-7, (Sun. 12-5 during Sept.-June)

 From I-495: Take Rte. 28 south 4 miles into Andover center. Take a left onto Chestnut St. and store's 100 yards up on left. From I-93: Take 125 north to Rte. 28 north (goes into downtown Andover). At first light, make a right onto Chestnut. Store's 100 yards up on left.

BEVERLY

A NEW LEAF

261 Cabot Street, 01915 • (978)927-5955

No produce.

M-Sat. 9:30-6 (Th. 'til 8)

 From I-95, get on Rte. 128 north. Turn right on Rte. 62 (Elliott St.) and follow it to end. Turn right on Cabot St. Store's on left.

BOSTON

Located in the Fenway area, the Westland Avenue Bread & Circus sits in one of Boston's cultural havens. Home to 2 art and 5 music schools, this district is known for Symphony Hall (where the Boston Symphony and Boston Pops perform), the Museum of Fine Arts, Copley Place, Newbury Street and Fenway Park (where the Red Sox play).

Chuck at this Bread & Circus suggests Cena, a restaurant on Westland Avenue which serves mostly vegetarian fare. Check out the Brighton recommendations.

BREAD & CIRCUS WHOLE FOODS MARKET

15 Westland Avenue, 02115 • (617)375-1010

Store is round!

Sun.-Sun. 9-10

 From I-93, take the Massachusetts Ave. exit and drive less than 2 miles (7-8 traffic lights) into the Fenway section. Store's kitty corner from Symphony Hall on Massachusetts Ave. in the center of Boston.

NATURE FOOD CENTER

545 Boylston Street, 02116 • (617)536-1226

Occasional produce.

M-F 8-8, Sat. 9-7, Sun. 10-7

 Store's in Copley Square in middle of city, less than one mile south of the Boston Common.

BRIGHTON

Emily at the Brighton Bread & Circus has a host of outstanding recommendations for the Boston area. In Brookline, check out Jera's Juice, get sandwiches at Underwrap, Ginza on Beacon Street for fabulous sushi, Vietnamese restaurant Pho Pasteur and celebrated vegetarian restaurant, Buddha's Delight (very yummy).

Kendall Cinema and Coolidge Corner are artsy movie houses that Emily says attracts "really neat, interesting looking crowds." She also recommends the Nickelodeon for movies.

BREAD & CIRCUS WHOLE FOODS MARKET
15 Washington Street, 02146 • (617)738-8187
Store has a lunch bar. Cafe has seasonal seating only.
Sun.-Sun. 9-9

From I-90, take Brighton/Allston exit and get on
Cambridge St. (one direction). Turn left on Washington St. and store's on left.

CAMBRIDGE

Koreana on Prospect serves "great everything," (but they're famous for their Korean barbecue). There's also Masao's and Pho Republique, a hip nouveau Vietnamese spot in Central Square (Emily says it's a "totally amazing vegetarian restaurant with great vegetarian entrees"). We also had many recommendations for both 5 Seasons restaurants in Brighton & Jamaica Plains.

BREAD & CIRCUS WHOLE FOODS MARKET
115 Prospect Street, 02139 • (617)492-0070
One of the oldest Bread & Circus', this store retains a neighborhood feel.
M-Sat. 9-10, Sun. 9-9

From I-90, take Cambridge exit, cross bridge and continue straight on River St. (River becomes
Prospect). Cross Massachusetts Ave. Store's on left.

HARVEST CO-OP SUPERMARKET
581 Massachusetts Avenue, 02139 • (617)661-1580
Sun.-Sun. 9-9

From I-90, take Cambridge exit, cross bridge and continue straight on River St. Cross
Massachusetts Ave. and turn right on Bishop Allen Dr. to park.

CENTERVILLE

CAPE COD NATURAL FOODS
1600 Falmouth Road, 02636 • (508)771-8394
M-Sat. 8-7, Sun. 12-5

From Rte. 3, take exit 5 and cross Rte. 149. Go right to
Craigville Beach and take a left on Old Stage Road at intersection. Go left at next
intersection/traffic light and store's in second strip mall (Bell Tower Mall) on left.

CHATHAM

CHATHAM NATURAL FOODS
1291 Main Street, 02633 • (508)945-4139
Sun.-Sun. 9-5:30 (9-6 in summer)

From Rte. 6, take exit 11. Go left onto Rte. 128 and store's 3.5 miles up on left.

CONCORD

CONCORD SPICE & GRAIN
93 Thoreau Street, 01742 • (978)369-1535
M-Sat. 9-6:30 (Th. 'til 8), Sun. 12-6

 From Rte. 2 (east), take Sudbury Rd. (Sudbury is first right after signs for Rte. 126). Take a left at first set of lights onto Thoreau. Store's on right.

FALMOUTH

AMBER WAVES NATURAL FOODS
445 Main Street, 02540 • (508)540-3538
M-Sat. 9-7, Sun. 12-5

 Store's on Rte. 28 (Main St.) in center of Falmouth.

GARDNER

HAPPY TRAILS
24 Main Street, 01440 • (508)632-4076/(800)550-4076
No produce.
M-W 9-6, Th. & F 9-7, Sat. 9-5

 From Rte. 2, take Rte. 68 exit north. Rte. 68 becomes Main St. Store's on right.

GLOUCESTER

 Check out the Glass Sail Boat Cafe.

CAPE ANN FOOD CO-OP
26 Emerson Avenue, 01930 • (978)281-0592
M-Sat. 9-7:30, Sun. 12-5

 Heading north on Rte. 128, come to the first rotary in Gloucester. Take first exit off rotary, then turn right on Centennial Ave. and right on Emerson Ave. Store's one block down on left.

GREAT BARRINGTON

 Check out Martin's on Railroad St. for breakfast and lunch.

BERKSHIRE CO-OP MARKET
37 Rosseter Street, 01230 • (413)528-9697
M-F 9-7:30, Sat. 9-6, Sun. 12-5

 From Rte. 7, go west on Rosseter. Store's on left in the heart of Great Barrington.

GUIDO'S FRESH MARKETPLACE
760 S. Main Street, 01230 • (413)528-9255
M-Sat. 9-6 (F 'til 7), Sun. 10-7

 From Rte. 90, take a left on ramp. Make 1st right onto Rte. 102 and drive to Rte. 7 south. Store's on Rte. 7 (Main St.) on right.

LOCKE, STOCK AND BARREL
265 Stockbridge Road, 01230 • (413)528-0800
Produce in summer only.
M-Sat. 9-6, Sun. 11-4

 From I-90, take Lee exit (2) to Rte. 7. Go south on Rte. 7 to Great Barrington. Store's on Rte. 7, diagonally across from McDonald's on right.

GREENFIELD

GREEN FIELDS MARKET
144 Main Street, 01301 • (413)773-9567
M-F 8-8, Sat. 9-6, Sun. 10-5

 From I-91, take southern Greenfield exit (of 2) and head into town on Main.

Store's west of Rte. 5 on left and has a large green awning.

HADLEY

BREAD & CIRCUS WHOLE FOODS MARKET
Route 9 (Russell Street), 01035 • (413)586-9932
Sun.-Sun. 9-9

From I-91 south: Take exit 19 and turn right off ramp onto Rte. 9 east. Go over bridge and drive 4 miles. Store's on right. From I-91 north: Take exit 20 and follow signs for Rte. 9 east. After the ramp turn left at light, then go left at next light onto Rte. 9. Drive 4 miles and store's on right.

HARWICH PORT

WILD OATS NATURAL FOODS
509 Route 28, 02646 • (508)430-2507
M-Sat. 9-6, Sun. 12-6

 From Rte. 124, take exit 10 and make a right at end of ramp. Go to Main St. in Harwich and make a left. Take first right onto Bank St., drive to Rte. 28 and make a right. Store's on left.

HYANNIS

SANDY'S NATURAL MARKETPLACE
605 Main Street, 02601 • (508)790-1580
M-Sat. 10-6

 From Rte. 6, take exit 7 and at end of ramp, go left. Drive to end and make a right onto Main St. Store's 8 blocks up on right.

LEE

SUNFLOWER'S NATURAL FOOD MARKET
42 Park Street, 01238 • (413)243-1775
M-Sat. 10-6 (F 'til 7), Sun. 12-5:30

 From I-90, take exit 2 and follow Rte. 20 west for one mile. Store's on north side of street.

LENOX

 Head over to the Kripalu Center for delicious vegetarian, natural food (buffet) and a peaceful environment. While you're there, take a yoga class or stroll this retreat's beautiful grounds.

CLEARWATER NATURAL FOODS
11 Housatonic Street, 01240 • (413)637-2721
M-Sat. 9:15-6, Sun. 11-3

 From I-90, take exit 2 (Lee). Go north on Rte. 20 (merges with Rte 7). Turn left after light onto Walker St. in center of Lenox (about 1 mile). Turn right at Monument onto Main, then right onto Housatonic. Store's on left.

LEVERETT

VILLAGE CO-OP
180 Rattlesnake Gutter Road, 01054 • (413)367-9794
Dar's local co-op. An unpretentious cross between a co-op and a general store. Pizza night is Friday and the staff is very nice!
Sat.-Th. 7-7, F 7-8

   From I-91, take Deerfield exit onto Rte. 116 south about a mile. Turn left on Rte. 47 (watch out for sharp right turn!) and follow road as it curves and weaves. Rte. 47 becomes N. Leverett Rd. after you cross Rte. 63. Drive a few miles, then store's on right. Drive down Rattlesnake to park. (Additional locating tip: Store's about 11 miles from I-91).

MELROSE

GREEN STREET NATURAL FOODS
164 Green Street, 02176 • (781)662-7741
M-F 9-6 (Th. open 'til 7), Sat. 9-5

From I-95, take exit 40A (Rte. 28 - Stoneham) and follow to center of town. Go left onto Franklin St. and follow into Melrose (becomes Green St.). Store's 100 yards down on right.

NEWTON

BREAD & CIRCUS WHOLE FOODS MARKET
916 Walnut Street, 02161 • (617)969-1141
Sun.-Sun. 8-9

From I-90, take I-95/128 south. Head east on Rte. 9 and take Center St. exit (just past Dunkin Donuts). Bear right at bottom of exit and turn left on Walnut. Store's on right.

NORTHAMPTON

 In Northampton, check out Fire & Water Cafe for plentiful local music, open mike nights and great vegetarian chili. Also, the mostly vegan restaurant, Bela, on Mason Street comes recommended, as does natural food restaurant Paul & Elizabeth. There's Haymarket cafe and Cha Cha Cha's serves Mexican food with "a California/Asian accent." Very delicious!

CORNUCOPIA
150 Main Street, 01060 • (413)586-3800
Well-stocked, small store (Can't beat the location!).
M-F 9:30-7 (Th & F 'til 9), Sat. 9:30-9, Sun. 12-6

 From I-91, take exit #18 (Northampton) and head north on Rte. 5. Turn left on Main St. (Rte. 9). Store's on left in basement of Thornes Market (green awning).

ORLEANS

ORLEANS WHOLE FOOD STORE
46 Main Street, 02653 • (508)255-6540
Lots of stuff with small town, old fashioned ambiance.
M-Sat. 8:30-6, Sun. 9-6 (open 'til 9 in summer).

 Rte. 6, from east: Take Rte. 6A exit at rotary and turn left on Main St. Store's on left. From west: Take Rte. 6A exit, turn right on 6A and right on Main St. Store's on right.

PITTSFIELD

PITTSFIELD HEALTH FOOD CENTER
407 North Street, 01201 • (413)442-5662
No produce.
M-Sat. 9:30-5:30

 From I-91, exit in Lee and take Rte. 7 north. Go through the rotary and bear right onto North St. Go through about 2 traffic lights and store's on left across from a large church.

GUIDO'S
1020 South Street, 01201 • (413)442-9912
M-Sat. 9-6, Sun. 10-5

 Take Rte. 7 south into Pittsfield. Store's on right.

QUINCY

GOOD HEALTH NATURAL FOODS
1627 Hancock Street, 02169 • (617)773-4925
M-Sat. 9-6, Sun. 12-7

 Take I-93 to Furnace Brook Parkway exit. Follow Furnace Brook to Hancock St. Go right on Hancock and store's on left.

SEEKONK

THE GOOD SEED
138 Central Avenue, 02771 • (508)399-7333
M-Sat. 10-6 (W & Th. 'til 8), Sun. 12-5

 From I-195, take Neort Ave./Rte. 1A exit toward Pawtucket. Turn left on Benefit St. (Benefit becomes Central). Store's on left on corner of Central and Rte. 152.

SHELBURNE FALLS

MCCUSKER'S MARKET
3 State Street (at the Bridge of Flowers), 01380 • (413)625-2548

A sort of country store in a lovely, river straddling town. Cross the bridge and check out the natural potholes. A wonderful summer swimming spot!

Sun.-Sun. 6-7 (winter), 6-9 (summer)

 From I-91 north, take Rte. 2 west (exit 26) about 7 miles. Turn left onto 2A by blinking light (at Sweetheart Restaurant), go into town and store's across iron bridge.

SHREWSBURY

BINKERMAN'S
558 Main Street, 01545 • (508)845-2087

Small on-premises restaurant.

M & T 10-5, W-F 10-7, Sat. 10-5, Cafe: T 12-5, W-F 12-7, Sat. 10-5

From south: Get on I-290 and take exit #22 on to Main St. Store's on right. From north: Take Rte. 140 south exit and drive for 1.5 miles. Turn right at first light onto Main St. Store's on left.

WELLESLEY

 Check out Carrots, a juice and sandwich place across from Bread & Circus. Folks at Bread & Circus say Wellesley College is a neat place to walk and ride your bike.

BREAD & CIRCUS WHOLE FOODS MARKET
278 Washington Street, 02481 • (781)235-7262

One of the oldest Bread & Circus'.

Sun.-Sun. 8-9

 From I-95/128 take Rte. 16 west exit. Store's on left, just past intersection of Rte. 16 and Washington.

WILLIAMSTOWN

 Suggested stops: Clark Art museum and in the summer, the Williamstown Theater Festival.

WILD OATS CO-OP
Colonial Shopping Center, Rte. 2, 01267 • (413)458-8060

M-Sat. 9-7, Sun. 9-6

Just west of North Adams town line and east of Williamstown Center, store's on north side of Rte. 2 in Colonial Shopping Center.

WORCESTER

LIVING EARTH
232 Chandler Street, 01609 • (508)753-1896

M-F 9-9, Sat. 9-6, Sun. 11-5

 Store's on the west side of Rte. 122 (Chandler St.), just south of Rte. 9 at the intersection of Park Ave. and Chandler.

Michigan

Most Michigan natural food stores are cooperatives!!!

1. ANN ARBOR
2. CANTON
3. DETROIT
4. EAST LANSING
5. GRAND RAPIDS
6. HANCOCK
7. HILLSDALE
8. KALAMAZOO
9. MARQUETTE
10. MOUNT PLEASANT
11. PAW PAW
12. PETOSKEY
13. RICHMOND
14. SAGINAW
15. TRAVERSE CITY
16. TROY
17. WOODLAND
18. YPSILANTI

ANN ARBOR

In Ann Arbor, check out Saginaw woods and vegetarian restaurant, Seva (on E. Liberty). The Gypsy Cafe features local music, School Kids is a great Indie record store and the Ark is a folk club of epic proportions.

PEOPLE'S FOOD CO-OP
216 North 4th Avenue, 48104 • (313)994-9174
Sun.-F 9-10, Sat. 8-10

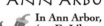 From I-94, take Ann Arbor/Saline Rd. exit north (will become Main). Turn right on Ann St. and left on 4th. Store's on right.

WHOLE FOODS MARKET
2398 East Stadium Boulevard, 48104 • (313)971-3366
Sun.- Sun. 9-10

 From I-94, take US 23 north to Washtenaw/Ann Arbor exit (#37B). Head west on Washtenaw about 2 miles. When road splits to right, bear left on Stadium. Store's on left in Lamp Post Plaza.

CANTON

GOOD FOOD COMPANY WEST
42615 Ford Road, 48187 • (313)981-8100
M-Sat. 9-9, Sun. 10-6

From I-275, take Ford Rd. exit west one mile. Store's on left in Canton Corners Shopping Center.

DETROIT

 Visit Traffic Jam and Snug on W. Canfield St. (great food) and the Greek restaurants downtown.

CASS CORRIDOR CO-OP
4201 Cass Avenue, 48201 • (313)831-7452
M-F 10-7, Sat. 10-6, Sun. 12-5

From I-10, take Forest/Warren St. exit and drive east on Forest. Turn right on Cass and go south. Store's on right.

EAST LANSING

 Recommendations: Visit Beamer's coffee house, Small Planet Food and Spirits on Mac Avenue and the Traveler's Club & Tuba Museum (an international cafe which features specialties from around the world). Both Woody's Oasis and Sultan's serve Middle Eastern fare.

EAST LANSING FOOD CO-OP
4960 Northwind Drive, 48823 • (517)337-1266
Store is strongly committed to providing environmentally friendly products and stocking local produce.
M-F 10-8, Sat. 9-8, Sun. 12-7

From Hwy. 127, take Michigan/Kalamazoo exit. Go east on Michigan Ave. (becomes Grand River) and turn right on Northwind Dr. Store's on right. (Store's about 1 mile past Michigan State University).

GRAND RAPIDS

 Stop by Gaia, one of the few vegetarian restaurants in West Michigan.

EASTOWN FOOD CO-OP
1450 Wealthy Street SE, 49506 • (616)454-8822
M-Sat. 9-9, Sun. 11-8

From I-96, take Hwy. 131 south. Take the Wealthy St. exit toward town. Store's on right in Eastown.

HANCOCK

KEWEENAW CO-OP
1035 Ethel Avenue, 49930 • (906)482-2030
M-Sat. 9-9, Sun. 12-6

Traveling north on US 41, turn left on Ethel. Store's 2 blocks down on right.

HILLSDALE

HILLSDALE NATURAL GROCERY
31 North Broad, 49242 • (517)439-1397
M-Th. 9-6, F 9-6:30, Sat. 9-5

 Rte. 34/99 is Broad St. Store's on east side.

KALAMAZOO

 In case you've wondered, Kalamazoo is a Native American word for "Bubbling Waters."

KALAMAZOO PEOPLE'S FOOD CO-OP
436 S. Burdick, 49007 • (616)342-5686
M-Sat. 9-7, Sun. 12-5

 From I-94, take Westnedge exit north and drive a few miles, then turn right on Cedar. Store's on left at corner of Cedar and Burdick.

SAWALL HEALTH FOODS
2965 Oakland Drive, 49008 • (616)343-3619
Store's been open since 1936! Cafe serves delicious, homemade natural & organic food (no cans opened!). Beer and wine available in cafe.
M-Sat. 9-8, Sun. 12-5, Cafe: M-F 10:30-9, Sat. 7:30-9:30, Sun. 9-2

     From I-94, take exit 75 and travel 1 mile north. Store's on right.

MARQUETTE

 Organic Food Co-op staffers say Marquette is a beautiful town with lots of outdoor activities available around Lake Superior. Check out Marquette's urban area for coffeeshops and to meet the local folk.

MARQUETTE ORGANIC FOOD CO-OP
325 West Washington Street, 49855 • (906)225-0671
M-F 10-6, Sat. 10-5

From Rte. 41, (either direction), turn/bear left on Washington. Store's between 4th & 5th.

MOUNT PLEASANT

 Check out the Northern Trading Post, they feature a few vegetarian entrees.

GREEN TREE NATURAL GROCERY
214 North Franklin, 48858 • (517)772-3221
M-F 9-7, Sat. 10-6

From Hwy. 27, take Mt. Pleasant Business 27 exit. Head west on Broadway and turn right on North Franklin. Store's on right.

PAW PAW

Paw Paw's fertile farmland is ideal for grapes, so visit some of the area wineries (many offer free tours).

PAW PAW FOOD CO-OP
39239 Red Arrow Highway, 49079 • (616)657-5934
This store was once a wine tasting room!
M-F 9-6, Sat. 9-4

 Store's on Red Arrow Highway, one mile north of I-94 between Paw Paw exits 60 & 56.

PETOSKEY

GRAIN TRAIN NATURAL FOODS CO-OP
421 Howard, 49770 • (616)347-2381
M-F 8-8, Sat. 8-5, Sun. 11-5

 From Rte. 131 (becomes 31 North, then Mitchell), bear right on Mitchell and turn right on Howard. Store's on left.

RICHMOND

 Check out Richmond's apple orchards and various U-pick berry farms.

RAINBOW HEALTH FOOD STORE
66783 Gratiot Avenue, 48062 • (810)727-5475
M-F 10-6, Sat. 10-3

 From I-94, take 26 Mile exit west. Take Gratiot north about 6 miles. Store's on left in Lenox Square Shopping Mall.

SAGINAW

 In the Saginaw-Bay City area, try Nino's Cafe (has vegetarian options) and Tommy V's serves great pizza!

GRAINS & GREENS
3641 Bay Road, 48603 • (517)799-8171
No produce.
M-F 9-8, Sat. 9-6, Sun. 12-5

 From 675, take Tittabawsee exit and go 1 mile to Bay Rd. Make a left on Bay and store's on left.

HERITAGE NATURAL FOODS
717 Gratiot, 48602 • (517)793-5805
Limited organic produce.
M-Sat. 9:30-5:30

From I-75, take Holland Ave. exit (Rte. 46) west. Rte. 46 runs into Gratiot. Store's on right, two blocks past Michigan.

TRAVERSE CITY

Poppycock's on East Front Street serves mostly vegetarian food with an Italian flair.

ORYANA FOOD CO-OP
260 E. 10th, 49684 • (616)947-0191
M-Sat. 8-8 (Winter 8-7), Sun. 12-5

 From Rte. 31/37, turn east on 10th and drive to end. Store's on south side of street at corner of Lake and 10th.

TROY

GOOD FOOD COMPANY EAST
74 West Maple Road, 48084 • (248)362-0886
M-Sat. 9-9, Sun. 10-6

From I-75, take 14 Mile exit west and turn right on Main St. (becomes Livernois).
Store's on left at corner of Livernois and Maple.

WOODLAND

WOODLAND CO-OP
116 North Main Street, 48897 • (616)367-4188
Conventional produce only.
M-W 12-5, Sat. 9-12

Store's half a block north of Rte. 43 on Main St.

YPSILANTI

YPSILANTI FOOD CO-OP
312 North River Street, 48198 • (313)483-1520
*This Co-op has been in business for over 20 years! Visit the Depot Town
Bakery next door... highly recommended.*
M-F 10-8 (W 'til 9), Sat. 9-8, Sun. 12-5

From I-94, take Huron St. exit and drive north to Michigan
Ave. Take Michigan to River St. Go north on River and
store's on east side of street.

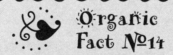

**Organic
Fact №14**

REDUCE POTENTIAL
HEALTH RISKS

Many EPA-approved pesticides
were registered long before
extensive research linked these
chemicals to cancer and other
diseases. Now, the EPA
considers 60% of all herbicides,
90% of all fungicides, and 30% of
all insecticides as potentially
cancer causing.

Minnesota

SP <u>SAINT PAUL AREA</u>
27, 29, 31

1. ALBERT LEA	19. MINNEAPOLIS
2. ALEXANDRIA	20. MINNETONKA
3. ANOKA	21. MORRIS
4. BAXTER	22. OAK CENTER
5. BEMIDJI	23. OWATONNA
6. BLUE EARTH	24. PRESTON
7. BRAINERD	25. ROCHESTER
8. BURNSVILLE	26. ST. CLOUD
9. CAMBRIDGE	27. ST. PAUL
10. DULUTH	28. ST. PETER
11. ELY	29. STILLWATER
12. GRAND MARAIS	30. VIRGINIA
13. GRAND RAPIDS	31. WHITE BEAR LAKE
14. HASTINGS	32. WILLMAR
15. ISLE	33. WINDOM
16. LITCHFIELD	34. WINONA
17. LONG PRAIRIE	
18. MANKATO	

ALBERT LEA

WINTERGREEN NATURAL FOODS
1442 West Main Street, 56007 • (507)373-0386
M-F 10-5:30, Sat. 9-5

 Albert Lea is at crossroads of I-35 and I-90. Store's one mile west of downtown on Main St., north of the Skyline Mall.

ALEXANDRIA

VILLAGE PANTRY
2020 Fillmore Street, 56308 • (320)763-4240
In 1994, the failing Village Pantry Cooperative was sold to the Alexandria school district. The store is now staffed by students from the High School's Marketing Class and run by the management team of Beth, a former co-op board member, and two students. Next door is a volunteer-run used clothing store and the store's parking lot plays host to summertime farmer's markets. No organic produce.
School year: M-F 12-7, Summer: M-F 10-6, Sat. 8-4

 From I-94, go north on MN 29 toward Alexandria. Turn left at traffic light on 22nd Ave., then make an immediate right. Store's on left.

ANOKA

Check out Downtown Anoka for Cafes, ethnic food, bars and coffee houses.

ANOKA FOOD CO-OP
1917 2nd Avenue South, 55303 • (612)427-4340
M-F 8-8, Sat. 8-6, Sun. 12-4

 From I-94, take 169 north to Anoka. Go across bridge, make a left on Main and a left on Second.

BAXTER

LIFE PRESERVER
875 Edgewood Drive, 56425 • (218)829-7925
Store has a naturopath on staff.
M-F 9:30-6, Sat. 9:30-5

 Store's on Hwy. 371 (parallel to 371N) on west side of street, 1 mile north of Paul Bunyan Amusement Center.

BEMIDJI

Bemidji recommendations: Head over to local microbrewery, Union Station (walking distance from the Harmony Co-op), and the "Lost Forty," a forty acre parcel of old growth forest. Also explore the headwaters of the Mississippi River at Lake Itasca State Park.

HARMONY FOOD CO-OP
117 3rd Street NW, 56601 • (218)751-2009
M-F 9-7, Sat. 9-6, Sun. 12-5

 Harmony Co-op worker Greg insists you'll find the store if you "go half a block west of Paul and Babe." Paul and Babe are on Hwy. 197 on the Bemidji waterfront.

SUNRISE NATURAL FOODS AND CRAFTS
802 Paul Bunyan Drive SW, 56601 • (218)751-9005
No produce.
M-F 9-7 Sat. 10-5

 On south side of Lake Bemidji, about a mile southeast of Paul and Babe.

BLUE EARTH

RAINBOW FOOD CO-OP
103 South Main Street, 56013 • (507)526-3603
M-F 10-5:30, Sat. 10-3

 From I-90, take Rte. 169 exit south. Turn right onto 7th and right on Main Street. Store's on right.

BRAINERD

CROW WING FOOD CO-OP
823 Washington Street, 56401 • (218)828-4600
According to Crow Wing Co-op staffer, Phil, the store has an excellent collection of glass snow globes. Phil's message to the masses... "Organic is where it's at!"
M-F 10-5:30, Sat. 10-4

 Store's 3 blocks east of the "water tower," intersection of 371 and 210 (also known as Washington St.), on the left.

BURNSVILLE

VALLEY NATURAL FOODS CO-OP
14015 Grand Avenue South, 55337 • (612)892-6667
Store has an information booth with a helpful reference section.
M-Sat. 9-9

 From north: off I-35W, take county road 42/ Burnsville Ctr. exit east. Turn left on Nicollet Ave., then left on Grand. Store's on right in McAndrew's Center. From south: off I-35, split on to I-35E. Take County Road 42 exit and turn left. Turn right on Nicollet. Same as above.

CAMBRIDGE

MINNESOTA ORGANIC MERCHANT (M.O.M.'S) FOOD CO-OP
1709 East Highway 95, 55008 • (612)689-4640
M-Sat. 9-6 (W-F 'til 8)

 Mom's Food Co-op is on State Hwy. 95, 1/4 mile east of bypass, near Cambridge exit signs.

DULUTH

 On the panoramic drive from Duluth to Canada, check out the Scenic Cafe on North Shore Dr., a restaurant that features whole foods cuisine with an organic emphasis.

WHOLE FOODS CO-OP
1332 East 4th Street, 55805 • (218)728-0884
Staffer Diana says their produce is "98% organic!" Picnic in the undeveloped park across from the store (complete with stream).
Sun.-Sun. 8-8

 From I-35, take Mesaba Ave. exit to 2nd St. Go right on 2nd St. and turn left on 14th Ave. Store's on left corner of 4th St. and 14th Ave.

ELY

 Pronounced "e-lee," this is the canoe capital of the world, on the edge of the Boundary Waters Canoe area.

NORTHWOODS WHOLE FOODS CO-OP
125 North Central, 55731 • (218)365-4039
Summer produce only. A small store in a small town, this co-op has an old-fashioned atmosphere. Member owned and operated for over 20 years.
M-Sat. 10-5:30

 Store's off of main intersection in town, four doors down from the Moose Restaurant.

GRAND MARAIS

COOK COUNTY WHOLE FOODS CO-OP
10 1st Avenue West, 55604 • (218)387-2503
Right on Lake Superior, they carry hand-harvested wild rice and local maple syrup. The only place in town to get organic produce!
M-F 10-5, Sat. 10-4

 From Hwy. 61, follow signs to downtown Grand Marais. Store's on left, across from the Blue Water Cafe.

GRAND RAPIDS

COVE WHOLE FOODS CO-OP
204 1st Avenue NW, 55744 • (218)327-1088
As of this printing, this store is for sale. Brewed Awakenings, the coffeehouse on-site, will remain and continue to offer prepared natural and vegetarian foods. However, the co-op will close and the name of the store will be Brewed Awakenings. The retail space will be more dedicated to vitamins and supplements, so call ahead to make sure they have what you need.
M-Sat. 10-6

 From Hwy. 2, turn south onto NW 1st Ave. Store's on left in Old Mill Place.

HASTINGS

SPIRAL FOOD CO-OP
307 East 2nd Street, 55033 • (612)437-2667
Features local produce (summer) and a frozen yogurt machine.
M-Th. 9-8, F 9-6, Sat. 9-5, Sun. 11-5

 From Rte. 61 north, make the first right after bridge to 3rd street. Take two quick rights onto 2nd street, and store will be on left. From Rte. 61 south turn onto 3rd St. (before bridge), then left on Ramsey and right on 2nd St. Store's on left.

ISLE

MILLE LACS AREA FOOD CO-OP
P.O. Box 233 Main Street, 56346 • (320)676-3813
One of the only volunteer run co-ops left in the state.
M-Sat. 10-5

 Store's on Main St. in Isle.

LITCHFIELD

NATURAL FOODS CO-OP
230 North Sibley Street, 55355 • (320)693-7539
M-F 10-6, Sat. 10-5

 West of Minneapolis on Hwy. 12. Store's right in town on Main St.

LONG PRAIRIE

EVERYBODY'S MARKET FOOD CO-OP
11 1st Street North, 56347 • (320)732-3900
Going on their 20th year.
M-F 9-5:30, Sat. 9-1

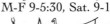 From Rte. 71, go east on Central St. for one block. Store's on left at corner of Central and 1st St.

MANKATO

CAYOL'S NATURAL FOODS
1400 Madison Avenue, Suite 600, 56001 • (507)389-9863
No produce. Store is soon expanding.
 M-F 9-8, Sat. 9-5, Sun. 12-5
From Hwy. 169, take Madison Ave. exit. Store's in Madison East Center mini-mall on left.

MINNEAPOLIS

Check out the City Pages, an alternative newspaper which highlights local happenings. Head downtown to natural food restaurant, Cafe Brenda or visit the Bella Luna Cafe in Old Riverside. There's also the French Meadow Bakery & Cafe for great soup, salads and sandwiches, Odaa, an East African restaurant on Cedar Ave., Kinhdo, an Asian restaurant on Hennepin Ave. and Organica Deli, an all organic (and mostly vegetarian) deli on Central Ave.

CAYOL'S NATURAL FOODS
811 La Salle Avenue, 55402 • (612)339-2828 (800)658-4804
No produce. Store has a frozen yogurt bar and grocery section will be expanding.
M-F 8:30-6:30, Sat. 9:30-4:30, (Sun. 12-5 during school year)

Take 394 to downtown, then take 11th or 12th (depending on direction you are coming from). Turn north on La Salle. Store's on right, across from Dayton's.

LINDEN HILLS FOOD CO-OP
4306 Upton Avenue South, 55410 • (612)922-1159
Sun.-Sun. 9-9

From 35W north: Take 6th street exit. Go right and drive until you run into Lake Calhoun. Make a left and drive to Sheridan (turns into Upton). At 43rd, take a right and store will be on left. If on Crosstown, get off on Xerxes and go north. Make a right on 43rd and store will be on right.

NORTH COUNTRY FOOD CO-OP
1929 South 5th Street, 55454 • (612)338-3110
A neighborhood co-op. Unpretentious with a helpful staff, the store is down the street from public radio station KFAI, the Free Wheel Bike Co-op and other kindred spirits.
 M-Sat. 9-9, Sun., 9-8

From I-94 west: Take the 25th St. exit and turn west on Riverside. Store's on corner of 20th and Riverside. From I-94 east: Take Riverside exit west. Store's on left at corner of 20th and Riverside. (Store has parking on west side of building).

PEOPLE'S COMPANY BAKERY CO-OP
1534 Lake Street E • (612)721-7205
O.K., O.K., they're not a natural foods store. Check out this 25+ year old cooperative-run bakery that uses organic flours. They sell baked goods at wholesale prices, day-old bread and "goodies."
M-F 9-5, Sat. 9-2

SEWARD COMMUNITY CO-OP
2111 East Franklin Avenue, 55404 • (612)338-2465
Sun.-Sun. 9-9

From I-94, take Riverside exit south and turn right on Franklin. Store's on left.

TAO NATURAL FOODS AND BOOKS
2200 Hennepin Avenue South, 55405 • (612)377-4630
M-Th. 9-8, F & Sat. 9-7, Sun. 12-6 (open 1 hour later in summer)
Cafe: closes 1 hour earlier than rest of store
A very small grocery with no produce or tofu. Store has a variety of vegetarian food, vegan soups, and fruit and vegetable juices.

One block south of Franklin on Hennepin Ave., in the uptown area.

WEDGE COMMUNITY CO-OP
2105 Lyndale Avenue South, 55405 • (612)871-3993
Award-winning, famous co-op (but they're all great in Minneapolis!). Recently expanded in 1997, the store is now a full service natural food supermarket complete with juice bar and a meat/seafood department.
M-F 9-10, Sat. & Sun. 9-9

From I-94, take Lyndale exit south. The Wedge is on left.

MINNETONKA

LAKEWINDS NATURAL FOODS
17523 Minnetonka Boulevard, 55345 • (612)473-0292
M-Sat. 8-9, Sun. 9-8

Corner of Hwy. 101 and Minnetonka Boulevard.

MORRIS

POMME DE TERRE FOOD CO-OP
25 East 7th Street, 56267 • (320)589-4332
"Going out of business since 1971!" Produce by special order only.
M-Sat. 10-6 (Th. 'til 8)

From Rte. 28, head south into the town on Atlantic. Turn left on 7th. Store's 2 blocks down on left.

OAK CENTER

OAK CENTER GENERAL STORE FOOD CO-OP
Route 1 Box 52BB/Highway 63, 55041 • (507)753-2080
A unique store in an old building. Organic produce from the store's farm is featured in the summer, but produce is limited in the winter. Live music featured November through April. Call ahead for details.
M-Sat. 8-6, Sun. 12-5

Ten miles south of Lake City or 25 miles north of Rochester on Hwy. 63.

OWATONNA

HARVEST FOOD CO-OP
137 East Front Street, 55060 • (507)451-0340
M-F 9:30-5:30, Sat. 9-1

On North end of town, across the street from a big grain elevator.

PRESTON

COMMUNITY MARKET & DELI
110 St. Anthony Street • (507)765-5245
Seasonal organic produce.
M-F 8-7, Sat. 9-5, Sun. 10-4
(Dec.-April, store closes M-F at 6 and is closed Sun.)

 Across from Courthouse Square, 1.5 blocks from Route River Trail Head.

ROCHESTER

THE GOOD FOOD STORE (CO-OP)
1001 6th Street NW, 55901 • (507)289-9061
Recently expanded, store features an impressive bulk section.
M-F 9-9, Sat. 9-8, Sun. 10-6

 From Hwy. 52, exit at Civic Center Drive. Turn left on 11th Ave. and right on 6th St. NW. Store's first building on left.

ST. CLOUD

GOOD EARTH FOOD CO-OP
2010 8th Street North, Centennial Plaza, 56303 • (320)253-9290
M-F 8:30-9, Sat. 8:30-8, Sun. 11-6

 From I-94, take exit for Hwy. 15 N and turn right on 8th St. Store's 15 blocks down on right.

INEZ NATUREWAY FOODS
3715 3rd Street North, 56303 • (320)259-0514
No produce. They cater to those with food sensitivities.
M-F 9-7, Sat. 9-3

 From I-94, take exit for Hwy. 15 N and turn right on 3rd St. Store's on left, across from Northwest Fabrics.

ST. PAUL

Recommended St. Paul restaurants: Khyber Pass Cafe (Afgani) on St. Clair Ave. has a cool atmosphere, Caravan Serai on Ford Parkway features Middle Eastern and White Lily on Grand Ave. serves Vietnamese fare.

CAPITAL CITY CO-OP GROCERY
26 West 10th Street, 55102 • (612)298-1340
M-F 9-9, Sat. & Sun. 9-6

 From I-94 east: Take 10th St. exit and the co-op is on corner of 10th and St. Peter. From I-94 west: Take 12th St. exit and make a left on St. Peter. Store's on corner of 10th and St. Peter.

HAMPDEN PARK FOOD CO-OP
928 Raymond Avenue, 55114 • (612)646-6686
One of the few co-ops still staffed by volunteers.
M-F 9-9, Sat. 9-7, Sun. 10-7

 3 blocks north of University Ave. on Raymond.

MISSISSIPPI MARKET
1810 Randolph Avenue, 55105 • (612)690-0507
Sun.-Sun. 8:30-9

 From I-94, take Snelling Ave. exit south and turn right on Randolph. Store's on left at corner of Randolph and Fairview.

WHOLE FOODS MARKET
30 Fairview Avenue South, 55105 • (612)690-0197

 Sun.-Sun. 9-10
On corner of Grand and Fairview.

ST. PETER

ST. PETER FOOD CO-OP
119 West Broadway, 56082 • (507)931-4880
Store has a large bulk and produce section. Local produce in season.
M-Sat. 8-8, Sun. 9-7

 From Hwy. 169, go east on Broadway. Store's at corner of Broadway and Hwy. 169.

STILLWATER

VALLEY CO-OP
215 North William Street, 55082 • (612)439-0366
A friendly place to stop for good food.
M-F 8:30-9, Sat. 8:30-6, Sun. 11-6

 3 miles north of 36, just off Myrtle.

VIRGINIA

NATURAL HARVEST WHOLE FOOD CO-OP
505 3rd Street North, 55792 • (218)741-4663
On Bailey's Lake (check out the lake's walking path). Store has a small cooperative garden.
M-F 8-8, Sat. 8-6, Sun. 11-5

 From Hwy. 169, turn north on Hwy. 53 and drive to first set of lights. Turn right on 9th Ave., go all the way past hospital and at second set of lights, make a right on 6th Ave. Go to 2nd St. North and drive around block to get on 3rd. Store's right on Bailey's Lake.

WHITE BEAR LAKE

SASSAFRAS
4746 Washington Square, 55110 • (612)426-0101
M-Th. 9-8, F 9-7, Sat. 9-6, Sun. 12-5

 From I-694, go north on 61. Once in White Bear Lake, go east (right) on 4th St., then take next right on Washington Square. Store's right there.

WILLMAR

KANDI CUPBOARD FOOD CO-OP
412 Litchfield Avenue SW, 56201 • (320)235-9477
M-F 9-6, Sat. 9-5

 From Hwy. 12, turn south on 3rd then drive west on Litchfield. Store's on right.

WINDOM

PLUM CREEK FOOD CO-OP
183 10th Street, 56101 • (507)831-1882
No produce.
M-F 9:30-5 (M 'til 8), Sat. 9:30-3

 Across from the town square.

WINONA

BLUFF COUNTRY FOOD CO-OP
114 East 2nd Street, 55987 • (507)452-1815
M-W 9-6, Th. & F 9-8, Sat. 9-6, Sun. 11-5

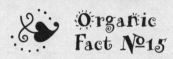 From I-90, take Hwy. 43 exit north and drive about 7 miles. Cross Hwy. 61 (road becomes Mankato Ave.) and stay on Mankato. Turn left on 2nd. Store's on right.

Organic Fact Nº15

PESTICIDE USAGE

According to the EPA's Office of Prevention, Pesticides and Toxic Substances, about 2.2 billion pounds of pesticides are used annually in the U.S. Pesticides are not just used for conventional crops, but also in homes, gardens, schools, offices, grocery stores, golf courses and parks.

Mississippi

1. GULFPORT
2. JACKSON
3. LONG BEACH
4. OCEAN SPRINGS

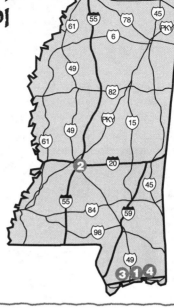

GULFPORT

RENAISSANCE NATURAL FOODS
1702 West Pass Road, 39501 • (228)864-4898
Limited organic produce.
M-F 9:30-5:30, Sat. 10-5

   Store's 8 blocks east of Hwy. 49 on Pass Rd. in an older white house with green trim (connected to a strip mall).

JACKSON

In Jackson, check out Le Fluer's Bluff State Park and the National Science Museum.

FOR HEALTH'S SAKE
235 Highland Village, 39211 • (601)981-2838
"The largest complete health food store in Mississippi" Owner loves to help people find local spots to visit.
M-Sat. 10-6

     From I-55, get off at the Northside Dr. exit. Store faces I-55, right under the highway.

RAINBOW WHOLE FOODS CO-OP
2807 Old Canton Road, 39216 • (601)366-1602
M-Sat. 9-7

     From I-55, take Lakeland Dr. exit west about 3 blocks. The road dead-ends at Old Canton Rd. and store's right there!

LONG BEACH

RENAISSANCE NATURAL FOODS
104 West Railroad, 39560 • (228)865-9911
Limited organic produce.
M-F 9:30-5:30, Sat. 10-5

 From Hwy. 90 in Long Beach, go north on Jeff Davis. Store's at intersection of Jeff Davis & Railroad.

OCEAN SPRINGS

 Check out The Walter Anderson Museum of Art.

FIVE SEASONS WHOLE FOODS MARKET
601 Washington Avenue, 39564 • (601)875-8882
M-Sat. 9:30-5:30

 From I-10, take exit #50 south on Washington Ave. Store's past Hwy. 90 on right.

Organic Fact №16

ORGANIC SHOPPER STATISTICS

According to the 1996 Fresh Trends Report, published by The Packer:

Percentage of those who buy organic produce are satisfied with the quality: 97%

Percentage of shoppers who have bought natural or organic produce in the previous six months: 23%

Purchases of organic are highest among those aged 40-49 at 28%; followed with the age group 18-29 at 27%; Age 60+ had the lowest level of purchases.

Missouri

1. COLUMBIA
2. KANSAS CITY
3. ST. LOUIS
4. SPRINGFIELD
5. WEBSTER GROVES

COLUMBIA

Recommendations: Vegetarian restaurant The Main Squeeze, Bangkok Gardens features yummy Thai food and Ozark Mountain Bar and Grill is a friendly, authentic place to hang out. Also check out Devil's Icebox in Rockbridge State Park (an underground cavern).

CLOVERS NATURAL FOOD
802 Business Loop 70E, 65201 • (573)449-1650
"The narrowest, longest store in existence. Kinda pie shaped."
M-Sat. 9-7, Sun. 12-5

 From I-70, take Rangeline exit south one block and turn right on Business Loop. Store's on left.

KANSAS CITY

In the basement of the Unity Temple on the Plaza, check out the funky vegetarian restaurant, Eden Alley.

CITY GARDEN & BLUEBIRD CAFE
1700 Summit Street, 64108 • (816)221-7559
Small natural food convenience store attached to vegetarian cafe.
M-Sat. 8:30-7, Sun. 10-4

From I-70 west, take the Broadway exit and go south on Broadway to 17th. Turn west onto 17th and store's 3 blocks down on the southwest corner. From I-35 north, take the Broadway exit, go south on Broadway and follow above directions.

WILD OATS MARKET
4301 Main Street, 64111 • (816)931-1873
M-Sat. 8-9, Sun. 9-8

 From I-35, take Southwest Trafficway exit south. Turn left on 43rd. Store's on right, corner of 43rd and Main.

131

ST. LOUIS

 The arch lives up to its image. Designed by Eero Saarinen with a curvaceous elegance that gives the Washington Monument a run for its money. Visit Ethiopian restaurant, the Red Sea, on Delmar and Sunshine Inn on S. Euclid Ave.

GOLDEN GROCER
335 North Euclid Avenue, 63108 • (314)367-0405
M-Sat. 10-7, Sun. 12-5

 From I-40, take Kings Hwy. north. Turn right on Maryland and left on Euclid. Store's on left, set back a bit.

GOLDEN GROCER
559 North & South Road, 63018 • (314)862-0777
M-Sat. 10-7, Sun. 12-5

From I-40, get on I-70, then take Delmar exit east. Turn right on North & South Rd. Store's on right.

THE NATURAL WAY
12345 Olive Boulevard, 63141 • (314)878-3001
M-F 9:30-8, Sat. 9:30-6:30, Sun. 12-5

 From 270, take Olive St. exit west. Store is 2 blocks down on north side of Olive in Woodcrest Center.

WILD OATS MARKET
8823 Ladue Road, 63124 • (314)721-8004
Sun.-Sun. 8-10

 Store's 1/2 mile east of I-70, on east side of Ladue Rd.

SPRINGFIELD

 Check out vegetarian restaurant, Well Spring Cafe.

AKIN'S NATURAL FOODS
1330 East Battlefield Road, 65804 • (417)887-5985
M-Sat. 9-8, Sun. 12-5

 From I-44, head south on I-65 to Battlefield Rd. Take Battlefield west. Store's on corner of Battlefield and Fremont in Fremont Shopping Center.

AU NATUREL
1135 East St. Louis, 65806 • (417)866-1337
Store sells lots of ethnic goodies in their cafe.
M-F 10-6, Sat. 9-5, Cafe: M-Sat. 11-2

 From I-44, take Business 65 (Glenstone Ave.) south. Turn right on Saint Louis St., cross National St. and store's in pink building on right.

SPRING VALLEY
1738 South Glenstone Avenue, 65804 • (417)882-1033
No produce.
M-Sat. 10-10

 From I-44, go south on Business 65. Take Sunshine exit west (turns into Glenstone). Store's on the right, next to the Park Inn.

Check out **The Natural Fact**, a natural food deli down the street from The Natural Way.

THE NATURAL WAY
8110 Big Bend, 63119 • (314)961-3541
M-F 9-9, Sat. 9-7, Sun. 10-6

 From I-270, take I-44 exit east and get off at La Clede Station Rd./Murdock exit. Go over highway and go right onto Laclede Station, then make another right onto Murdock. Take a left onto Big Bend. Store's on left.

Organic Fact №17

PESTICIDE CROP USAGE

According to the EPA's Report on Conventional Pesticides Applied to Agricultural Crops in 1994-1995, each year an estimated 911 million pounds of synthetic pesticides are applied to conventional agricultural crops throughout the United States.

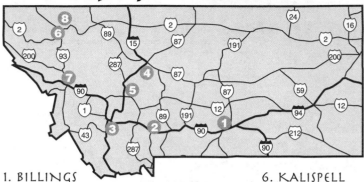

Montana

1. BILLINGS
2. BOZEMAN
3. BUTTE
4. GREAT FALLS
5. HELENA
6. KALISPELL
7. MISSOULA
8. WHITEFISH

BILLINGS

Evergreen Health Foods staffers recommend Japanese restaurant, the Great Wall. For coffee and light vegetarian fare, check out Cafe Jones.

EVERGREEN HEALTH FOODS
1507 14th Street West, 59102 • (406)259-4603
M-Sat. 9:30-5

From I-90, take City Center exit and follow signs to Billings. Turn right on King Ave., left on 24th St. W., right on Grand Ave. and left on 14th St. W. Store's on right in Evergreen Shopping Center.

GOOD EARTH MARKET
3115 10th Avenue, 59715 • (406)259-2622
M-Sat. 10-7, Sun. 12-5

From I-90/94, take 27th St. north exit. Go north and drive to 10th Ave. Take a right and store's at corner of 31st and 10th.

BOZEMAN

Lots of outdoor activities in Bozeman (they have 4 seasons... June, July, August and Winter!). Check out the Emerson Cultural Center in a converted school house. The space features art and Cafe International (recommended).

COMMUNITY FOOD CO-OP
908 West Main Street, 59715 • (406)587-4039
This Co-op has a large outdoor lawn and seating area and features spectacular views. And in the spirit of Bozeman's new glitterati residents, this Co-op has an espresso bar. As for those sub-zero winter temps...
Sun.-Sun. 8-10 (Closes 1 hour earlier in Winter)

From I-90 take Bozeman MSU exit and follow signs to Bozeman. Turn right onto Main St. Store's on left.

BUTTE

 Check out the Butte Hill Bakery and Northwest Noodles & Wraps.

DANCING RAINBOW NATURAL GROCERY
9 South Montana Street, 59701 • (406)723-8811
M-F 10-5:30, Sat. 10-5

 From I-90, take Montana exit and head north on Montana (uphill). Store's on left, next to (natural) Butte Hill Bakery.

NATURAL HEALING
1875 Harrison Avenue, 59771 • (406)782-8314
M-Sat. 9-6:30

 Take I-90 exit - Harrison Ave. Go up a few blocks and you'll find the store.

GREAT FALLS

2-J'S PRODUCE INC.
105 Smelter Avenue NE, 59404 • (406)761-0134
Store offers free coffee while you shop!
M-Sat. 9-7

 From I-15, take Central Ave. exit west about 1 mile and curve right onto Smelter. Store's on left.

HELENA

 The No-Sweat Cafe serves organic food and lots of ambiance. "It's a funky little place with great food," say Real Food staffers.

REAL FOOD STORE
501 Fuller Avenue, 59601 • (406)443-5150
"Largest health food store in Montana!" Deli is all vegetarian.
M-F 8-7, Sat. 9-6, Sun. 9-3

 From I-15, take Capital exit and go down Prospect. Go left on Montana and then right on 11th
Ave. Follow 11th to downtown and through 'malfunction junction'. After this kooky intersection you'll be on Neal Ave. Take a left onto Fuller and store's on left.

KALISPELL

 Kalispell is 30 minutes from Glacier National Park and Flathead Lake, the largest freshwater lake west of the Mississippi. Check out Montana Coffee Traders, their bakery and restaurant which features vegetarian fare.

MOUNTAIN VALLEY FOODS
404 1st Avenue East, 59901 • (406)756-1422
M-Sat. 9-5:30

From Rte. 93, take 4th St. E. and turn right on 1st Ave. E. Store's on right.

MISSOULA

Good Food Store staffer, Carey, has Missoula recommendations. Check out the Black Dog Cafe on Broadway and The Hob Nob Cafe on East Main (both feature yummy vegetarian options). For hiking, he recommends the Rattlesnake Recreation Area and the 'M' Trail (to view the city from above).

Head over to the Ironhouse microbrewery or try some of the local microbrews from Big Sky Brewery and Bear Grass brewing. Carey says, "if you're into beer and cruising through Missoula, you gotta try em all..."

FREDDY'S FEED & READ
1221 Helen Avenue, 59801 • (406)549-2127
Some organic produce.
M-F 7:30-9, Sat. & Sun. 9-7

From I-90, take Van Buren exit south. Turn right on Broadway, left on Madison St., right on University and left on Helen. Store's on right.

GOOD FOOD STORE
920 Kensington Avenue, 59801 • (406)728-5823
M-Sat. 8-9, Sun. 10-6

From I-90, take Orange St. exit south (Orange becomes Stephens). Store's on left at corner of Kensington and Stephens.

WHITEFISH

"This place is cool!" says Macaroni & Chreese aficionado, Matt, about the area. Check out the Direwolf Pub for great homebrews and Glacier National Park. It's just 20 minutes from Whitefish.

THIRD STREET MARKET
244 Spokane Avenue, 59937 • (406)862-5054
M-Sat. 9-6

Take Rte. 40 to Hwy. 93 to Whitefish. Store's at corner of Hwy. 93 and Third St.

Nebraska

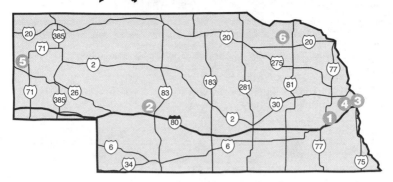

1. LINCOLN
2. NORTH PLATTE
3. OMAHA
4. RALSTON
5. SCOTTSBLUFF
6. WINNETOON

LINCOLN

In downtown Lincoln, visit Crane River Brewpub and Cafe (they serve decadent vegetarian dishes). Open Harvest Co-op staffer Jackie recommends Wilderness Park and the Nature Center at Pioneer's Park.

AKIN'S NATURAL FOODS
6900 "O" Street, 68510 • (402)466-5713
Store began as a small buying club in the 40's.
M-Sat. 9-9, Sun. 12-6:30

 From I-80, take exit 409 and head west on Cornhusker Hwy./Hwy. 6. Go south on 84th, then take a right on "O" Street. Store's in Meridian Park Shopping Center on right.

OPEN HARVEST CO-OP
1618 South Street, 68502 • (402)475-9069
Sun.-Sun. 9-9

 From I-80, take West "O" St. exit and drive east. Turn right on 16th and go about 20 blocks to South St. Store's on left, at corner of 16th and South.

NORTH PLATTE

HAPPY HEART SPECIALTY FOODS
301 S. Jeffers, 66101 • (308)532-1505
Store grinds its own flour for baked goods.
M-F 9-5:30, Sat. 9-5

 From I-80, get off at North Platte exit. Go right onto Dewey St. and right onto "C" St. Store's at corner of "C" and Jeffers.

NATURAL NUTRITION HOUSE
203 West 6th Street, 69101 • (308)532-9433
Occasional seasonal organic produce.
M-Sat. 9-5:30

 From I-80, take Rte. 83 exit north, turn left on 5th St. then right on Vine. Store's on left in large white house, corner of Vine and 6th.

OMAHA

 Folks at Community Natural Foods Co-op recommend McFoster's Natural Cafe and Daisy Maze (vegetarian). They also suggest Fontedelle Forest for hiking.

COMMUNITY NATURAL FOODS CO-OP
10801 Blondo Street, 68164 • (402)431-8494
M-F 12-7 (Th. 10-7), Sat. 12-5:30

 From I-680, take Maple St. west to 108th. Go south on 108th to Blondo. Store's on corner.

RALSTON

GRAINERY WHOLE FOODS MARKET & RESTAURANT
7409 Main Street, 68127 • (402)593-7186
M-F 10-6:30, Sat. 10-6, Sun. 1-4:30

 From I-80, take 72nd St. exit to Main (second light south of L St.). Turn right on Main St. and store's on left.

SCOTTSBLUFF

TAMARAK'S FOODS OF THE EARTH
1914 Broadway, 69361 • (308)635-1514
This store serves the only Tofu Burger in town! Try the bakery next door for coffee, pie and lunch.
M-Sat 9-5:30 (Th. 'til 6)

 From Rte. 26, take 20th St. west to Broadway and go left on Broadway. Store's 1/2 block down on right.

WINNETOON

WINNETOON MINI MALL CO-OP
Main Street, 68789 • (402)847-3368
Serving a community of 68, this small cooperative grocery is also a post office and antique store. Very nice folks, but no produce. If you're in northeast Nebraska, stop by for bulk, herbs, spices and dairy.
M-F 8-4, (F eves. 6-9) - Other times open by appt.

 Winnetoon is 4 miles north of Hwy. 59 or 14. Follow sign that points to Winnetoon and drive 4 miles into center of town.

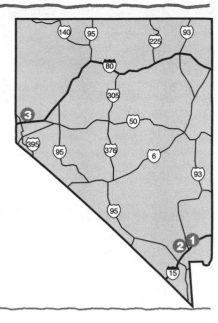

Nevada

1. HENDERSON
2. LAS VEGAS
3. RENO

HENDERSON

TRADER JOE'S CO.
2716 North Green Valley Parkway, 89014 • (702)433-6773
Limited organic produce.
Sun.-Sun. 9-9

On corner of Green Valley and Sunset Road in Henderson.

LAS VEGAS

Well, this town can be a toughie for vegetarian food. Consult an area phone book for Indian restaurant listings and check out the mostly vegetarian Pneumatic Diner on W. First Street (downtown). If you decide to do it Vegas style, we highly recommend the very delicious (and cheap) pancakes available 24 hours a day at the Pink Pony Cafe in the Circus Circus Hotel and Casino.

RAINBOW'S END NATURAL FOODS
1100 East Sahara Avenue, 89104 • (702)737-7282
One of the oldest natural food stores in Las Vegas.
M-Sat. 9-9, Sun. 11-6

Six blocks east of the strip on E. Sahara.

WILD OATS MARKET EAST
3455 East Flamingo, 89121 • (702)434-8115
A comprehensive natural food market.
Sun.-Sun. 8-9

From I-15, take E. Flamingo Rd. exit east about 3 miles. Store's on right.

NEVADA

WILD OATS MARKET WEST
6720 West Sahara, 89102 • (702)253-7050
Wild Oats staffer James says, "Our organic produce is second to none!"
Their salad bar is 85% organic, the juice bar is all organic and the cafe serves
organic coffee and tea.
Sun.-Sun. 8-9 (Cafe closes at 8)

From I-15, take West Sahara exit about 3.5 miles. Store's on right.

RENO

 **In Reno, check out the Blue Heron Natural Food Restaurant and Bakery.**

WASHOE-ZEPHYR FOOD CO-OP
314 Broadway Boulevard, 89502 • (702)323-0391
Open since 1975, this store is Reno's natural food source.
M-Sat. 10-7, Sun. 12-6

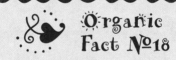

From I-80, take Wells Ave. south about 2 miles and turn left on Broadway. Store's 1/2 block down on left.

Organic Fact №18

PESTICIDE EXPORTS

According to the Foundation for Advancements in Science and Education, a non-profit research organization in Los Angeles, over 344 million pounds of potentially dangerous pesticides were legally exported by the U.S. from 1992 through 1994.

New Hampshire

1. CONCORD
2. DOVER
3. EXETER
4. HAMPTON
5. HANOVER
6. KEENE
7. LEBANON
8. LITTLETON
9. MANCHESTER
10. NEW LONDON
11. NEW MARKET
12. PETERBOROUGH
13. PLAISTOW
14. PORTSMOUTH
15. PLYMOUTH
16. SALEM
17. TILTON
18. WOLFEBORO

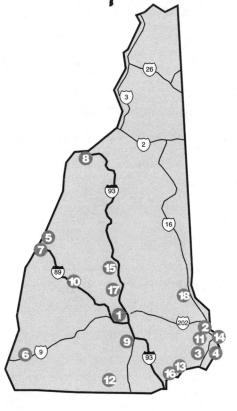

CONCORD

 Check out The Sandwich Depot on Hall Street, a relaxed spot for breakfast, lunch or dinner.

CONCORD FOOD CO-OP
24 1/2 South Main Street, 03301 • (603)225-6840
M-F 9-7, Sat. 9-6, Sun. 11-5

 From I-93, take Rte. 3 exit and head toward downtown. Store's behind Mailboxes Etc., and is close to Pleasant St.

GRANITE STATE NATURAL FOODS
164 N. State Street, 03301 • (603)224-9341
Store stocks homebrew supplies.
M-F 9-7, Sat. 9-5, Sun. 10-5

 From I-93, take 15 west to I-393. At second set of lights, stay to right (will be North Main which turns into State St.). Store's on right across from City Park. (Store has a funky mural on the side... hard to miss!)

DOVER

 Check out the Goodwill Thrift shop across from Dover Natural Foods.

DOVER NATURAL FOODS AND CAFE
24 Chestnut Street, 03820 • (603)749-9999
Deli's vegan cook, Diane (also a huge fan of the Tofu Tollbooth), says this riverside spot is a great place to get out, stretch and walk the dog. It's also a short walk from downtown Dover.
M-Sat. 9:30-7, Sun. 12-4

 From I-95, north or south, get onto
Spaulding Turnpike (Rte. 16) north to Dover. Take exit 8A - Silver St. and at second light (Locust St.) turn left. After Police station, road will fork. Bear left and it will become Chestnut St. Go through next light, over bridge and store's on right.

EXETER

 The Loaf & Ladle serves some vegetarian fare.

THE BLUE MOON MARKET
8 Clifford Street, 03833 • (603)778-6850
M-F 10-6, Sat. 10-4, Sun. 12-4

 In Stratam, take Portland Ave. and follow to its end in Exeter. At light, go right. The road splits. Go left onto Clifford and store's 100 yards up on left.

HAMPTON

HAMPTON NATURAL FOODS
321 Lafayette Road, 03842 • (603)926-5950
M-Sat. 9:30-7, Sun. 12-4

 Lafayette Rd. is Rte 1. Store's just east of I-95 in same building as Hampton Cinemas.

HANOVER

Hanover is home to Dartmouth College, the Appalachian trail (runs 1000 yards from the Co-op entrance) and The Hopkins Center which regularly brings artists, dancers and musicians to the area. Ryan at the Lebanon Co-op recommends renting a canoe from the Ledyard Canoe Club to paddle up the Connecticut River.

HANOVER CONSUMER CO-OP
45 South Park Street/P.O. Box 633, 03755 • (603)643-2667
Since 1979, the Hanover & Lebanon Co-ops have offered child car seat rentals in 4 different sizes... from infant to boosters. 50 cents a month for co-op members, $1 per month for non-members.
Sun.-Sun. 8-8

From I-89, take exit 18 (Hanover). Drive Rte. 120 into Hanover. Store's on right as you enter town.

KEENE

 Keene suggestions: Country Life has a vegetarian buffet and small natural food store, Brewbakers serves coffee, pastries, soup and sandwiches (Blueberry Fields Market folks love relaxing there on the couch) and Colony Mill, the town brew pub, also comes recommended. Also check out Keene Bagelworks for yummy bagels.

BLUEBERRY FIELDS MARKET
48 Emerald Street, 03431 • (603)358-5207
M-F 9-7, Sat. 9-6. Sun. 11-5

 Take I-91 to Rte. 9 north (9 turns into 101). In Keene, take a left at third light onto Main St. Go about 8 blocks, then turn left onto Emerald St. across from the Bagelry. Store's on left.

THE VITALITY SHOP
116 Main Street, 03431 • (603)357-3639
No organic produce, but a very nice store.
M-Th. 9-6, F 9-7, Sat. 9-5, Sun. 11-4

 From Rte. 9, get onto 12 south and go left at stoplight onto Main St. Store's on right near Keene Bagelworks.

LEBANON

THE LEBANON CO-OP FOOD STORE
12 Centerra Parkway, 03766 • (603)643-2667
Store offers child car seat rentals and self-guided tours for unfamiliar shoppers. The Lebanon & Hanover Co-ops (affiliated) are 2 miles from each other.
Sun.-Sun. 7-9

 From I-89, take exit 18 (Hanover) and drive on Rte. 120 into Hanover. Store's two miles from interstate on right in Centerra Marketplace.

LITTLETON

 Franconia Notch Brewery comes recommended.

HEATLHY RHINO
106 Main Street, 03561 • (603)444-2177
M-Sat. 9-6, (F 'til 8), Sun. 11-5

From I-93, take exit 41 (Hospital/Littleton). Go east on Cottage St. past Hospital and then left at first stoplight onto Main. Store's 2 blocks down on right in Parker's Marketplace.

MAGOON'S
103 Main Street, 03561 • (603)444-6634
M-Th. 10-5:30, F 10-6, Sat. 10-5, Sun. 11-3

 From I-93 north, take exit 41 and go to light. Take a right onto Main St. Store's on right next to Thayer's Inn.

MANCHESTER

A MARKET
125 Loring Street, 03103 • (603)668-2650
M-Sat. 9:30-6 (Th. 'til 9), Sun. 11-5

From I-293, take S. Willow St. exit (#1) north for one mile. Turn left on Loring and store's on left.

NEW LONDON

FOURTEEN CARROTS NATURAL FOODS MARKET
New London Shopping Center, 03257 • (603)526-2323
M-Sat. 9-5:30 (Th. & F til 6), Sun. 11-3

From I-89 north, take exit 11. Go right at end of ramp, drive a mile up the hill, then take a left onto Main St. Drive a few miles, bear to left when road bends and store's a few blocks up on left in New London Shopping Center. From I-89 south, take exit 12 and go left at end of ramp. Drive a few miles into New London and store's on right behind a bank in New London Shopping Center.

NEW MARKET

CORNERSTONE NATURAL FOODS
170 Main Street, 03857 • (603)659-8209
Area resident Dan says Cornerstone Natural Foods is, "a bit of an alternative student center, despite its tiny size." Cafe open for lunch, breakfast and dinner. Every Wednesday is all-you-can-eat pasta night. No produce.
M 6:30-1, Tu. 6:30-7, W 6:30-9, Th. 6:30-7, F & Sat. 6:30-9, Sun. 6:30-7

Take I-95 to last exit before tollbooth. In Exeter, take 108 north into New Market. At blinking light, look for store on left.

PETERBOROUGH

Check out the Toadstool Bookshop.

MAGGIE'S MARKETPLACE
14 Main Street, 03458 • (603)924-7671
M-F 9-6 (Th. 'til 7), Sat. 9-5, Sun. 11-3

From Rte. 101, head north on Grove and turn right on Main St. Store's on right.

PLAISTOW

BREAD AND HONEY
18 Plaistow Road, Plaza 125, 03865 • (603)382-6432
M-F 9-5:30, Sat. 9-5

From Rte. 495, take exit 51B (still in Mass). Take 125 north a few miles into Plaistow (just over MA/NH border). Store's on left.

PORTSMOUTH

Portsmouth is a beautiful coastal town which offers plentiful swimming in its nearby rivers and sea. Recommendations: Nektar juice bar, Ceres Street Bakery on Penhallow St. serves delicious lunches and visit the ever-quirky restaurant, the Friendly Toast!

PORTSMOUTH HEALTH FOODS

151 Congress Street, 03801 • (603)436-1722
Established in 1968.
M & T 9-6:30, W & Th. 9-7, F 9-6:30, Sat. 9-6, Sun. 11-5

From I-95, get off at exit 7 - Market St. From north, take a left onto Market, from the south, go right onto Market. Either way, head into downtown. At blinking yellow light, bear right. Take a right at stop sign onto Deer St. and first left onto Maplewood Ave. Go through light and take a left into parking lot. Store's on corner of Maplewood Ave. and Congress. (Rear and front entrances).

PLYMOUTH

PEPPERCORN NATURAL FOODS

43 Main Street, 03264 • (603)536-3395
Seasonal produce only.
M-Th. 9-5:30, F 9-7, Sat. 9-5

From I-93, take exit 25 into Plymouth. Store's on south Main on left, next to movie theater.

SALEM

Check out Field of Dreams, an open park with trails to get away from it all!

NATURAL MARKETPLACE

419 South Broadway, 03079 • (603)893-2893
Organic carrots only.
M-W 10-6, Th. & F 10-8, Sat. 10-5:30

From Rte. 93, take exit 1 to 28 south. Store's 2 miles down on left.

TILTON

SWAN LAKE NATURAL FOODS

266 Main Street, 03276 • (603)286-4405
M-Th. 9-6, F 9-8, Sat. 9-6, Sun. 1-5

From 93, take exit 20 and take a right toward downtown. Drive 1.5 miles and store's on left.

WOLFEBORO

EVERGRAIN

45 N. Main Street, 03894 • (603)569-4002
Check out Lydia's Cafe next to Evergrain!
M-Sat. 9:30-5:30, Sun. 11-4 (open one hour later every day in summer)

Take exit 15 off Spaulding Turnpike. Take Rte. 11 to Rte. 28 and follow signs to Wolfeboro. Store's on Main St. on left.

New Jersey

1. BAYONNE
2. CHESTER
3. DENVILLE
4. EAST RUTHERFORD
5. EMERSON
6. FREEHOLD
7. HOBOKEN
8. LINDENWOLD
9. LITTLE SILVER
10. MANAHAWKIN
11. MANALAPAN
12. MILLBURN
13. MONTCLAIR
14. MORRISTOWN
15. MOUNT LAUREL
16. NEW BRUNSWICK
17. NEWTON
18. NORTH ARLINGTON
19. PARSIPPANY
20. POINT PLEASANT BEACH
21. PRINCETON
22. RED BANK
23. RIDGEWOOD
24. SCOTCH PLAINS

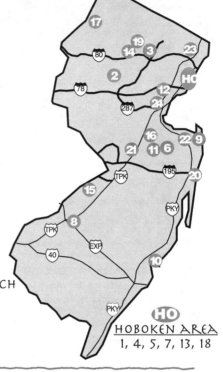

HO HOBOKEN AREA
1, 4, 5, 7, 13, 18

BAYONNE

JOHN'S NATURAL FOODS
486 Broadway, 07002 • (201)858-0088
M-Sat 9:30-6 (M, Th. & F 'til 9), Sun. 10-5

 From NJ Turnpike, take exit 14A and head south on Ave. E. Turn right on 22nd and right on Broadway. Store's in middle of block on right.

CHESTER

THE HEALTH SHOPPE
201 Route 206 South, 07930 • (908)879-7555
M-F 9-9, Sat. 9-6, Sun. 9-6

      Store's on north side of Rte. 206 in Chester Springs Shopping Center.

DENVILLE

Check out Metro Cafe for vegetarian fare.

MRS. ERB'S GOOD FOOD

20 First Avenue, 07834 • (973)627-5440
Mrs. Erb's offers in-store massages & facials.
M-F 9-8, Sat. 9-7, Sun. 10-5

 From I-80 west: Take
exit 37 (Denville). Get
on Rte. 46 east and drive 200 feet. Get in left lane, turn left, then take a quick right
onto Broadway. Drive straight and take first left onto First Ave. Store's on right.

EAST RUTHERFORD

THE THIRD DAY

220 Park Avenue, 07073 • (201)935-4045
M, Tu., Sat. 10-6, W-F 10-8,

 From NJ Turnpike, take exit 16W west to
Rte. 3. Take Ridge Rd. exit and turn right
(becomes Park Ave.) through Rutherford.
Go around traffic circle and cross RR tracks. Store's on right.

EMERSON

OLD HOOK FARM

650 Old Hook Road, 07630 • (201)265-4835
A grocery and farm!
Tu.-Sat. 9-6, Sun. 9-4

 From Garden State Parkway, take exit 165. Head toward
Oradell. Turn left on Kinderkamack Rd. and drive about 5 miles.
Turn right on Old Hook Rd. Store's on left.

FREEHOLD

PAULINE'S HEALTH FOODS

3585 Route 9 North, 07728 • (732)303-0854
M-F 9:30-7, Sat. 9:30-6, Sun. 11:30-5

 From New Jersey Turnpike, take exit 7A to 33 east to
Rte. 9 south. Store's about 2 miles down on north side
of highway.

HOBOKEN

HOBOKEN FARM BOY

229 Washington Street, 07030 • (201)656-0581
M-Sat. 8-10, Sun. 8-9

 From Rte. 1 & 9, take Hoboken exit. Before
Holland tunnel, go right to Observer Highway into
Hoboken. Take a left onto Washington Street. Store's between 2nd & 3rd on right.

LINDENWOLD

NATURAL HEALTH

Blackwood-Clementon & Laurel Roads, 08021 • (609)784-1021
M-F 9-8, Sat. 10-5, Sun. 12-5

 From NJ Turnpike, take exit 3 (Rte. 168/ Black Horse Pike)
south. Turn right on Rte. 42 toward Atlantic City. Take
Clementon exit and turn right on Clementon. Store's three miles down on right.

LITTLE SILVER

HEALTHFAIR
625 Branch Avenue, 07739 • (732)747-3140
M-F 9-7, Sat. 9-6, Sun. 10-5

From Garden State Parkway, take Redbank/Newman Springs Rd. exit (#109). Take Rte. 520 east. Turn right on Rte. 35, left on White Rd. and right on Branch. Store's 2 miles down on right.

MANAHAWKIN

EARTH GOODS NATURAL FOOD MARKET
777 East Bay Avenue, 08050 • (609)597-7744
M-F 10-7, Sat. 10-6, Sun. 11-4

From Garden State Parkway, take Manahawkin exit (#63). Get onto Rte. 72 east and then north on Rte. 9. From Rte. 9, turn right on Bay Ave. Store's on right.

MANALAPAN

PAULINE'S HEALTH FOODS
303 Route 9 South, 07726 • (732)308-0449
M-F 9:30-8:30, Sat. 9:30-6, Sun. 11-5

From Garden State Parkway, take exit 123 (Sayreville exit for Rte. 9). Drive south on Rte. 9 for 11 miles. Store's on south side of highway.

MILLBURN

FRESH FIELDS WHOLE FOODS MARKET
187 Millburn Avenue, 07041 • (973)376-4668
M-Sat. 8-9, Sun. 8-8

From Rte. 78 west, take exit 50B-Millburn onto Vauxhall Road. Go west and take a left onto Millburn Ave. Store's 2 blocks down on right.

MONTCLAIR

 Check out Eagle Rock Reservation for a nifty view of Manhattan from the beautiful hills of Montclair.

FRESH FIELDS WHOLE FOODS MARKET
701 Bloomfield Avenue, 07042 • (973)746-5110
M-Sat. 8-9, Sun. 8-8

From Garden State Parkway, take exit 128 - Bloomfield Ave. north and drive 3.5 miles into Montclair. Store's on right, just before Montclair ends and Verona begins.

MORRISTOWN

 Visit Chan Palace for great Indian food or the Mayflower for vegetarian Chinese.

THE HEALTH SHOPPE

66 Morris Street, 07960 • (973)538-9131

Organic produce only! One Tofu Tollbooth reader reports, "The Health Shoppe is the most fabulous health food store I've ever seen!"

M-F 9-9, Sat. 9-7, Sun. 9-6

 From I-287 north: Take Lafayette exit, bear right and come to a light. Continue through light and drive under railroad tracks. At next light, turn right onto Morris St. Store's on right in a shopping center (next to Burger King). From I-287 south: Take exit 36, go straight through 2 lights and make a right at second light. Store's on right.

MOUNT LAUREL

GARDEN OF EDEN NATURAL FOODS & COUNTRY KITCHEN

1155 North Route 73, 08054 • (609)778-1971

M-F 9-9, Sat. 9-6, Sun. 10-4, Restaurant: M-F 11-8, Sat. 11-5, Sun. 10-2

 From NJ Turnpike, take exit 4. Head south on Rte 73. Store's 1 mile down at intersection of Church Rd. and Route 73, in Ramblewood Center.

NEW BRUNSWICK

 This metropolitan New Joisey city features a rich cross section of folks from all walks of life. Stroll down George Street to the Cedar (by the fountain) for the best Lebanese food in a town full of Lebanese restaurants (we especially recommend the baba ganouj, baklava and rose lemonade). Also, the Old Bay has a large array of beer selections on tap. Need to escape into the forest? Helyar Woods off Rte. 1 toward Milltown is a nice break from the urban scene.

GEORGE STREET CO-OP

89 Morris Street, 08901 • (732)247-8280

New Jersey's beloved co-op. A very small store, yet community minded, friendly & welcoming.

M-F 10-8, Sat. 10-6, Sun 11-6

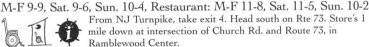 From NJ Turnpike, take exit 9 - New Brunswick. Bear right after toll and take Rte. 18 north through 2 lights (bear left whenever road curves). Exit right on New Street. At third light, make a left onto Livingston. Take first left onto Morris and find store on left. (Hint: The George Street Co-op is not on George St.)

NEWTON

SUSSEX COUNTY FOODS

30 Moran Street, 07860 • (973)579-1882

Seasonal produce.

M-Th. 9:30-5:30, F 9-9, Sat. 9:30-5:30, Sun. 1:15-5

Store's in center of Newton, twenty minutes north of I-80. From I-80, take 2nd Sparta exit (Rte. 15 north). Drive straight and look for the intersection with a Shell station and Grand Union. Go straight and the Racket Center will be on right. (You'll be on Newton-Sparta Rd. or Sparta Ave., it changes). Drive through Andover, then Newton and road will bear left. Go past Movie Theater, then turn right on Moran St. Store's a block and a half down on right in a brown building.

NORTH ARLINGTON

SURREY INTERNATIONAL NATURAL FOODS
33 Ridge Road, 07031 • (201)991-1905
M-F 9-7:30, Sun. 9-3

From NJ Turnpike, take exit 15W and stay on right. Take Kearny exit straight, then turn right on Schuyler Ave. (first light). Turn left on Belleville Turnpike and right on Ridge Rd. Store's on left and has a green awning.

PARSIPPANY

THE HEALTH SHOPPE
1123 Route 46 East, 07054 • (973)263-8348
M-F 9-9, Sat. 9-6, Sun. 11-6

From I-80, take Lake Hiawatha exit west, go over I-80 and take first left into Whippany Shopping Center.

POINT PLEASANT BEACH

WILD OATS NATURAL FOODS
1300 Richmond Avenue, 08742 • (732)899-2272
M-Th. & Sat. 9:30-5:30, F 9:30-7

Richmond Ave. is Rte. 35S, and it only goes south. Store's on left.

PRINCETON

WHOLE EARTH CENTER
360 Nassau Street, 08540 • (609)924-7429
M-F 10-7, Sat 10-6, Deli: M-F 10-6

From Rte. 1, head west on Harrison. Make a right at Nassau St. (Rte. 27). Store's at back of first driveway on left (hidden next to another store).

RED BANK

 Check out Red Bank's celebrated vegetarian restaurants, The Garden and also the Eurasian Eatery. The Basil Tea Leaf is a good brewery and tap room.

SECOND NATURE
65 Broad Street, 07701 • (732)747-6448
Nice people who work here... equally nice store. Organic, vegan soup featured every day.
M-F 10-8, Sat. 10-6, Sun. 10-5

Take Garden State Parkway to exit 109 - Red Bank. Get on Rte. 520 east until it dead ends at railroad tracks on Broad St./Rte. 35. Make a left and drive through 3 lights. Store's just past third light on right.

NEW JERSEY

150

RIDGEWOOD

NATURE'S MARKETPLACE
1 West Ridgewood Avenue, 07450 • (201)445-9210
M-Sat. 10-6 (Th. 'til 8)

 From Hwy. 17, take Ridgewood/Oradell exit and follow signs to Ridgewood to end. Take a right, then go to light and take a left. Go under railroad and take a right at next light. Store's on corner.

SCOTCH PLAINS

AUTUMN HARVEST HEALTH FOODS
1625 2nd Street, 07076 • (908)322-2130
M & F 9:30-7:30, T-Th. 9:30-8:30, Sat. 9:30-5, Sun. 10:30-3:30

 From Hwy. 22, go south on Terrill Rd., then turn left on 2nd St. Store's on left.

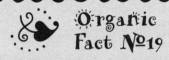

Organic Fact № 19

ORGANIC SHOPPING STATISTICS

Of all shoppers, 23 percent buy natural or organic foods at least once a week from supermarkets. 42 percent of mainstream stores carry organic products and average 12 items (Food Marketing Institutes 1995 Industry Speaks Report).

New Mexico

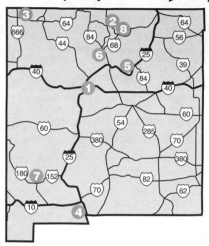

1. ALBUQUERQUE
2. EL PRADO
3. FARMINGTON
4. LAS CRUCES
5. LAS VEGAS
6. SANTA FE
7. SILVER CITY
8. TAOS

ALBUQUERQUE

 Visit Robin's Natural Cafe and 20 Carrots Juice & Cafe on Central.

LA MONTANITA FOOD CO-OP
3500 Central SE, 87106 • (505)265-4631
This Co-op has a great sense of community.
M-Sat. 7-10, Sun. 8-8

 From I-40, take Carlisle exit south and drive about 2 miles. Store's on right at corner of Central and Carlisle in Nob Hill Shopping Center. Extra parking in back.

WILD OATS MARKET
6300-A San Mateo NE, 87109 • (505)823-1933
"We have a sushi bar, a masseuse and a floral department."
Sun.-Sun. 7:30-10

From I-25, take San Mateo exit. Head south on San Mateo. Store's about 100 yards down in Far North Shopping Center.

EL PRADO

CID'S
822 Paseo Del Pueblo Norte, 87529 • (505)758-1148
Largest selection of natural and organic food in town.
M-Sat. 8-7

 One mile north of the main town plaza.

FARMINGTON

WILDLY NATURAL FOODS
Hutton Plaza, 2501 E. 20th Street, Suite 1, 87401 • (505)326-6243
Natural facials now available in store.
M-F 9-6:30, Sat. 9-6, Sun. 11-5

 Take Main St. east to Hutton, turn left (north) on Hutton. Go left on 20th St. and store's on first block on left.

LAS CRUCES

 Nestled in the Nesilla Valley of the Rio Grande River and in view of the beautiful Organ Mountains. Area is a renowned Alien sighting hotspot.

CO-OP MARKET
1300 El Paseo Street, Suite M, 88001 • (505)523-0436
Produce is 100% organic or locally grown without pesticides. Store has a "grab and go" deli.
M-Sat. 8-8, Sun. 10-6

 From I-25, take Hwy. 70 exit west toward Las Cruces (becomes Main). Turn left on El Paseo. Store's on right at light in Idaho Crossings Shopping Center.

LAS VEGAS

 The original Las Vegas. Many beautiful areas to hike and camp.

SEMILLA NATURAL FOODS
510 University Avenue, 87701 • (505)425-8139
M-F 10-6, Sat. 10-5

 From I-25, take University exit (2nd Las Vegas exit) west. Store's on right.

SANTA FE

 As the spiritual and kitschy art capital of the Southwest, Santa Fe is great! Check out 10,000 Waves for a soak in their outdoor hot tubs, the Cloud Cliff Bakery and don't miss the Cowgirl Hall of Fame, a fun spot for food and drink (drinks come complete with horse and rider toy figurines).

Santa Fe has lots of great food but in general it is quite expensive. For cheap eats, try one of the natural food store deli-cafes (Alfalfa's is recommended).

ALFALFA'S
333 West Cordova Road, 87501 • (505)986-8667
M-Sun. 7:30-10

 From I-25, take St. Francis exit and head north. Take a right on Cordova and the store is a half mile up on left.

THE MARKETPLACE
627 West Alameda, 87501 • (505)984-2852
Santa Fe's only locally owned store. Great selection of organic produce.
M-Sat. 7:30-9, Sun. 9-8

 From I-25, take St. Francis exit north about 3 miles and turn right on Alameda. Store's on left.

WILD OATS MARKET
1090 St. Francis Drive, 87501 • (505)983-5333
Sun.-Sun. 7-11

From I-25, take St. Francis Drive exit. Store's about 3 miles up on left.

WILD OATS MARKET
1708 Llano Street, 87505 • (505)473-4943
Sun.-Sun. 7-9

 From I-25, take Cerrillos Rd. exit (one direction).

Turn right on St. Michael's. Store's on right at corner of St. Michael's and Llano.

SILVER CITY

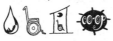 Check out the Gila Wilderness area for amazing hiking and also San Francisco Hot springs. (* Please remember to be gentle around these geothermal hot spots*).

SILVER CITY FOOD CO-OP
520 North Bullard Street, 88061 • (505)388-2343
Check out area museums and coffee shops.
M-F 9-6, Sat. 9-5

 From Rte. 180, head south on Hudson, turn right on College and left on Bullard St. Store is on left.

TAOS

AMIGO'S NATURAL GROCERY
326 South Santa Fe, 87571 • (505)758-8493
"We are a 20+ year old Co-op!"
M-Sat. 8:30-7, Sun. 11-5

 Store's on Hwy. 64 (Santa Fe), three lights south of Taos Plaza, on west side.

Organic Fact №20

THE BUCK STARTS HERE

Households with incomes exceeding $50,000 and Westerners are more likely to purchase organic food (1996 Hartman Report).

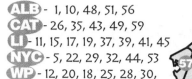

New York

ALB - 1, 10, 48, 51, 56
CAT - 26, 35, 43, 49, 59
LI - 11, 15, 17, 19, 37, 39, 41, 45
NYC - 5, 22, 29, 32, 44, 53
WP - 12, 20, 18, 25, 28, 30,
            31, 33, 36, 50, 54, 58

1. ALBANY
2. AMHERST
3. BINGHAMTON
4. BOONVILE
5. BROOKLYN
6. BUFFALO
7. CAMBRIDGE
8. CANTON
9. CHESTNUT RIDGE
10. CLIFTON PARK
11. COMMACK
12. CROSS RIVER
13. DELHI
14. ENDICOTT
15. GLEN COVE
16. HAMILTON
17. HICKSVILLE
18. HIGH FALLS
19. HUNTINGTON
20. HYDE PARK
21. ITHACA
22. JAMAICA
23. JEFFERSONVILLE
24. JOHNSON CITY
25. KATONAH
26. KINGSTON
27. LITTLE FALLS
28. MAHOPAC
29. MANHATTAN
30. MIDDLETOWN
31. MT. KISCO
32. MUNSEY PARK

33. NEW CITY
34. NEW HARTFORD
35. NEW PALTZ
36. NYACK
37. OCEANSIDE
38. ONEONTA
39. PLAINVIEW
40. PLATTSBURGH
41. PORT WASHINGTON
42. POTSDAM
43. POUGHKEEPSIE
44. QUEENS
45. RIVERHEAD
46. ROCHESTER
47. SARANAC LAKE
48. SARATOGA SPRINGS
49. SAUGERTIES
50. SCARSDALE
51. SCHENECTADY
52. SOUTH FALLSBURG
53. STATEN ISLAND
54. SUFFERN
55. SYRACUSE
56. TROY
57. WATERTOWN
58. WHITE PLAINS
59. WOODSTOCK

ALBANY

 Visit vegetarian restaurants, Mother Earth Cafe and Shades of Green.

HONEST WEIGHT FOOD CO-OP
484 Central Avenue, 12206 • (518)482-COOP (2667)
M-F 9-8, Sat. 9-6, Sun. 10-6

 From I-90: take
exit 5/Everett Rd.
south into city and
turn left on Central Ave./Rte. 5. Store's about 1 mile up from exit on right.

MILES NATURAL FOODS
28 Central Avenue, 12210 • (518)462-1020
Limited produce. No produce in winter.
M-F 10-6:30 (Th. 'til 8), Sat. 10-6

 From I-90, take Arborhill exit and drive five lights south on Henry
Johnson/Northern Blvd. Turn left on Central and park.

AMHERST

FEEL-RITE FRESH MARKET
3912 Maple Road, 14226 • (716)834-3385
Part of the largest chain in western New York. Store has an extensive selection.
M-Sat. 9-10, Sun. 11-7

 From 290: Take Niagara Falls
Blvd. exit south. Make a left on Maple Rd. and store's less than one block up on left.

BINGHAMTON

 Check out natural food restaurant, Hole in the Wall, on Washington St.

SUNRISE HEALTH FOODS
219 Main Street, 13905 • (607)798-6231
M-F 9-8, Sat. 10-6, Sun. 12-5

 Located in downtown Binghamton, on west side, near Foundry Plaza.

SUNY BINGHAMTON CO-OP
Student Union, SUNY, Binghamton, 13905 • (607)777-4258
Completely student run, this store was started in the mid-70's and began as a cafe.
M-F 11-4 (closed during summer)

 From Rte. 17 take exit 20S and follow signs to SUNY
Binghamton. (Ask for directions at info booth). Store's
located on 2nd floor of the Student Union.

BOONVILE

 Town has groomed cross-county ski trails nearby.

FOR GOODNESS SAKE
17 Schuyler, 13309 • (315)942-4585
Seasonal produce. Nestled in the foothills of the Adirondacks, this is the only natural food store around. Occasional free coffee.
T-Th. 10-5, F 10-7, Sat. 10-3

 In downtown Boonville, by the village park.

BROOKLYN

 Check out the all vegan, Cafe Love, on Court Street (cross St. is Warren).

APPLETREE NATURAL FOODS
7911 3rd Avenue, 11209 • (718)745-5776
M-F 9:30-6:30 (Th. 'til 7:30), Sat. 9:30-6

 Store's in Bay Ridge area. From I-278, take Ft. Hamilton exit onto 4th Ave. Turn left on Shore and right on 3rd. Store's on right, between 79 & 80.

BACK TO THE LAND NATURAL FOODS
142 7th Avenue, 11215 • (718)768-5654
Store has been around for 24 years and is now expanding!
Sun.-Sun. 9-9

 Store's 2 blocks west of Prospect Park, near Garfield Place.

FLATBUSH FOOD CO-OP
1318 Cortelyou Road, 11226 • (718)284-9717
"No pets allowed."
Sun.-Sun. 8-9

 From Ocean Parkway, head east on Cortelyou. Store's two blocks from D train Cortelyou stop.

BUFFALO

 Look for the Art Voice, Buffalo's local newspaper to what's happenin'! Recommendations: The Ujima Theater, Spot Coffee House and the Elmwood Strip.

FEEL-RITE FRESH MARKET
5425 Transit Road, 14221 • (716)636-1000
Store has a large selection of organic produce.
M-Sat. 9-10 Sun. 11-7

 1/4 mile north of Eastern Hills Mall.

FEEL-RITE NATURAL FOOD SHOPPES
720 Elmwood Avenue, 14222-1602 • (716)885-7889
Limited organic produce.
M-Sat. 9-9 Sun. 12-5

 On the Elmwood Strip.

OTHER BUFFALO FEEL-RITE NATURAL FOOD SHOPPES

No or limited produce.
1694 Sheridan Drive, 14223 • (716)877-6095
1451 Hertel Avenue, 14216 • (716)837-7661
Main Place Mall, 14202 • (716)842-1120
247 Cayuga Road, 14225 • (716)633-5472
4018 Seneca Street • (716)675-6620

LEXINGTON REAL FOODS COMMUNITY CO-OP

230 Lexington Avenue, 14222 • (716)884-8828
Near Elmwood, "The hip street in Buffalo."
Sun.- Sun. 9-9

 From I-90, take Rte. 33 exit west and get off on East Ferry. Go west and turn left on Elmwood, then right on Lexington. Store's on left.

NORTH BUFFALO FOOD CO-OP

3144 Main Street, 14214 • (716)836-8058
Store will soon be wheelchair accessible.
M-Sat. 9-9, Sun. 10-6, Cafe: M-Sat. 11-8

 From I-90, turn north on I-290 and take Main St. exit west about 2.5 miles. Store's on right.

CAMBRIDGE

VILLAGE STORE CO-OP

25 East Main Street, 12816 • (518)677-2765
M-Sat. 10-5, (Th. 'til 8)

 Cambridge is between Saratoga and Bennington, Vermont. Store's in center of Cambridge, next to Hubbard Hall.

CANTON

NATURE'S STOREHOUSE

21 Main Street, 13617 • (315)386-3740
"In this desert of St. Lawrence County, we are a mecca for natural foods."
M-Th. 9-5, F 9-6, Sat. 9-5

 Store's on Main St. (Rte. 11), across from the Mobil station.

CHESTNUT RIDGE

HUNGRY HOLLOW CO-OP

841 Chestnut Ridge Road, 10977 • (914)356-3319
Hungry Hollow is all about freshness and it shows in their soups!
M-Th. 10-7, F & Sat. 10-6

 From Garden State Parkway north, take last New Jersey exit (#172). Turn right, then left on Chestnut Ridge Rd. and drive for 5 miles into New York State (becomes Rte. 45). Store's on left.

CLIFTON PARK

THE GREEN GROCER
1505 Route 9, 12065 • (518)383-1613
"Largest selection of organic produce and herbal tinctures around."
M-F 10-8, Sat. 10-6, Sun. 10-6

 From I-87, take exit 8A (Grooms Rd.). Drive Grooms Rd. east for 2 miles to Rte. 9. Go left onto Rte. 9, then take first right into Half Moon Plaza.

COMMACK

THE MUNG BEAN
6522 Jericho Turnpike, 11725 • (516)499-2362
M-F 9-8, Sat. 9-6, Sun. 11-5

 From LIE, take Commack Rd. exit (#52) and head north to Jericho Turnpike. Store's in Commack Corners Shopping Center at corner of Commack Rd. and Jericho Turnpike.

CROSS RIVER

NATURE'S TEMPTATIONS
D'agostino Shopping Center, PO Box 639, 10518 • (914)763-5643
M-F 9:30-7, Sat. 9-5, Sun. 10-3

 From 684, take 35 east to 121. Store's in D'agostino Shopping Center/Cross River Plaza at Rte. 121/35 intersection.

DELHI

 This historic town is nestled in the scenic Catskills and its downtown area still maintains an old feel (buildings built circa 1800s). Organic farming, both vegetable and dairy, is prominent in the area.

GOOD CHEAP FOOD (CO-OP)
53 Main Street, 13753 • (607)746-6562
Store also houses a bookstore and sells clothing. They have a licensed acupuncturist who has in-store office visits once per week.
M-Sat. 10-5 (F 'til 6), Cafe: M-F 11:30-2:30, Sat. 12-3

 From Oneonta, take Rte. 28 north into Delhi and go right onto Rte. 10. Go through 2 lights and store's just beyond the second light on the left.

ENDICOTT

DOWN TO EARTH WHOLE FOODS CO.
305 Grant Avenue, 13760 • (607)785-2338
"The area's largest selection of food and products for those with food allergy-sensitivities".
M-F 9-9, Sat. 10-6, Sun. 12-6

 From Hwy. 17, take Endicott exit and get on Rte. 26 (north). Take ramp onto overpass where sign says Owego. Take first left onto Grant Ave. and find store on left.

GLEN COVE

RISING TIDE NATURAL MARKET
42 Forest Avenue, 11542 • (516)676-7895
M-F 9-8, Sat. 9-7, Sun. 10-6

 From Rte. 25A (LIE), take
39N/Glen Cove Rd. north to end
(fire station) and turn right. Store's five traffic lights down on right.

HAMILTON

 **Visit Hamilton's Saturday Farmer's Market on the village green (summer).**

HAMILTON WHOLE FOODS
28 Broad Street, 13346 • (315)824-2930
Frozen produce only. A sunny, airy, full-service store - a real oasis in the area. Staffer Monica recommends picking up a styly store T-shirt.
M-Sat. 10-5:30

 Across from the Village Green.

HICKSVILLE

GOOD LIFE NATURAL FOODS
9 West Marie Street, 11801 • (516)935-5073
This locally owned store has been in business for 20+ years.
M-F 9-7, Sat. 10-5, Sun. 11-3

 From LIE, take exit #41S. Stay on Rte. 107
about 2 miles. Store's on right.

HIGH FALLS

 High Falls is home to an art community, the Pottery Trail. Almost all restaurants in the small downtown area have good vegetarian options.

HIGH FALLS FOOD CO-OP
1098 State Road 213, 12440 • (914)687-7262
Twenty + years old, this is the only storefront co-op in Ulster County with a full line of organic produce. Local produce in season.
M-Sat. 10-7, Sun. 10-6

 Store's on corner of Lucas Ave. and Rte. 213.

HUNTINGTON

Check out the Cinema Arts Center, the IMAC Center, and the Hecksher Museum in the downtown area.

STRAIGHT FROM THE HEART
80 East Main Street, 11743 • (516)549-3750
Store's bulk section is entirely organic.
M-Sat. 9:30-7, Sun. 11-6

East of Huntington Village, 1/8 mile east of Park Ave.

SWEET POTATOES ORGANIC MARKET & PEOPLE'S CO-OP

35B Gerard Street, 11743 • (516)423-6424

This community store has a vegan deli.

M-W 9:30-7, Th. & F 9:30-9, Sat. 9:30-7, Sun. 12-6

Rte. 25A becomes Main St. in Huntington. Turn north on Wall St. and right on Gerard. Store's on left.

HYDE PARK

MOTHER EARTH'S STOREHOUSE

Route 9, 12538 • (914)229-8593

Recently rated the best health food store in Hudson Valley by a regional magazine.

M-Sat. 9-8, Sun. 12-5

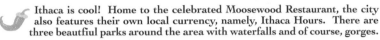

One Rte. 9, store's in plaza across from Shoprite (in the back, look for sign).

ITHACA

Ithaca is cool! Home to the celebrated Moosewood Restaurant, the city also features their own local currency, namely, Ithaca Hours. There are three beautfiul parks around the area with waterfalls and of course, gorges.

Visit Four Chimneys Winery, the first organic winery in North America, or check out the Cornell Plantations (flower gardens and an open space preserve open to the public). Pick up a copy of the Ithaca Times, the local free weekly to find out what's going on around town. Staffer recommendation: The ABC Cafe serves great natural food.

GREENSTAR COOPERATIVE MARKET

701 West Buffalo Street, 14850 • (607)273-9392

"Ithaca's best source for natural and organic foods, alternative health care products and an all natural deli." - Greenstar staffer, Allison.

M-Sat. 9-9, Sun. 10-7

From Rte. 13, take Buffalo St. east. Store's half a mile from downtown center, across from bus station. (8 blocks from Oasis).

LUDGATE PRODUCE FARMS

1552 Hanshaw Road, 14850 • (607)257-1765

Natural and specialty foods, fresh cut flowers, etc. Family owned and operated since 1973.

Sun.-Sun. 9-9

Just outside Ithaca, store's off Rte. 13 between 366 and Warren Rd. Take Hanshaw toward Ithaca. Go right at stop sign and store's one mile down on right.

OASIS

215 North Cayuga, DeWitt Mall, 14850 • (607)273-8213

This friendly store has been around for 20 years. They bake bread for the Moosewood restaurant and prepare homemade granola and pastries.

M-F 9:30-7, Sat. 9:30-6, Sun. 12-5

From Rte. 13 take Buffalo St. east. The mall is on right corner of Buffalo and Cayuga, with a maroon awning.

JAMAICA

GURU'S HEALTH FOOD
86-18 Parson's Boulevard, 11432 • (718)291-7406
M-F 9:30-7:30, Sat. 10:30-7, Sun. 11:30-6

 Guru's is 2 blocks from Hillside Ave., between Hillside Ave. and Grand Central Parkway.

JEFFERSONVILLE

THE GOOD EARTH
448 Main Street, 12748 • (914)482-3131
M-Sat. 10-6

 From Rte. 17, take exit 100/Liberty to Rte. 52W. Follow 10 miles to Jeffersonville. Store's on right, across from post office in center of town.

JOHNSON CITY

HEALTH BEAT NATURAL FOODS
214 Main Street, 13790 • (607)797-1001
Store offers vegetarian cooking classes.
M-F 9-8, Sat. 10-6, Sun. 12-5

 From I-81, take Johnson City exit and head east on Main. Store's on right.

KATONAH

KATONAH NATURAL MARKET
202 Katonah Avenue, 10536 • (914)232-7574
Sushi available on Wednesday and Saturday.
M-F 8:30-6:30 (Th. 'til 7), Sat. 8:30-6, Sun. 10-5

 From Saw Mill Parkway: Take Katonah exit. From south: Follow signs to Harris Rd. Turn left on Harris, right on Bedford Rd. (117) and bear right on Katonah Ave. Store's on right. From north: Take 684 south to exit 6. Turn right at end of ramp. Take first left onto Woodsbridge Rd., then left onto Parkway. Drive 1 block, then take a right at stop sign onto Katonah. Store's on left.

KINGSTON

MOTHER EARTH'S STOREHOUSE
1200 Ulster Avenue, 12401 • (914) 336-5541
M-F 9-9, Sat. 10-6, Sun. 12-5

 One mile from Rte. 209 on Ulster Ave.

LITTLE FALLS

 This scenic, historic canal town is situated on the Mohawk River and the Old Erie Canal.

COMMUNITY CO-OP
515 Garden Street, 13365 • (315)823-0686
This friendly store welcomes travelers and is the area's source for natural food.
Tu. - F 9:30-5 (Th. 'til 8), Sat. 9:30-1

 From west: Take Rte. 5 into Little Falls. Go left on Albany St. and left on 2nd St. Store's on left after crossing Main. From east: Take Rte. 5 into town, turn right on Main, then right on 2nd St. Store's half a block up on left.

MAHOPAC

MRS. GREEN'S
Lake Plaza Shopping Center, 10541 • (914)628-0533
M-Sat. 9-7, Sun. 11-5

 From I-84, take exit #19 and turn right off ramp onto Rte. 312 toward Carmel. Turn right at first light and left on Rte. 6. Store's about 5 miles on left in Lake Plaza Shopping Center.

MANHATTAN

*Since Manhattan is basically a big numbered grid (and most people don't drive there), the cross streets are given, but not full directions. By all means, spend a buck or two and get a small map!

Decadent food options are bountiful in Manhattan, but Angelica's Kitchen, Spring Street Natural and Zen Palate are exceptionally good!

COMMODITIES EAST
165 1st Avenue, 10003 • (212)260-2600
Sun.-Sun. 9-9

 Cross streets are 10th St. and 1st Ave.

COMMODITIES NATURAL
117 Hudson, 10013 • (212)334-8330
M-F 9-8, Sat. & Sun. 10-8

 On Hudson, at Northmore (Franklin stop on the 1 or 9 subway).

GOOD EARTH FOODS
1330 1st Avenue, 10021 • (212)472-9055
M-F 9-7:30, Sat. 9-6, Sun. 12-6

 Store's between 71st and 72nd Sts.

GOOD EARTH FOODS
169 Amsterdam Avenue, 10023 • (212)496-1616
M-F 9:30-7:30, Sat. 9:30-6:30, Sun. 12-6

 Store's at 68th St.

GRAMERCY NATURAL
427 2nd Avenue, 10010 • (212)725-1651
M-F 10-8, Sat. 10-6, Sun. 12-5

 Between 24th and 25th Sts.

THE HEALTH NUTS
1208 2nd Avenue, 10021 • (212)593-0116
M-F 9:30-8:30, Sat. 10-8, Sun. 11-8

Store's between 63rd and 64th Sts.

THE HEALTH NUTS
2611 Broadway, 10025 • (212)678-0054
Only this Health Nuts has a nutritionist, but the nutritionist is accessible by phone from any of the other stores.
M-Sat. 9-9, Sun. 11-7

Store's between 98th and 99th Sts.

THE HEALTH NUTS
2141 Broadway, 10023 • (212)724-1972
M-Sat. 9-9, Sun 11-7

Store's between 75th and 76th Sts.

THE HEALTH NUTS
835 2nd Avenue, 10017 • (212)490-2979
M-F 8:30-8:30, Sat. 10-7

Between 44th and 45th Sts.

HEALTHY PLEASURES
93 University Place, 10003 • (212)353-3663 (FOOD)
Beautiful, splashy store. Great salad bar is the central element. The somewhat pricey food makes a Washington Square picnic seem like a catered affair.
Sun.-Sun. 7:30-11:30

Store's between 11th and 12th Sts.

INTEGRAL YOGA
229 West 13th Street, 10011 • (212)243-2642
Drop in Yoga classes next door.
M-F 10-9:30, Sat. 10-8:30, Sun. 12-6:30

Store's between 7th and 8th Aves., near Down to Earth. Both are great!

ORGANIC MARKET #1
229 7th Avenue, 10011 • (212)255-1288
M-F 10-9, Sat. 10-7

Between 23rd and 24th Sts.

ORGANIC MARKET #2
432 Park Avenue South, 10016 • (212)532-2644
M-F 8:30-8, Sat. 10-7

Between 29th and 30th Sts.

PRANA FOODS
125 1st Avenue, 10003 • (212)982-7306
M-Sat. 9-9, Sun. 10-7

 Store's between 7 St. and St. Marks (8th St.). St. Mark's Place is young, hip and fairly trendy.

WHOLE FOODS MARKET UPTOWN
2421 Broadway, 10021 • (212)874-4000
Rated #1 in the country by Zagat.
Sun.-Sun. 8-11

 Corner of 89th and Broadway.

WHOLE FOODS NATURAL SUPERMARKET
117 Prince Street, 10012 • (212)982-1000
Rated #1 in New York by Zagat.
M-F 8-10, Sat. 9-10, Sun. 9-9

 Store's between Greene and Wooster.

YOUNG'S NATURAL MARKET
250 Mercer Street, 10012 • (212)260-3353
M-F 10-9, Sat. 10-7

 Between 3rd and 4th Sts., near New York University.

MIDDLETOWN

THE ROSE GARDEN
19 West Main Street, 10940 • (914)342-4007
This is an old-school, independent, traditional, health food store. On the web at www.rosehealth.com. No produce.
Tu.-Sat. 9:30-5:30

 From Rte. 17, take exit 120 to Rte. 211 west and drive to end of commercial strip. Four lane road becomes 2 lanes. Drive through 2 lights and go left at third light onto North St. Take a right at 2nd light onto North and then take 1st left into city parking lot and go to the back. Walk up private parking lot to back door of store.

MT. KISCO

GOOD EARTH HEALTH FOODS
13 Main Street, 10549 • (914)241-3500
M-F 9-6:30, Sat. 10-5:30

 From Saw Mill River Pkwy, take Kisco Ave. exit. Turn left on Kisco and left on Rte. 133. Store's on left.

MRS. GREEN'S
666 Lexington Avenue, 10549 • (914)242-9292
M-F 9-8, Sat. & Sun. 10-7

 From Saw Mill River Parkway, take Reader's Digest exit, cross RR tracks and bear right at light. Follow to first light, make a left on 117, go to first light and make a right on Lexington Ave. Turn right into shopping center.

MUNSEY PARK

FRESH FIELDS WHOLE FOODS MARKET
2101 Northern Boulevard, 11030 • (516)869-8900
Sun.-Sun. 9-9

From LIE, take exit 36. As you approach lights, make a left on Searingtown Rd.
Drive to intersection and store's across road on left in first building past intersection.

NEW CITY

BACK TO THE EARTH NATURAL FOODS
306A South Main Street, 10956 • (914)634-3511
M-F 9-7:30, Sat. 9-6, Sun. 10-6

From I-87, take Palisades Parkway exit north (#13N). Once on Palisades, take exit
10 and turn left off ramp. Turn right on Little Tor Rd. and drive about 1.5 miles.
Turn right on Collyer and left on Main. Store's on right.

NEW HARTFORD

PETER'S CORNUCOPIA
52 Genesee Street, 13413 • (315)724-4998
M-F 9:30-8, Sat. 9:30-6, Sun. 12-5 (Closed Sun. - July & Aug.)

 From I-90, take Genesee exit and drive on S.
Genesee for about three miles. Store's on right.

NEW PALTZ

EARTHGOODS
71 Main Street, 12561 • (914)255-5858
M-F 10-8, Sat. 9-9, Sun. 10-6

 From I-87, take New Paltz exit, go left and drive 1.5 miles west. Store's
on Main St. on left.

NYACK

BORN OF EARTH
1 South Broadway, 10960 • (914)353-3311
M-Sat. 10-6 (Th. 'til 7:30), Sun. 11-5

 From 287 north: Take exit 11 and go
through a stop sign. Make a right at next
light (which is 9W). Drive and make a
left on Rte. 59 east (59 turns into Main St.). Store's at corner of Main and Broadway.
From 287 south: Take exit 11. Make a left at traffic light onto Rte. 59. Same as above.

OCEANSIDE

JANDI'S NATURE WAY, INC.
24 Atlantic Avenue, 11572 • (516)536-5535
Store has a vegetarian take-out deli which they say is "the best food anywhere!"
M-F 10-7 (Th. 'til 9), Sat. 10-6, Sun. 11-5

 From Rte. 27, go south on Longbeach Rd. Store's
on right in Great Lincoln Shopping Center at
corner of Atlantic and Longbeach.

ONEONTA

 In this cool little town, check out natural food restaurant, Autumn Cafe, Elena's Italian Bakery and India House of Tandoori (don't miss the palak paneer).

DEER VALLEY
19 Ford Avenue, 13820 • (607)432-0172
M-Sat. 9:30-6

 From I-88, take exit 15 onto Lettis Hwy. Extension. Take left at light, go across extension. Take left at next light and then right onto Ford Ave. Store's on left.

THE GREEN EARTH
7 Elm Street, 13820 • (607)432-7160
Store has a great selection of organic produce. Stop by and say hello to Annie, the Tofu Tollbooth's biggest fan!
M-F 10-6 (Th. 'til 8), Sat. 10-5

 From I-88, take exit 15. Go into Oneonta, take first left on Main and first right on Elm. Store's on corner.

PLAINVIEW

DR B. WELL NATURALLY
8 Washington Avenue, 11803 • (516)932-9355
Store takes major credit cards.
M-F 9-8, Sat. 9-7, Sun. 9-6

 From LIE west: Take exit #45 and go onto Manetto Hill Rd. south. Turn left on Washington. Store will be on left. From east: Take exit #48 and turn left on Round Swamp Rd.. Bear right on Old Country, turn right on Manetto Hill Rd. and right on Washington. Store's on right.

PLATTSBURGH

 In the heart of historic Champlain Valley, right on the lake.

NORTH COUNTRY CO-OP
25 Bridge Street, 12901 • (518)561-5904
A good combination of natural food and unusual gifts. Store has a second floor library and the "Co-op Coffeehouse" is upstairs.
M-F 10-7, Sat. 10-4, Sun. 12-5 (soon to expand hours)

 From I-87, take exit 37 (Plattsburgh/Rte. 3) east and follow signs to Rte. 9 - Plattsburgh and historic district. Store's in downtown Plattsburgh across from city parking lot.

PORT WASHINGTON

TWIN PINES CO-OP
382 Main Street, 11050 • (516)883-9777
The only food co-op left on Long Island! They offer work experience for the handicapped and have a food pantry. A real community service organization!
T 1-5, W, F, Sat. 11-5, Th. 11-6

From LIE, take exit 36 going north. Get onto Searingtown Rd., pass first intersection and take a right into Port Washington. Make a left on Main, go down 1.25 mile. Store's on left, at corner of Prospect and Main. Park on town dock on right.

POTSDAM

 On Monday nights from Sept.-June, check out Cinema 10 (they show independent and foreign films). Visit Taste of India for great Indian food.

POTSDAM CONSUMER CO-OP
24 Elm Street, 13676 • (315)265-4630
"We have an awesome, varied produce selection with several local farms represented."
M-F 9-7, Sat. 9-6, Sun. 12-4

 Take Rte. 81 to Rte. 11 into Potsdam. Take a left on Union St., and then a right on Elm. Store's on left. From Rte. 56 south: Take a left onto Elm St. and store's on right. From 56 north, take a left onto Elm St., store's on left. The Coop is kitty-corner from the Big M Market, across from the Village Offices.

POUGHKEEPSIE

HUDSON VALLEY FEDERATION
6 Noxon Road, 12603 • (914)473-5400
M-Sat. 10-7

 Right off Rte. 5. From Taconic Parkway, take Arthursburg Rd. turnoff.

MOTHER EARTH'S STOREHOUSE
804 South Road Square, 12601 • (914)296-1069
Opening Summer of '98.
M-Sat. 9-9, Sun. 12-5

 At entrance to the Galleria Mall on Rte. 9.

QUEENS

QUANTUM LEAP NATURAL GROCERY
6560 Fresh Meadow Lane, 11365 • (718)762-3572
Restaurant attached.
Sun.-Th. 10-10, F & Sat. 10-11

 From LIE, take exit 25 and drive two blocks south. Turn right on 67th Ave. Store's on right at corner of 67th and Fresh Meadow Lane.

QUEENS HEALTH EMPORIUM
15901 Horace Harding Expressway, 11365 • (718)358-6500
M-Sat. 9:30-8, Sun. 10-6

 From LIE west: Take exit 24 and head for 164th St. Make a full U-turn. Store's on corner of 159th and Horace Harding Exp. From east: Take exit 24 and store's immediately on right.

RIVERHEAD

THE GREEN EARTH GROCERY
50 East Main Street, 11901 • (516)369-2233
M-F 9:30-6, Sat. 10-6, Sun. 11-5

 Take the LIE to exit 72. Go east on Rte. 25 (becomes Main St.). Store's on north side of street.

ROCHESTER

 These restaurants serve natural and vegetarian fare: The Mission Cafe, Spice of Life Cafe and Savory Thyme.

GENESEE CO-OP FOODSTORE
713 Monroe Avenue, 14607 • (716)244-3900
"Rochester's natural food store." Located in a funky little neighborhood.
M-F 10-7 (Th. 'til 8), Sat. 10-6, Sun. 10-5

 From Rte. 490, take Monroe Ave. exit west two blocks. Store's on left, one mile east of downtown, in the old firehouse.

LORI'S NATURAL FOODS
900 Jefferson Road, 14623 • (716)424-2323
M-Sat. 8-8, Sun. 12-6

 From I-390, take Jefferson Rd. exit. Go north to intersection of Jefferson and E. Henrietta Rd. Proceed west 1/4 mile. Store's on north side of street.

SARANAC LAKE

 Bring your mountain bike.

NORI'S WHOLE FOODS
70 Broadway Avenue, 12983 • (518)891-6079
M-F 9-7, Sat. 10-5

 From I-87, take exit 30 to Rte. 73 north to 86 west into Saranac Lake. Store's in a 3-story brick building next to post office.

SARATOGA SPRINGS

FOUR SEASONS NATURAL FOODS
33 Phila Street, 12866 • (518)584-4670
Down the block from the legendary Cafe Lena. Four Seasons has a comprehensive hot & cold buffet for weary travelers.
Sun.-Sun. 9-8 (Store closes 1 hour later in summer).

 From I-87, take exit 15. Go south on Rte. 9 about 2 miles. Once in center of town, go left on Phila St. Store's on left.

SAUGERTIES

MOTHER EARTH'S STOREHOUSE
249 Main Street, 12477 • (914)246-9614
M-Th. 9-6, F 9-8, Sat. 10-6, Sun. 12-5

 From I-87 north: Make a right on exit 20 - Ulster Ave. Follow to end, at light go left and store's on left. From I-87 south: Take exit 20. Make a left (takes you up to Ulster Ave). Same as above.

SCARSDALE

MRS. GREEN'S NATURAL MARKET
780 White Plains Road, 10583 • (914)472-0111
M-F 9-8 (Th. 'til 9), Sat. 9-7, Sun. 10-7

From George Washington Bridge, take Major Degan (upstate) to exit 4 to Bronx River Parkway North. Take exit 10 - Harney Rd. (right) to White Plains Rd. (22) right. Store's 1.5 blocks on left.

MRS. GREEN'S NATURAL MARKET
365 Central Park Avenue, 10583 • (914)472-9675
M-Sat. 9-7, Sun. 11-6

From George Washington Bridge, take Major Degan (upstate) to exit 4 to Bronx River Parkway North. Take exit for Senimore Rd. which brings you into Hartsdale, then East Hartsdale. Make a left on Central Park Ave. and store's one half mile on right.

SCHENECTADY

EARTHLY DELIGHTS NATURAL FOOD
162 Jay Street, 12305 • (518)372-7580
Take-out food available. Made fresh daily.
M-Sat. 9-6 (Th. 'til 8)

From I-90, take exit 25 (becomes I-890 west). Take exit 5 - Broadway. Go right onto Broadway. At 2nd traffic light, go right onto Clinton St. After 2nd light, drive 1/2 block and park on left in free 2 hour parking lot. Walk left on brick walkway on Jay St. Store's about 4 stores down on right.

SOUTH FALLSBURG

PRATT'S FARMER'S HARVEST
Main Street, 12779 • (914)436-8581
M-Sat. 10:30-6

From Rte. 17, follow signs for South Fallsburg (exit 107). Take to Thompson Rd. and follow to Rte. 42. Make a right onto Rte. 42 and store's on left.

STATEN ISLAND

TASTEBUDS NATURAL FOOD
1807 Hylan Boulevard, 10305 • (718)351-8693
M-Sat. 9-8, Sun. 11-7

On I-278, from Brooklyn: Take Hylan Blvd. exit and get on Richmond Rd. Turn left on Buel and right on Hylan. Store's on right. On I-278 from New Jersey: Take Clove Rd./Richmond Rd. exit and turn right on Richmond. Same as above.

SUFFERN

NEW HARVEST NATURAL FOODS
41 Lafayette Avenue, Route 59, 10901 • (914)357-9200
M-F 9:30-5:30, Deli: M-F 11:30-2:30

5 miles west of Tappan Zee Bridge on Rte. 59.

SYRACUSE

DISCOUNT NATURAL FOODS
2120 Burnet Avenue, 13206 • (315)437-4542
M-Sat. 9-8, Sun. 9-6

 From 690, take Midler Exit. "You can't miss it."

SYRACUSE REAL FOOD COOPERATIVE
618 Kensington Road, 13210 • (315)472-1385
M-Sat. 8-8, Sun. 10-6

 From I-81, take Adams St. exit and take E. Adams St. east. Turn right on Ostrom Ave. then left on Euclid. Turn right on Westcott, go 3 blocks, then left on Kensington Rd. Store's on right.

TROY

UNCLE SAM'S GOOD NATURAL PRODUCTS
77 4th Street, 12180 • (518)271-7299
M-F 10-6:30, Sat. 10-5

From I-87, take Rte. 7 exit east. Take Downtown Troy exit (will put you on 6th St. south). Turn right on Congress and right on 4th. Store's on left.

WATERTOWN

THE MUSTARD SEED
1304 Washington, 13601• (315)788-2463
M-F 9-7, Sat. 9-5 Sun. 10-2

From Rte. 81, follows signs to Watertown Center. Turn left on Washington. Store's across from high school behind Pizza Hut.

WHITE PLAINS

MANNA FOODS, INC.
171 Mamaroneck Avenue, 10601 • (914)946-2233
M-W & F 9-6, Th. 9-7, Sat. 9-5, Kitchen: M-F 11:30-2:30

 From Hutchinson River Parkway: Take exit 23N. Store's 4-5 miles up on right.

WOODSTOCK

 Home to lots of museums, cafes, the Golden Notebook and Tofu Tollbooth publishers, Ceres Press.

SUNFLOWER NATURAL FOODS
Bradley Meadows Shopping Center, 12498 • (914)679-5361
M-Sat. 9-9, Sun. 10-7

      From I-87 south: Take Rte. 28 exit (#19) west about 5 miles. Turn right on Rte. 375 (to end) and left on Rte. 212. Store's on right. From north: Take Saugerties exit (# 20), and take Rte. 212 west about 8 miles. Store's on right.

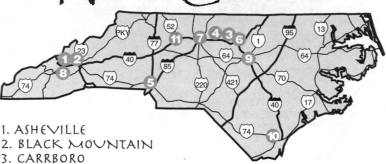

North Carolina

1. ASHEVILLE
2. BLACK MOUNTAIN
3. CARRBORO
4. CHAPEL HILL
5. CHARLOTTE
6. DURHAM
7. GREENSBORO
8. HENDERSONVILLE
9. RALEIGH
10. WILMINGTON
11. WINSTON-SALEM

ASHEVILLE

Residents and visitors alike speak of Asheville with great reverence. They love the hip, downtown area and beautiful mountains near-by. One French Broad Co-op staffer told us she visited on vacation and has never left.

Most Asheville restaurants offer vegetarian selections. ("It's just that kind of town," say French Broad Co-op staffers... "very veggie friendly!") Check out vegan-macrobiotic restaurants, the Laughing Seed and Max & Rosie's.

Asheville's beer spot is Barley's tap room, Bean Street has great coffee and Be Here Now features live music. Also, the Duckett House is a youth hostel located 1 hour from Asheville (in Hot Springs). A visit to the Biltmore Estate was also recommended.

EARTHFARE
66 Westgate Parkway, 28806 • (704)253-7656
M-Sat. 8-9, Sun. 9-8

Store's off I-240 loop (exit 3B/Westgate- Holiday Inn) on right in parking lot after exit.

FRENCH BROAD CO-OP
90 Biltmore Avenue, 28801 • (704)255-7650
Soon expanding to include a deli & cafe.
M-F 9-8, Sat. 9-7, Sun. 12-6

 From I-240, take the Broadway or Merrimon exit (depending on which way you're coming from). Drive south toward downtown on Broadway. Broadway turns into Biltmore in front of the Vance Mounument. Drive 2 blocks and store's on left. Co-op parking lot is on corner of Hillyard and Biltmore.

BLACK MOUNTAIN

HEALTHY HARVEST
115 Black Mountain Avenue, 28711 • (704)669-9813
M-Sat. 10-6

 From I-40, take Black Mountain exit #64 (there are two, make sure you take western exit) and drive north. Turn left on Vance Ave. Store's on right.

CARRBORO

 Check out Basaimi Burro for Mexican fare.

WEAVER STREET MARKET
101 East Weaver Street, 27510 • (910)929-0010
One of Dar's favorite stores. They know their food politics and educate accordingly.
M-F 9-9, Sat. & Sun. 9-8 (coffee bar opens at 7:30)

 From I-40, take Bypass 15-501 south to Hwy. 54. Head west on 54. Take Greensboro St. exit and drive north one mile. Store's on right in Carr Mill Mall, at corner of Greensboro and Weaver.

CHAPEL HILL

 Visit The Carolina Brewery on Franklin Street for good beer and a number of vegetarian selections. The Pyewacket serves an array of vegetarian dishes and the Aurora features Mexican fare. Duke Forest north of town (off Whitfield Rd.) is recommended for hiking.

WELLSPRING GROCERY WHOLE FOODS MARKET
81 South Elliott Road, 27514 • (919)968-1983
Sun.-Sun. 8-9, Cafe: M-Sat. 7:30-8, Sun. 7:30-8

 From I-40, take Rte. 15/501 south for about 3 miles (toward Chapel Hill). At fork in the road, stay to right to get onto Franklin St. Take a left onto Elliot and store's on left.

CHARLOTTE

 Take the trolley to Charlotte's uptown district and check out the Discovery Place, a highly recommended science museum for kids (we learned about fractals there). Also, in the newly revitalized South End, stop by the South End Brewery. Store staffers recommend Freedom Park and Latta Park to relax.

BERRYBROOK FARM NATURAL FOOD PANTRY
1257 East Boulevard, 28203 • (704)334-6528
M-F 9-7, Sat. 9-6, Deli: M-Sat. 11-4 daily

 From I-277, take Kennilworth exit (away from Charlotte) to East Blvd. Turn left on East. Store's at corner of East Blvd. and Kennilworth.

TALLEY'S GREEN GROCERY

1408-C East Boulevard, 28203 • (704)334-9200

Store has a great salad bar/deli. Food is served on non-disposable plates!

M-Sat 9-9, Sun. 10-7

From I-277, take Kennilworth exit away from town to East Blvd. Turn left on East. Store's a block down on right in Dilworth Gardens Shopping Center.

DURHAM

Durham recommendations: Duke Forest and the Eno River are great outdoor spots, The Lounge is a suggested martini bar and The Cosmic Canteen is an L.A. style burrito joint. Store workers tell us that 9th Street is Groovy. Better check it out!

DURHAM FOOD CO-OP

(a.k.a. People's Intergalactic Food Conspiracy No. 1, Inc.)

1101 West Chapel Hill Street, 27701 • (919)490-0929

Store features free coffee while you shop!

M-Sat. 10-8, Sun. 11-7

 From I-85, take Gregson St. exit. Drive on Gregson about two miles, then turn right onto West Chapel Hill. Store's on left, at corner of Carroll and West Chapel Hill.

WELLSPRING GROCERY WHOLE FOODS MARKET

621 Broad Street, 27705 • (919)286-0371

Sun.-Sun. 9-9

 From I-85, take Guess Rd. exit south. Veer right over tracks onto Broad St. Store's on right side of Broad. From Durham Freeway, take Swift Ave. exit, cross Main and store's directly on left.

GREENSBORO

Check out recommended vegetarian restaurant, The Grapevine (next to Joel's Natural Foods). The Sunset Cafe serves natural food, but is not completely vegetarian.

DEEP ROOTS CO-OP MARKET

3728 Spring Garden Street, 27407 • (910)292-9216

M-F 9-9, Sat. 9-8, Sun. 12-7

 From I-40, take Wendover exit and turn east off ramp onto Wendover Ave. Drive about 1 mile and at first overpass, make a left onto Spring Gardens. Store's on left.

JOEL'S NATURAL FOODS

435C Dolley Madison Road, 27410 • (910)855-6500

M-Sat. 10-9, Sun. 1-6

 From I-40, take Gilford College Rd. exit and drive north 2 miles on Gilford College Rd (changes name to College Rd). Store's behind Pizza Hut on the right.

HENDERSONVILLE

Nestled in the mountains, Hendersonville is a very pretty little town. Check out Chimney Rock Park and also Fruity Rooty Juice Bar on Main (3 blocks from the co-op).

HENDERSONVILLE COMMUNITY CO-OP - LIFE'S BEST MARKET
715-B Old Spartanburg Highway, 28792 • (704)693-0505
M-F 9-6:30, Sat. 9-6, Sun. 12-5

 From I-26, take Upward Road exit. Turn right onto 176/Spartanburg Hwy. Go through several lights, over a bridge and right onto Old Spartanburg Hwy. Store's one block down on left.

RALEIGH

HARMONY FARMS
5653 Creedmoor Road, 27612 • (919)782-0064
M-F 10-7, Sat. 10-6, Sun. 1-6

 From I-40, take Glenwood Ave. exit past Crabtree Valley Mall. Go right on Creedmoor Rd. and drive 1 mile. Store's in Creedmoor Crossing Shopping Center.

HARMONY FARMS
2710 Hillsborough Street, 27607 • (919)832-3237
Carrots only.
M-F 9-6, Sat. 10-6, Sun. 1-6

 Take I-440 Beltline to Hillsborough St. exit. Turn left and store's two miles down on left.

WELLSPRING GROCERY WHOLE FOODS MARKET
3540 Wade Avenue, 27607 • (919)828-5805
Sun.-Sun. 9-9

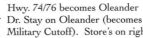 From I-40 Beltline, get off at Wade Ave. exit. Store's one block east of Interstate at corner of Ridge Rd. and Wade Ave. in the Ridgewood Shopping Center.

WILMINGTON

DOXIE'S MARKET
1319 Military Cutoff Road, 28405 • (910)256-9952
M-Sat. 9-7

 Hwy. 74/76 becomes Oleander Dr. Stay on Oleander (becomes Military Cutoff). Store's on right in Landfall Center. Or, go to end of Rte. 40. Follow signs to Wrightsville Beach and take Eastwood Rd. to Military Cutoff. Go left into Landfall Center to find store.

TIDAL CREEK FOODS CO-OP
4406 Wrightsville Avenue, 28403 • (910)799-2667
M-F 9-8, Sat. 9-6

 I-40 becomes College Rd. (Hwy. 132). Take a right on Wrightsville Ave. Store's on left.

WINSTON-SALEM

FRIENDS OF THE EARTH
114 Reynolda Village, 27106 • (919)725-6781
M-F 10-6:30, Sat. 10-5

 From I-40, take Silas Creek Parkway exit north. Take Reynolda Rd. exit and turn right onto Reynolda Rd. Turn left into the byway of Reynolda Village. Store's in a barn.

North Dakota

1. BISMARCK
2. DICKINSON
3. FARGO
4. GRAND FORKS
5. MINOT

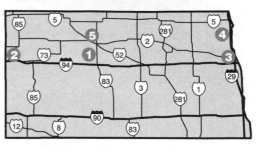

BISMARCK

 Check out the Green Earth Cafe, a natural food & ethnic restaurant.

EARTH PANTRY
738 Kirkwood Mall, 58504 • (701)258-7987
No produce. In Bismarck since 1981.
M-F 10-9, Sat. 10-6, Sun. 12-6

 Store's off Bismarck Expressway in Kirkwood Mall Shopping Center.

STOREFRONT FOOD CO-OP
609 Memorial Highway, 58504 • (701)255-7757
No produce. A completely volunteer operated store.
M-W 12-6, F 12-6, Sat. 11-3

 From I-94, take one of the Bismarck exits south into town. Turn west on Main and head west toward river. Turn left on Washington and right on Memorial Hwy. Store's on left.

TERRY'S HEALTH PRODUCTS
801 East Main Avenue, 58501 • (701)223-1026
Terry's has a huge selection of bulk herbs and spices. Seasonal produce.
M-F 9-6, Sat. 9-3

 From I-94, take Hwy. 83 exit south. Turn left on Main Ave. Store's on right.

DICKINSON

NATURAL HEALTH
32 1st Avenue West, 58601 • (701)225-6614
No produce.
M-F 9-6, Sat. 9-5

 From I-94 take 3rd Ave. West, south to lights. Go right onto Willard St. and right on 1st Ave. Store's on east side.

FARGO

 In Fargo, check out the community-run Fargo Theater.

SWANSON HEALTH PRODUCTS
109 North Broadway, 58102 • (701)293-9842
Open for 20+ years.
M-F 9-6, Sat. 9-5

 From I-94, take University Dr. exit north. Turn east on 2nd Ave. and left on Broadway. Store's on left.

TOCCHI PRODUCTS
1111 2nd Avenue North, 58102 • (701)232-7700
Limited organic produce. In business for over 26 years, this store is a great place to stock up for the road.
M-Sat. 10-6 (Th. 'til 8)

 From I-94: Take University Ave. north exit to 13th Ave. south. Take a right on 13th and drive to 10th St. south. Go left (west) on 10th and drive under an underpass. Go two more blocks, then make a left (west) on 2nd Ave north. Store's 1.5 blocks on right.

GRAND FORKS

AMAZING GRAINS NATURAL FOOD MARKET
1602 9th Avenue North, 58203 • (701)775-4542
M-Sat. 10-7, Sun. 1-5

 From Hwy. 2, turn south on N. Washington and right on 9th Ave. North. Store's on right.

MINOT

THE MAGIC MILL
115 South Main, 58701 • (701)852-4818
No produce.
M-Sat. 10-5:30

 From Hwy. 83, turn east onto Burdock, then north onto Main. Store's in downtown center, just north of Trinity Hospital.

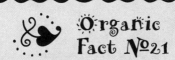

Organic Fact № 21

KILLER TAP WATER

In their study, the Environmental Working Group found that in 28 of the 29 cities tested, weed killers were found in tap water.

Ohio

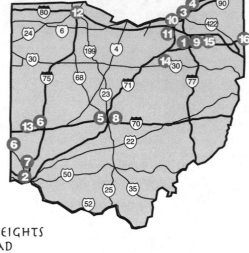

1. AKRON
2. CINCINNATI
3. CLEVELAND
4. CLEVELAND HEIGHTS
5. COLUMBUS
6. DAYTON
7. FAIRFIELD
8. GAHANNA
9. KENT
10. MIDDLEBURG HEIGHTS
11. NORTH OLMSTEAD
12. TOLEDO
13. TROY
14. WOOSTER
15. YELLOW SPRINGS
16. YOUNGSTOWN

AKRON

CO-OPERATIVE MARKET
1596 West Market Street, 44313 • (330)869-2590
M-W 9-7, Th.-Sat. 9-9, Sun. 12-6

 From I-77, take White Pond exit. Go north over railroad tracks, take a right on Frank and another right on Market. Store's 1/2 mile down on right.

MUSTARD SEED MARKET & CAFE
3885 West Market Street, 44333 • (330)666-7333
M-Th. 9-9, F- Sat. 9-10, Sun. 10-6, Restaurant: M-Th. 11-8, F & Sat. 11-9, Sun. 11-5

From I-77, take 137A or Rte. 18 east to Fairlawn. Store's on left in West Market Plaza.

CINCINNATI

Vegetarian restaurant recommendations: Spatz Natural Health Food Deli on Main St., Floyd's in Clifton and Malane's in downtown Cincinnati.

CINCINNATI NATURAL FOODS
9268 Colerain Avenue, 45251 • (513) 385-9622
M-F 10-8, Sat. 10-6, Sun. 12-5

 From I-275, take Colerain exit and drive south. Store's 1/4 mile south of Northgate Mall, on left. (Look for a yellow sign with red apple).

CINCINNATI NATURAL FOODS

6911 Miami Avenue, 45243 • (513)271-6766
M-F 9-8, Sat. 9-6, Sun. 12-5

From I-71 north: Take Kenwood Rd. exit, turn right onto Kenwood and at first light, turn left onto Euclid. Turn right at next light onto Miami. Go over railroad tracks and store's on right. From I-71 south: Take Montgomery exit and turn right on Montgomery, then left onto Kenwood. Same as above.

HEALTHY'S HEALTH FOODS

9525 Kenwood Road, 45242 • (513)984-1333
M-Sat. 9:30-7:30, Sun. 12-4

From I-71, take Pfeiffer Rd. exit. Go west on Pfeiffer, then south on Kenwood. Store's on right.

NEW WORLD FOOD SHOP

347 Ludlow Avenue, 45220 • (513)861-1101
The oldest natural food store in Cincinnati. Staffers say it's a small store with "gourmet touches." Seasonal produce.
M-Sat. 10-9, Sun. 12-6

From I-75, take Hopple St. exit and go left on Hopple. Turn left on Central Parkway and bear to right (road becomes Ludlow). Store's on right.

TWIN PINES NATURAL FOODS CO-OP

1051 North Bend Road, 45224 • (513)681-3663
M-F 10-8, Sat. 9-8

Take I-75 north to I-74 west and exit at Colerain Ave. Take a left and go north to North Bend Rd. Turn right on North Bend and store's 2.8 miles down on right.

CLEVELAND

 Check out Aladdin's (Lebanese) and the Little Italy area for yummy Italian fare.

FOOD CO-OP

11702 Euclid Avenue, 44106 • (216)791-3890
High-ceilinged and roomy, even more impressive is its support of the community. With "green stamps" and their memberships, this co-op works to make their food affordable to all. Store is near the museum-filled University Circle.
M-Sat. 9-8, Sun. 10-6

From I-90, take Martin Luther King exit south and continue south to Euclid. Store's on right, one mile before underpass. (Store's 3 miles east of downtown).

CLEVELAND HEIGHTS

FOOD CO-OP

1807 Coventry Road, 44118 • (216)321-9292
Staffers highly recommend vegetarian restaurant, Tommy's, across from the Co-op
M-Sat. 9-8, Sun. 10-6

From I-271, take Cedar Rd. exit west five miles. Turn right on Coventry. Store's on right, adjacent to municipal parking garage.

COLUMBUS

 Check out Whole World Natural Bakery and the King Avenue Restaurant & Coffee House (serves organic and vegetarian food). Try the High Banks for hiking.

BEXLEY NATURAL MARKET - A COOPERATIVE GROCERY
508 North Cassady Avenue, 43209 • (614)252-3951
M-F 9-8, Sat. 9-6, Sun. 12-5

 From I-71, take 670 east. Get off at 5th Ave. At next light, turn right on Cassady and store's 1 block up.

NORTHWEST NATURAL AND SPECIALTY FOODS
1636 Northwest Boulevard, 43209 • (614)488-0607
M-Sat. 9-8, Sun. 11-6

 From I-70, take Grandview exit and follow street down. Turn right on King. Store's on left at corner of King and Northwest.

DAYTON

 Check out Christopher's Restaurant on E. Dorothy Lane.

WORLD OF NATURAL FOODS
2314 Far Hills Avenue, 45419 • (937)293-8978
M-Sat. 9-6

 From Rte. 48, take Kettering exit and head north on Main St. (becomes Far Hills Ave.). Store's on right in Oakwood Plaza.

HEALTHY ALTERNATIVES
8351 North Main Street, 45419 • (937)890-8000
Neat as a pin and close to the highway. Wine only.
M-F 10-8

From I-70, take Englewood exit (just west of I-75) south on Main St. Store's on right in Randolph Plaza.

HEALTHY ALTERNATIVES
6204 Wilmington Pike, 45459 • (937)848-8881
M-F 10-8, Sat. 10-5, Sun. 12-5

Off I-675, store's 1/4 mile south on Wilmington Pike on east side of street.

FAIRFIELD

JUNGLE JIM'S
5440 Dixie Highway, 45014 • (513)829-1919
Sun.-Sun. 8-10

 From I-275, take exit 41 and drive 4 miles north. Store's on right.

GAHANNA

Elise at Northwest Foods suggests La Rochelle, a French cafe she says is "straight out of France" (in the Stonerich Plaza Shopping Center) and also Jaba's Cyberspace Cafe, a groovy spot on Hamilton St. Elise also recommends Hoggy's across from the store. They feature blues bands, "down-home cookin'" and beer.

NORTHWEST NATURAL AND SPECIALTY FOODS
1387 East Johnstown Road, 43230 • (614)939-2500
"We have a beautiful view from our store, we're on the outskirts of town."
M-Sat. 9-8, Sun. 11-6

 Get on 270 and exit at Morse Rd. Go east on Morse about 4 miles. Store's on corner of Morse and East Johnstown Rd. in Market at Roger's Corner (big silo in front of this shopping strip).

KENT

 Visit the mostly vegetarian Zephyr Cafe on W. Main.

KENT NATURAL FOODS CO-OP
151 East Main Street, 44240 • (330)673-2878
The only grocery store in downtown Kent.
M-Sat. 10-6:30

 Main St. is Rte. 59. Store's one block east of Rte. 43 on north side.

MIDDLEBURG HEIGHTS

AMERICAN HARVEST
13387 Smith, 44130 • (216)888-7727
M-F 9:30-8:30, Sat. 10-6

 From I-71, take Bagley Rd. exit east. Turn left on Pearl and right on Smith. Store's on right in Southland Shopping Center.

NORTH OLMSTEAD

SUNRAY FOODS
4860 A Dover Center Road, 44070 • (216)779-8040
Carrots only. "We are about our customers. We put customers on a prayer list."
M-F 10-6, Sat. 10-5

From Cleveland, take I-90 west to Columbia Rd. Go south on Columbia to Center Ridge Rd. Go west to Dover Center and then south from Dover Center. Store's under water tower, just north of Route 10 (Lorraine Rd).

TOLEDO

BASSETT'S HEALTH FOODS
3301 West Central Street, 43606 • (419)531-0334
M-F 9:30-9, Sat. 9:30-8, Sun. 11:30-5

From I-475, take Secor exit south. Store's on right in West Gate Shopping Center, corner of Secor and Central.

BASSETT'S HEALTH FOODS
4315 Heatherdowns, 43606 • (419)382-4142
No produce.
M-Sat. 9:30-8, Sun. 11:30-5:30

From I-80/90, take exit 4 and go north on Reynolds Rd. Turn right on Heatherdowns. Store's on right.

PHOENIX EARTH FOOD CO-OP
1447 West Sylvania Avenue, 43612 • (419)476-3211
Store is "committed to promoting a philosophy of life that is nutritionally and environmentally sound."
M-F 9-8, Sat. 9-7, Sun. 11-5

From north/east side of I-475, take Willis Parkway exit and follow signs onto Willis. Turn left on Sylvania and store's on left.

TROY

Visit Taggart's for fresh and whole grain items. The Brewery and Dunaway's Pub (Cornerstone Natural Foods staffer Trish says they serve a mean vegetarian pizza there). Bruckner Nature Center is a recommended hiking spot.

CORNERSTONE NATURAL FOODS
110 East Main Street, 45373 • (937)339-8693
Small store with a large variety.
M-F 9:30-6, Sat. 10-4

From I-75, take 41 south about 2 miles. (Main St. is 41). The circular intersection in the center of town separates east and west Main. Go straight through this and store's 2 blocks down on right.

WOOSTER

WOOSTER FOOD CO-OP
247 West North Street, 44691 • (330)264-9797
Store's in an old house a comfortable atmosphere.
M-Sat. 10-6

From Hwy. 30, take Rte. 3 north exit. Turn right on North St. Store's on left.

YELLOW SPRINGS

Check out the Sunrise Cafe and Winds Cafe & Bakery, both serve great food. Outdoor recommendations: Visit Glen Echo and the Glen, a 1,000 acre parcel of woods. Organic Grocery staff say Yellow Springs is a funky town with lots of "weird people" rambling around.

ORGANIC GROCERY
230 Keith's Alley, 45387 • (937)767-7215
Ten miles from I-70, this funky little store is located in the same town as Antioch College.
M-F 10-7, Sat. 9-7, Sun. 11-6

From I-675, take Dayton/Yellow Springs Rd. - Yellow Springs exit. Head south on Dayton/Yellow Springs Rd. for eight miles to Yellow Springs. Turn right on Corry, then right into Keith's Alley.

YOUNGSTOWN

Check out Mill Creek Park, a beautiful spot in the middle of Youngstown.

GOOD FOOD CO-OP
62 Pyatt Street, 44502 • (330)747-9368
M-Sat. 10-6

From I-680, take Market St. (Rte. 7) exit south. Turn left on Pyatt St. Store's on left across from Pyatt Street Market.

Oklahoma

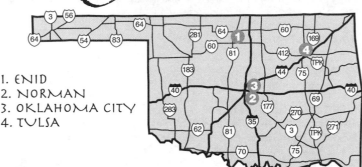

1. ENID
2. NORMAN
3. OKLAHOMA CITY
4. TULSA

ENID

NATURAL FOOD CENTER
131 West Garriott, 73701 • (405)234-5000
Carrots only.
M-F 9-5:30, Sat. 9-1

 From I-81, go east on Hwy. 412 (Garriott). Store's on right at corner of Garriott & Independence.

NORMAN

 Check out mostly vegetarian restaurant, Love Light, on Buchanan Street.

EARTH NATURAL FOODS
309 South Flood Avenue, 73069 • (405)364-3551
M-F 9-7, Sat. 9-6, Sun. 12-5

 From I-35, head east on Main St. Turn right on Flood and store's on left.

OKLAHOMA CITY

 Check out Sala Thai on NW 23rd Street for excellent Thai food.

AKINS NATURAL FOOD
2924 NW 63rd Street, 73116 • (405)843-3033
"Largest organic produce selection in the state."
M-Sat. 9-9, Sun. 10-6

  From I-44, take 63rd St. exit south/west about two miles. Store's on right.

EARTH NATURAL FOODS & DELI
49th & North Western, 73118 • (405)840-0502
M-F 10-8, Sat. 10-6, Sun. 10-5

   From I-244, go three blocks south on Western St. Store's on right in "The Iglesia."

TULSA

 Check out the Riverpark on Tulsa's west side for walking and biking (bike rentals available in the area) and Big Al's for vegetarian fare. Not too many vegetarian restaurants in the area though... "We're still in cattle country out here," says Maryann, the nutritionist at the East 31st St. Akins store. "That may be why Akins does so well."

AKINS NATURAL FOODS
7807 East 51st Street, 74145 • (918)663-4137
M-Sat. 9-9, Sun. 12-6

From I-44 or I-64, turn south on Memorial Drive. Turn right on 51st St. Store's on right in Fontana Shopping Center.

AKINS NATURAL FOODS
3321 East 31st Street, 74135 • (918)742-6630
M-Sat. 9-8, Sun. 12-6

From I-44, take Harvard exit north. Turn right on 31st. Store's on left in Neort Square Shopping Center.

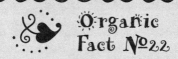

Organic Fact №22

ORGANIC CHEFS

In Food & Wine magazine's 1997 Chef's Survey administered by Louis Harris & Associates, 76 percent of those chefs surveyed responded "Yes" to the question, "Do you actively seek out organically grown ingredients?"

Oregon

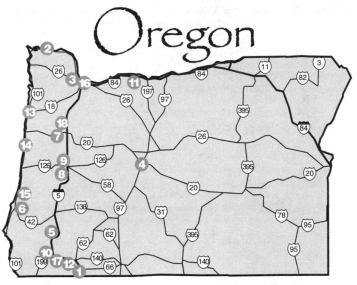

1. ASHLAND
2. ASTORIA
3. BEAVERTON
4. BEND
5. CANYONVILLE
6. COQUILLE
7. CORVALLIS
8. COTTAGE GROVE
9. EUGENE
10. GRANTS PASS
11. HOOD RIVER
12. JACKSONVILLE
13. LINCOLN CITY
14. NEWPORT
15. NORTH BEND
16. PORTLAND
17. ROGUE RIVER
18. SALEM

ASHLAND

 An adventurous little town with a plethora of outdoor activities available (check out the nearby Pacific Coast trail). Ashland is great!

Ashland Community Food staffer, Michelle, recommends: The House of Thai, 5 Rivers (Indian fare) and for breakfast, check out Brothers (Michelle says their tofu scramble is great!) At night, head over to Ashland Creek Bar and Grill, Daddy'O's and The Catwalk, a dance club that also serves Asian food.

If you're traveling in a van, bus or assorted motorized vehicle, keep in mind that Ashland ordinances prohibit overnight camping within city limits (tickets are issued often). Michelle recommends Jackson Hot Springs to park your rig.

ASHLAND COMMUNITY FOOD STORE
237 North 1st Street, 97520 • (541)482-2237
M-Sat. 8-9, Sun. 9-9

From I-5 south: Take Hwy. 66 exit, turn left off ramp and take Siskiyou Blvd. Turn right on 1st St. Store's on left. From I-5 north: Take Valley View exit and go right off ramp. Turn left on Hwy. 99. This will split and become Main, take Main. Turn left on 1st St. and store's on left.

ASTORIA

COMMUNITY STORE
1389 Duane Street, 97103 • (503)325-0027
M-Sat. 9-6

 From Hwy. 30 (26/101 from south), follow signs to downtown Astoria, and from there, take 12th St. away from river. Turn left on Exchange and left on 14th. Store's on left.

BEAVERTON

NATURE'S FRESH NW
4000 SW 117th Street, 97005 • (503)646-3824
Sun.- Sun. 9-9

From I-5, take Rte. 217 exit and follow signs to Beaverton. Take Canyon exit and turn left on Canyon. Turn right on 117th. Store's on right.

BEND

 Bend = outdoor fun! Check out Cafe Sante on NW Franklin Street.

DEVORE'S GOOD FOOD
1124 NW Neort, 97701 • (541)389-6588
M-Sat. 8-7, Sun 11-6

 From Hwy. 97, go west on Greenwood (becomes Neort). Store's on right.

NATURE'S
1950 NE 3rd Street, 97701 • (541)382-6732
M-F 9-9, Sat. 9-6, Sun. 10-6

 Hwy. 97 is 3rd St. Store's on north side in Wagner Payless Mall.

CANYONVILLE

PROMISE NATURAL FOOD & BAKERY
503 South Main, 97417 • (541)839-4167
M-F 9:30-6, Sat. 10-4 (depending on whim)

 From I-5 northbound, take first Canyonville exit (1 of 2). Take a right onto 5th St. Drive one block and store's at corner of 5th & Main St.

COQUILLE

NOSLER'S NATURAL GROCERY
99 East 1st Street, 97423 • (541)396-4823
M-F 10-6 (Th. 'til 7), Sat. 10-5

Take Rte. 42 into Coquille. Store's across street from Safeway on 1st St.

CORVALLIS

 Latin for "the heart of the valley." Check out Nearly Normal, a 100% vegetarian restaurant on NW 15th Street.

FIRST ALTERNATIVE INC. - A COOPERATIVE GROCERY
1007 SE 3rd Street, 97333 • (541)753-3115
Sun.-Sun. 9-9

 From I-5, take Hwy. 34 exit west into Corvallis. Turn left on 4th St. Store's 8 miles from I-5, on left.

COTTAGE GROVE

SUNSHINE GENERAL STORE
824 West Main Street, 97424 • (541)942-8836
M-Sat. 10-7

 From I-5, take exit 174 and follow signs to Rte. 99. Turn right on Main St. Store's on right.

EUGENE

 With 8 stocked natural food stores and a ton of vegetarian restaurants, this town is excellent for decadent (and cheap) dining!

Check out The Keystone Cafe (we highly recommend ordering the Powerhouse and eating in their outside dining area). "Everything they make is so phenomenally good," says one traveler. "Stay in Eugene long enough to try everything on their menu." Visit New Day Bakery for delicious breakfast, lunch, baked goods and most importantly, the best Tempeh sandwich ever (the carrot relish does it!). Pick up a bottle of Genesis juice, Eugene's cooperatively run fresh juice company. Great stuff!

Since most every Eugene visitor eventually happens upon Cougar Hot Springs, we thought we'd pass along a warning. This is a place to tread lightly. The forest, lagoon and springs themselves have a cathedral-like beauty, but the effects of human interference are clear. Be conscious as you enter any forest or hot spring area. Glass does not belong in a hot spring, nor does alcohol, trash or dogs. We need to protect the remaining places that still inspire us... and this is one of them.

FRIENDLY FOODS & DELI
2757 Friendly Street, 97405 • (541)683-2079
M-Sat. 8-10, Sun. 9-10

 From I-5, take 30th St. exit west toward town. It zigzags twice, becoming 29th, then 28th. Stay on 28th, then turn right onto Friendly. Store's on right.

KIVA
125 West 11th Avenue, 97401 • (541)342-8666
M-Sat. 9-8, Sun. 10-5

 From I-5, take Downtown/Civic Center exit onto 6th Ave. (one way). Turn right on Olive. Store's on right, corner of Olive and 11th Ave.

NEW FRONTIER MARKET - WEST
1101 W. 8th Avenue, 97402 • (541)345-7401
This neighborhood natural food store is housed in a turn of the century building.
M-F 7am-midnight, Sat. 8am-midnight, Sun. 8am-11pm

 From I-5, take exit 105 heading west into town. Drive to last exit (Jefferson St.). Drive down Jefferson and turn right on 8th St. Take that to Van Buren and store's on corner of 8th & Van Buren.

NEW FRONTIER MARKET - EAST
2390 Agate Street, 97403 • (541)343-4933
M-F 7-12, Sat. 8-12, Sun. 8-11

From I-5, take 30th Ave., go to Hilyard and make a right. Drive to 24th St. and go right. Drive to Agate(next stop sign). Store's on left corner.

OASIS FINE FOODS MARKETPLACE
2580 Willakenzie Road, 97401 • (541)334-6382
Sun.-Sun. 7-9

From I-5, take Beltway west to Coburg Rd. exit. Go south on Coburg Rd. Store's 1/2 mile up on right.

OASIS FINE MARKETPLACE SOUTH
2489 Willamette St., 97405 • (541)345-1014
This store has motorized shopping carts and an in-store post office.
Sun.-Sun. 7-11

From I-5, take 30th Ave. exit west, turn left on 29th and right on Willamette. Store's on right.

RED BARN
357 Van Buren, 97402 • (541)342-7503
Sun.-Sun. 9-10

From I-5, get on I-105/126 exit west. Take 6th St./Hwy. 99 exit and bear right. Turn right on Blair. Store's on right at corner of Blair and 4th.

SUNDANCE NATURAL FOODS
728 East 24th, 97403 • (541)343-9142
Everything a traveler needs!
Sun.-Sun. 7-11

From I-5, take 30th Ave. exit and head west. Turn right on Hilyard. Store's on right, corner of 24th and Hilyard.

GRANTS PASS

FARMER'S MARKET
603 Rogue River Highway, 97527 • (541)474-0252
M-Sat. 8:30-6:30, Sun. 10-5

From I-5, take the northern of the two Grants Pass exits and drive on 6th St. through town. Go over the Rogue River and when road splits, stay to left. After three stoplights, store is on right, just past Herb's La Casita.

SUNSHINE NATURAL FOOD MARKET
128 SW H Street, 97526 • (541)474-5044
Store's bakery is all organic, all vegan and uses no white sugar.
M-Sat. 8-7

From I-5, take southern Grants Pass exit (of 2) and get on Hwy. 199 (one direction). Turn right on 7th, left on H St. Store's on right.

HOOD RIVER

 20 minutes from majestic Mt. Hood, this area is popular for skiing, snowboarding and in the summer, windsurfing. "It's gorgeous. I love it!" says a Wy'east Naturals staffer.

WY'EAST NATURALS
110 5th Street, 97031 • (541)386-6181
M-Sat. 7:30-7, Sun. 10-5

 From I-84, take 2nd St. Hood River exit, go south on 2nd, right onto Cascade and left on 5th. Store's on west side of street.

JACKSONVILLE

RUCH NATURAL FOODS
181 Upper Applegate Road, 97530 • (541)899-1519
M-Sat. 10-7, Sun. 10-5

 From I-5, take Medford exit to Hwy. 238. Take that through Jacksonville to Ruch. Make a left onto Upper Applegate Rd. and store's 1/8 mile up on left.

LINCOLN CITY

TRILLIUM NATURAL FOODS
1026 SE Jetty Avenue, 97367 • (541)994-5665
M-Sat. 9:30-7, Sun. 11-6

 From Hwy. 101, turn east on East Devils Lake Rd. Turn left on Jetty. Store's on right at corner.

NEWPORT

 Famous for its tidal pools and whale watching opportunities.

OCEANA NATURAL FOODS CO-OP
159 SE 2nd Street, 97365 • (541)265-8285
Sun.-Sun. 8-7

   From Hwy. 101, turn east on Hwy. 20. Go 2 blocks to Benton, turn south and drive for 2 more blocks. Store's at corner of 2nd & Benton.

NORTH BEND

 In North Bend, find beaches, dunes, botanical gardens, nature walks and Sunset Bay, a must for watching sunsets.

COOS HEAD FOOD STORE
1960 Sherman Avenue (Hwy. 101 S), 97459 • (541)756-7264
M-F 9-7, Sat. 10-6, Sun. 12-5

 Store's on west side of Hwy. 101 south (1 block south of North Bend Library).

Check out Mount Hood, the Columbia River and Mount St. Helens. Portland is an hour from the shores of the Pacific Ocean, and close to the Cascade Mountains.

Restaurant recommendations: Visit The India Grill, Jarra's Ethiopian on SE Hawthorne, Indigine on SE Division, Old Wives Tales on East Burnside and the many McMenamin's Pubs (they brew their own beer, feature great food and one has a movie theater inside!). Prema, a worker at the Daily Grind says, "If you haven't been to McMenamin's Pub, you haven't been to Portland." Don't miss Powell's Books, an enormous bookstore located downtown!

THE DAILY GRIND BAKERY RESTAURANT & NATURAL FOODS
4026 SE Hawthorne Boulevard, 97214 • (503)233-5521
Sun.-Sun. 9-9

From I-84 west: Take 39th St. exit south and turn left on Hawthorne. Store's on right. From I-84 east: Take 43rd St. exit. Turn left at second light. Turn left on 39th and left on Hawthorne. Store's on right.

FOOD FRONT CO-OP
2375 NW Thurman, 97210 • (503)222-5658
Sun.-Sun. 9-9

From I-405, take Rte. 30 exit west. Take Vaughn St. exit and turn left on 23rd Place. Store's on right.

NATURE'S FRESH NW
3016 SE Division, 97202 • (503)233-7374
Sun.-Sun. 9-10

From I-205, take Division St. exit west about 60 blocks. Store's on left.

NATURE'S FRESH NW
6344 SW Capitol Highway, 97219 • (503)244-3110
Sun.-Sun. 9-10

From I-5, take Capitol Hwy. west. Store's on right in Hillsdale Shopping Center.

NATURE'S FRESH NW
5909 SW Corbett, 97201 • (503)244-3934
Sun.-Sun. 9-9

From I-205, take any Lake Oswego exit and drive south on Macadam St. Turn right on Pendleton. Store's on left, corner of Pendleton and Corbett.

NATURE'S FRESH NW
3449 NE 24th, 97212 • (503)288-3414.
Sun.-Sun. 9-9

From I-5, take Coliseum exit east on Weidler. Turn left on 24th and store's on left.

PEOPLE'S FOOD STORE
3029 SE 21st Avenue, 97202 • (503)232-9051
Store sells organic produce only!
Sun.-Sun. 9-9

 From I-5, take Ross Island Bridge exit. Take 26 east (Powell Blvd.) and store's one block north of Powell on 21st Ave.

ROGUE RIVER

 **Rafting is the major summer attraction!**

WILD BERRIES
106 East Main Street, 97537 • (541)582-3075
Local, family run business.
M-F 9:30-6, Sat. 9:30-5

 From I-5, take exit 48 and follow signs to Rogue River. Turn left on Main St. Store's on East Main.

SALEM

HELIOTROPE
2890 Market Street NE, 97301 • (503)362-5487
M-Sat. 8-9, Sun. 9-8

 From I-5, take Market St. exit and head west. Store's on right, 8 blocks from highway.

Organic Fact №23

ORGANIC CONSCIOUS COMPANIES

Leading companies are recognizing the importance of organic production. Patagonia has announced a new program for purchasing certified organic cotton with a goal to buy 100% organic cotton only.

PENNSYLVANIA

PH PHILADELPHIA AREA - 1, 2, 4, 5, 10, 11, 16, 18, 19, 21, 23, 26, 27, 29, 30

1. ALLENTOWN
2. BRYN MAWR
3. CLARKS SUMMIT
4. COLLEGEVILLE
5. EASTON
6. ERIE
7. EYNON
8. HARRISBURG
9. HONESDALE
10. HUNTINGTON VALLEY
11. KIMBERTON
12. LANSDALE
13. LUZERNE
14. MARSHALLS CREEK
15. NEW CUMBERLAND

16. NEW HOPE
17. NORTH WALES
18. PAOLI
19. PENNDEL
20. PENNS CREEK
21. PHILADELPHIA
22. PITTSBURGH
23. PLUMSTEADVILLE
24. STOVERSTOWN
25. STATE COLLEGE
26. WAYNE
27. WEST CHESTER
28. WILLIAMSPORT
29. WILLOW GROVE
30. WYNNEWOOD

ALLENTOWN

Check out the Green Cafe in nearby Bethlehem. They carry some grocery but mainly feature excellent food and music on weekends. Area resident Stacey says... "It has a great, liberal, crunchy atmosphere. It's a mostly vegetarian cafe with tons of vegan options including desserts and baked goods."

SIGN OF THE BEAR NATURAL FOODS
514 North Saint Cloud Street, 18104 • (610)439-8575
M-W 9:30-7, Th. & F 9:30-8, Sat. 9-5:30

From I-78, take 15th St. exit to Tilghman St. Turn right on Tilghman and left on Saint Cloud. Store's on right.

BRYN MAWR

 Once a country getaway for the Philadelphia upper crust, this college town is filled with mansions and old country estates from yesteryear.

Elizabeth at Arrowroot Natural Market recommends Marbles & the Big Fish, both restaurants feature vegetarian offerings.

ARROWROOT NATURAL MARKET
834 W. Lancaster Avenue, 19010 • (610)527-3393
M-F 9-9, Sat. 9:30-6, Sun. 10-5:30

From 476, take the St. David's exit - Rte. 30. Go east on Rte. 30 for 6 minutes. Store's in the center of town, near the movie theater.

CLARKS SUMMIT

EVERYTHING NATURAL
412 South State Street, 18411 • (717)586-9684
M-Sat. 10-8

 From I-81, take exit 58/Rte. 6 & 11 to Clark's Summit (approximately 1.5 miles). Store's downtown, on left.

COLLEGEVILLE

COOK'S NATURAL FOODS
222 West Main Street, 19426 • (610)489-6322
No organic produce.
M-Th. 9-8 (F 'til 9), Sat. 10-6

 From 422, take Collegeville exit. Go right (west) for two miles on old 422. Store's in Acme Shopping Center on left.

EASTON

NATURE'S WAY
143 Northampton Street, 18042 • (610)253-0940
M, W, Th. 9:30-5:30, Tu. & F 9:30-8, Sat. 9:30-5, Sun. 12-4

 From I-78, take Easton exit and follow to 611 north to Larry Holmes Dr. Make a left onto Northampton St. Store's one block up on right.

ERIE

WHOLE FOODS CO-OP
318 E. 6th Street, 16507 • (814)456-0282
Whole Foods Co-op has over 8600 members!
M-W 10-5, Th. 10-7:30, F 10-6, Sat. 10-5

 From I-90, take I-79 north (becomes Bayfront Hwy.). Once at the edge of downtown, continue to traffic light and make a right onto Holland. Go left at traffic light onto 6th St. Store's a block and a half down on left.

EYNON

AURORA NATURAL FOODS
784 Scranton-Carbondale Highway, 18403 • (717)876-4252
M-Th 10:30-5:30 (F. 'til 7:30), Sat. 10:30-5

 From I-81, take Carbondale exit east. Store's on right. (Eynon is near the town of Archibald).

HARRISBURG

GENESEE NATURAL FOODS
5405 Locust Lane, 17109 • (717)545-3712
M, Tu., Sat. 10-6, W-F 10-8

 From I-83, take Colonial Park exit and drive to Prince St. (a few lights). Go right on Prince, then left on Locust Lane at the T junction (end of Prince). Store's 1/4 mile down on right.

HONESDALE

NATURE'S GRACE
947 Main Street, 18431 • (717)253-3469
Take out only deli. Limited organic produce.
M-Sat. 10-6 (F 'til 8)

 From I-81, take Rte. 6 exit in Scranton. Drive 30 minutes on Rte. 6 to Honesdale. Store's on Main St. on left.

HUNTINGTON VALLEY

VALLEY HEALTH FOODS
25-71 Huntington Pike, 19006 • (215)947-4585
M-Sat. 9-6 (F 'til 7)

 On Rte. 232, just north of Rte. 63.

KIMBERTON

KIMBERTON WHOLE FOODS
Kimberton Road/P.O. Box 760, 19442 • (610)935-1444
M-F 8-8, Sat. 9-6, Sun. 10-5

 From I-76 east: Take King of Prussia exit and go west on Rte. 422. Take Rte. 23 exit west and turn left on Rte. 113 south. Bear right on Kimberton. Store's about one mile down on left.

LANSDALE

NORTH PENN HEALTH FOOD CENTER
1313 North Broad Street, 19446 • (215)855-1044
M-Sat. 9-6 (F 'til 9)

 From Rte. 309, take Rte. 63 exit. Rte. 63 becomes Main and crosses Broad St. Go north on Broad. Store's one mile up on right.

LUZERNE

HOUSE OF NUTRITION
140 Main Street, 18709 • (717)714-0436
M-Th. 10-6, F 10-8, Sat. 10-6, Sun. 12-4

 From I-81, take Wilkes-Barre exit (37) and you'll be on Cross Valley (309 north). Drive straight and take exit 6 - Luzerne. Turn right at light onto Union St. Go up 1 light, take a right over a bridge and an immediate left. Follow up to stop sign. Go left there onto Main St. Store's on left.

MARSHALLS CREEK

NATURALLY RITE
P.O. Box 1187/Route 209, 18335 • (717)223-1133
Store owns clinic next door. Clinic staff is comprised of a chiropractor, nutritionist and masseuse.
Sun.-Sun. 9-9 (open at 11 on Sun.)
Restaurant: Sun-Th. 11-9 (closed Tu.), F & Sat. 'til 10

 From I-80, take exit 52 (Marshalls Creek). Drive toward Marshalls Creek to Rte. 209. Take a right there and drive three miles. Store's on right.

NEW CUMBERLAND

Check out The Wire (a loved coffee house) and the Groove for used clothes and records. Both are in walking distance from Avatar's Natural Foods.

AVATAR'S NATURAL FOODS
321 Bridge Street, 17070 • (717)774-7215
Deli is take-out only.
M & Tu. 9-7, W-F 9-9, Sat. 9-5, Deli: M-Sat. 11-2

From Pennsylvania Turnpike, take I-83 exit north and get off at New Cumberland exit. Go east on Simpson Ferry Rd. Turn left on 4th St. and right on Bridge St. Store's 1/2 block up on left, next to movie theater.

NEW HOPE

Plentiful shopping nearby.

NEW HOPE NATURAL MARKET
415 B Old York Road, 18938 • (215)862-3441
The couple who run this store grow and sell their own organic produce in the summer.
M-F 10-7, Sat. 10-6, Sun. 12-6

 Store's at intersection of Rte. 202 and 179 (Old York Rd.).

NORTH WALES

FRESH FIELDS WHOLE FOODS MARKET
1210 Bethlehem Pike, 19454 • (215)646-6300
M-Sat. 8-9, Sun. 8-8

 From Pennsylvania Turnpike, take Fort Washington exit north (Rte. 309). Store's 3 miles up 309 on left.

PAOLI

ARROWROOT NATURAL MARKET
83 East Lancaster Avenue, 19301 • (610)640-2720
Store features live music on Friday & Saturday nights. Store also has a homeopathic pharmacy & pharmacist.
M-F 9-6, Sat. 9:30-6, Sun. 10-4

 On Rte. 30 in the heart of Paoli, store's across from shopping center.

PENNDEL

THE NATURAL FOODS STORE
131 Hulmeville Avenue, 19047 • (215)752-7268
No produce.
M-Th. 10-6:30, F 10-7:30, Sat. 10-5:30, Sun. 11-4

 From Rte. 1 (Roosevelt Blvd.), take Penndel exit onto Business Rte. 1 (Old Lincoln Hwy.). At third light, make a right. Store's directly on left.

PENNS CREEK

WALNUT ACRES
Walnut Acres Road, 17862 • (800)433-3998
These acclaimed mail-order organic growers also have a store! They give farm tours M-F 9:30, 11 & 1.
M-Sat. 9-5, Sun. 12-5

 From I-80, drive south on Rte. 15, then west on Rte. 45 at Lewisburg. Take 104 south at Mifflinburg and take first left after Penns Creek Bridge. Store's on left.

PHILADELPHIA

 Yum! Harmony on North 9th Street in Chinatown has some of the best vegetarian Chinese food we've tasted... beware, it's addictive! We recommend the sesame noodles, lemon beef and General Tsao's chicken. Essene's Cafe also serves up great food!

ARNOLD'S WAY
4438 Main Street, 19127 • (215)483-2266
Store donates all sales from tea, chai, hot chocolate and Roma to the local Waldorf School. But, they don't serve coffee. "We don't believe in coffee," says the owner. "Technically, it's not good for your health." No produce.
M-Sat. 10-6, Sun. 11-5

From I-76 east: Take Green Lane and Manyunk exit (exit 31). Turn right at light and right on Main St. Store's on right. From west: Take Roxborough and Manyunk exit, turn left at light and right on Main. Store's on right.

CENTER FOODS
1525 Locust Street, 19102 • (215)732-9000
M-F 8-8, Sat. 10-6, Sun. 12-5

 From I-295, take exit 676 west to B St., (which puts you onto 15th St.). Stay on 15th, then make a right onto Spruce and drive to 16th. Go right on 16th and drive to Locust St. Store's at 16th & Locust.

ESSENE, THE NATURAL FOOD MARKET

715-719 South 4th Street, 19147 • (215)922-1146

Good food here!

Sun.-Sun. 9-8, Cafe: M-F 9-9

From Vine St. Expressway, take Washington/Columbus Ave. exit. Turn right onto Delaware Ave. Turn west on Christian, right on 3rd and left on Monroe. Store's on right, corner of 4th and Monroe.

FRESH FIELDS WHOLE FIELDS MARKET

2001 Pennsylvania Avenue, 19130 • (215)557-0015

Sun.-Sun. 8-10

Take I-95 south to 676. Get off at museum area exit and cross over Parkway. At first light, make a right onto Hamilton Ave. Make another right at 21st St. Drive to Pennsylvania Ave. and make a left. Store's down the block.

MARIPOSA FOOD CO-OP

4726 Baltimore Avenue, 19143 • (215)729-2121

Store does not accept cash. Food stamps, money orders and checks only. If you're traveling through town, get a free 1 month trial membership to shop.

W 3-9, Th. 1:30-9, Sat. 12-4

From 76/Schykill Expressway, get off at South St. exit and go west (turns into Spruce St.). Head west on Spruce and drive to 47th. Turn left on 47th and drive to Baltimore Ave. (4 -5 blocks) and you'll find store. (Located in west Philadelphia).

WEAVER'S WAY COOPERATIVE ASSOCIATION

559 Carpenter Lane, 19119 • (215)843-2350

M-Th 10-8, F 9-8, Sat 9-6, Sun 10-4

Take I-76 to Lincoln Dr. and go left onto Greene St. Drive 2 stops to Carpenter Lane and make a right. Store's on right.

PITTSBURGH

Check out vegetarian restaurant, Zip, or stop by the East End Co-op's cafe. Sweet Basil Bar & Grille on Forbes Avenue is also recommended, as is Phnom Penh downtown on First Ave. (delicious Chinese and Cambodian fare).

EAST END FOOD CO-OP

7516 Meade Street, 15208 • (412)242-3598

This is a really nice, low-key co-op. And it's in this country's best kept secret, the lovely city of Pittsburgh.

M-F 10-8, Sat. 10-6, Sun. 10-6

From I-376, take exit 9 (Edgewood) and turn right onto Braddock Ave. Drive 2 miles and turn left at fourth light onto Meade St. Store's on left.

PLUMSTEADVILLE

PLUMSTEADVILLE NATURAL FOODS, INC.

Route 611, 18949 • (215)766-8666

M-F 9:30-6:30 (F 'til 7), Sat. 9:30-5

Plumsteadville is one hour north of Philadelphia. Rte. 611 runs through center of town. Store's in Plumsteadville Shopping Center on 611.

STOVERSTOWN

SONNEWALD NATURAL FOODS
RD1 Box 1510A - Lehman Road, 17362 • (717)225-3825
Store began in the 50's as a commercial grain mill and has since grown into a supermarket sized natural food store. "We have a loyal following," say staff members. Nutritional counseling is free, staffers will grind grain as customers need it and the bulk room is refrigerated.
Tu.-Th. 10-6, F 10-9, Sat. 8-5

 From I-30, head south on Rte. 616 for 2 miles. At York New Salem, turn right at light in square and go 2.3 miles to Lehman Rd. Take a right on Lehman. Store's on left, 150 yards down.

STATE COLLEGE

THE GRANARY
2766 West College Avenue, 16801 • (814)238-4844
Occasional organic produce.
M-Sat. 10-6

 From I-80, take Rte. 26 south. Store's three miles south of center of town.

WAYNE

FRESH FIELDS WHOLE FIELDS MARKET
821 Lancaster Avenue, 19087 • (610)688-9400
Store offers at least 80 organic produce items daily.
M-Sat. 8-9, Sun. 8-8

 From Pennsylvania Turnpike, take I-202 exit south to Rte. 252 south and head for "Paoli." Turn left on Rte 30. Store's about 3 miles up on left.

WEST CHESTER

 Check out beautiful Longwood Gardens, 15 minutes from Great Pumpkin Health Foods.

GREAT PUMPKIN HEALTH FOODS
607 East Market Street, 19382 • (610)696-0741
No produce.
M-F 9-8, Sat. 9-6, Sun. 10-3

 Rte. 3 is Market St. (one way street). Heading out of West Chester, store's on left.

WILLIAMSPORT

FRESHLIFE
2300 E. 3rd Street, 17701 • (717)322-8280
The only vegetarian spot in town!
M-F 9-8, Sat. 9-5, Cafe: M-F 9-3

 From State College, take Rte. 180 to 3rd St./Faxon exit (depending on direction). At light, make a right. Store's 3 lights down on right.

WILLOW GROVE

NATURE'S HARVEST INC. AND HORIZONS CAFE
101 East Moreland Road, 19090 • (215)659-7705
M 10-8, Tu.-Sat. 10-9, Sun. 11-6, Cafe: Tu.-F. 11:30-3 & 5-8:45, Sat. 11:30-8:45

 From Pennsylvania Turnpike, take exit 27 and head south on 611. Store's on corner of Rte. 63 and Rte. 611 in Moreland Plaza.

WYNNEWOOD

FRESH FIELDS WHOLE FIELDS MARKET
339 East Lancaster Avenue, 19096 • (610)896-3737
M-Sat. 8-9, Sun. 8-8

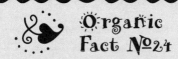 From Rte. 1 (City Ave.) make a right onto Rte. 30. Drive 1.5 miles. Store's just past Wynnewood Ave. on right.

Organic Fact №24

TREMENDOUS INDUSTRY GROWTH

For the seventh consecutive year, the organic industry has posted double digit sales growth of 20 percent or greater, with 24 percent growth reported for 1996.

RHODE ISLAND

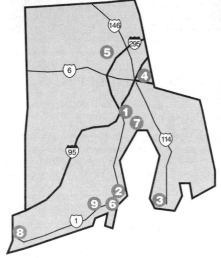

1. EAST GREENWICH
2. NARRAGANSETT
3. NEWPORT
4. PROVIDENCE
5. SMITHFIELD
6. WAKEFIELD
7. WARWICK
8. WESTERLY
9. WEST KINGSTON

EAST GREENWICH

 Got a hankerin' for falafel, hummus and other Middle Eastern specialties? Check out Pick Pockets in East Greenwich.

BACK TO BASICS NATURAL FOOD GROCERY
500 Main Street, 02818 • (401)885-2679
M-W 10-6, Th. & F 10-7, Sat. 10-5:30, Sun. 12-5

From I-95 north: Take Rte. 4 exit to East Greenwich exit. Turn right and go 2.5 miles, then turn left on Main St. to find store. From I-95 south: Turn right off East Greenwich. Take first left on Division Rd. then turn left on Main. Store's on right.

NARRAGANSETT

 The Crazy Burger has a number of meatless options.

FOOD FOR THOUGHT
140 Point Judith Road #32, 02882 • (401)789-2445
Seasonal organic produce.
M-Sat. 10-6 (F 'til 8), Sun. 12-5

From I-95, take Rte. 4 south (becomes Rte. 1). Take first north exit onto 108 south. Drive until Stop & Shop Mall on right. Store's on left in Mariner Square Mall.

NEWPORT

 Outdoor recommendations: Take the cliff walk near Salve Regina University, stroll down the rocks to Ocean Drive (an equally beautiful spot to play in the sun). The Norman bird sanctuary is a great place to hike.

Check out the old mansions of yesteryear on Bellvue Ave. and there's also the Newport Art Museum. The Salvation Cafe on Broadway serves vegetarian fare.

HARVEST NATURAL FOODS
1 Casino Terrace, 02840 • (401)846-8137
M-F 9-7, Sat. 9-6, Sun. 11-5

 From I-95, take Rte. 4 or Rte. 1 (depending on your direction) to get to Rte. 138 east. This will go over Jamestown bridge, then the Newport bridge. After Newport bridge, take first exit off Rte. 138 and go right onto Farewell Dr. At 2nd light, take a right onto America's Cup. Follow this along water to end when road turns into Memorial Blvd. Go up a hill and take a right at Bellvue. Make a left into Bellvue Shopping Center just past Tennis Hall of Fame to find store.

PROVIDENCE

BREAD & CIRCUS WHOLE FOODS MARKET
261 Waterman, 02906 • (401)272-1690
Seasonal cafe.
M-Sat. 8:30-9:30, Sun. 8:30-8:30

 From I-95, take Rte. 195 exit. Take exit #3 off I-195 (Gano St.) and turn right at bottom. Turn right on Waterman (2nd light). Store's on right.

SMITHFIELD

NATURE'S NEST
445 Putnam Pike, 02828 • (401)232-2410
No produce.
M-W 10-6, Th. & F 10-7, Sat. 9-6, Sun. 12-5

 From I-295, take exit 7B and get onto Rte. 44 west. Store's 1/4 mile on right in Apple Valley Mall.

WAKEFIELD

MOTHER NATURE'S
52 Main Street, 02879 • (401)789-0280
No produce.
M-F 10-5:30, Sat. 10-5

 From Rte. 1, take Wakefield exit and drive straight past mall and through light. Store's on left in same plaza as Wakefield Music (across from Citizen's Bank).

WARWICK

VILLAGE NATURAL
18 Post Road, 02888 • (401)941-8028
M-Sat. 10-6

From I-95, take exit for Rte. 37 east/Post Rd. north straight to end. Take a left onto Post. Store's one block down on left.

WESTERLY

ALLEN'S HEALTH FOOD
Franklin Street, 02891 • (401)596-5569
Organic carrots only.
M-Th. 9:30-5:30, F 9:30-6, Sat. 9:30-4

 From I-95, take Rte. 78 exit toward ocean/beach. Turn right on Rte. 1 (Franklin). Store's on right.

WEST KINGSTON

Spice of Life in Charlestown serves mostly organic fare.

THE ALTERNATIVE FOOD COOPERATIVE
3362 Kingston Road, 02892 • (401)789-2240
M-F 9-7, Sat. & Sun. 9-6

From I-95, take exit 3A toward University of Rhode Island. Drive east on 138 for several miles. Store's on right (corner of Liberty Lane and Rte. 138), 1 mile west of URI campus entrance.

> *"Sometimes its a little better to travel than to arrive."*
>
> —Robert Pirsig
> Zen & the Art of
> Motorcycle Maintenance

South Carolina

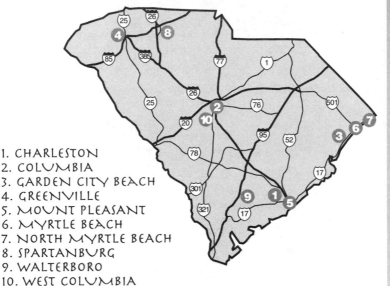

1. CHARLESTON
2. COLUMBIA
3. GARDEN CITY BEACH
4. GREENVILLE
5. MOUNT PLEASANT
6. MYRTLE BEACH
7. NORTH MYRTLE BEACH
8. SPARTANBURG
9. WALTERBORO
10. WEST COLUMBIA

CHARLESTON

In this historic beach town, check out recommended vegetarian restaurants, Mustard Seed and Angel Fish. Also try Doe's Pita Plus for Mediterranean fare and the East Side Bakery & Cafe.

BOOKS, HERBS & SPICES
480 H East Bay Street, 29403 • (803)722-9024
M-F 9-6, Sat. 9:30-5

From Hwy. 17, take East Bay St. exit and follow signs to East Bay St. Turn right on East Bay. Store's on left, across from Channel 5.

RASPBERRY'S NATURAL FOOD STORE
1331 Ashley River Road, 29407 • (803)556-0076
Some produce...
M-F 9:30-6:30, Sat. 9:30-5:30, Sun. 1-6

From I-26, take I-526 exit. Take Ashley River Rd. south exit. Store's 5 miles down on right.

COLUMBIA

Camille at 14 Carrot Whole Foods (see West Columbia) recommends The Basil Pot, the Blue Cactus (a Korean vegetarian restaurant) and the Middle Eastern Tea Room. She also suggests the Congaree Swamp National Monument for canoeing and hiking. "You have to search for things to do in Columbia, but they're there," says Camille.

COLUMBIA CONT.

ROSEWOOD MARKET & DELI
2803 Rosewood Drive, 29205 • (803)765-1083
Cafe has seasonal patio seating.
M-Sat. 9-7, Sun. 1-6

 Take I-26 toward Columbia (away from airport) and take Huger St. exit. Turn left on Blossom and drive to 5 Points (past USC and Carolina Coliseum). Take a right on Harden. Drive to end and go left on Rosewood. Store's on left at third light down, corner of Rosewood and Maple (across from a shopping center).

GARDEN CITY

NEW LIFE NATURAL FOODS
2712 Hwy. 17 S., 29576 • (803)651-5701
M-Sat. 9-6, Sun. 12-6

 Located on Business 17 in the Garden Gate Plaza.

GREENVILLE

Check out the Roper Mountain Science Center & Planetarium.

GARNER'S NATURAL MARKET & CAFE
60 E. Antrim Drive, 29607 • (864)242-4856
M-Sat. 9-9, Sun. 1-6

 From I-85, take South Pleasantburg exit. Go north on Pleasantburg Dr. about 1.5 miles. Take the next right onto E. Antrim and store's on right.

MOUNT PLEASANT

See Charleston for area info.

THE GOOD NEIGHBOR
423 Coleman Boulevard, 29464 • (803)881-3274
A natural food general store.
M-Sat. 10-6

 From I-26 S., take Mt. Pleasant exit, but stay on Business Mt. Pleasant. Once you're on bridge, stay in far right lane. After 3 lights, turn right into Peach Orchard Plaza.

MYRTLE BEACH

Lots of deep fried, southern food in these parts. Check out New Life Natural Foods for good eats.

NEW LIFE NATURAL FOODS
96-72 Hwy. 17 North, 29572 • (803)449-8533
Deli features Thai, Vietnamese and Indian fare.
M-Sat 9-8, Sun. 11-6

 From Hwy. 501, head north on Bypass 17 (connects into Business 17). Store's 1/2 mile up on right in Galleria mall.

NORTH MYRTLE BEACH

NEW LIFE NATURAL FOODS
3320 Hwy. 17 S., 29582 • (803)449-8533
M-Sat. 9-8, Sun. 11-5

 From Hwy. 501, take Rte. 17 Bypass north. Store's on left in Harris Teeter Shopping Center.

SPARTANBURG

 20 miles from the Smokies!

GARNER'S NATURAL FOODS
205 Blackstalk Road, 29301 • (864)574-1898
No produce.
M-Sat. 10-9, Sun. 1:30-6

 From I-26, head north on US 29. Store's on left in Westgate mall, at intersection I-26 and US 29.

GARNER'S NATURAL FOODS
1855 East Main Street (US 29), 29301 • (803)585-1021
M-Sat. 9:30-6

 From I-26, head north on US 29. Store's on right in Hillcrest Mall.

WALTERBORO

NO JUNK JULIE'S
301 Cooler's Dairy Road, 29488 • (803)538-8809
Nutritionist on staff, fun crowd, nice setting, seasonal outdoor cafe.
M, T, Th., F 9-5, W & Sat. 9-6

 From I-95, take exit 57 toward Walterboro. Turn left on Robertson Blvd., then left on Hwy. 17A north. Bear right at fork in road and take a left after Circle M Ranch (on the left w/ red barn). The next street on left is Cooler's Dairy Road. Take that and find store. * In the last edition we suggested following the big carrot to get to the store, but Julie tells us someone stole it!

WEST COLUMBIA

14 CARROT WHOLE FOODS
2250 Sunset Boulevard West, 29169 • (803)791-1568
M-Sat. 9-7, Sun. 1-6

 From I-20, go east on I-26 and turn left off exit 110 (Hwy. 378/ Sunset Blvd.). Store's on left in Westland Square.

South Dakota

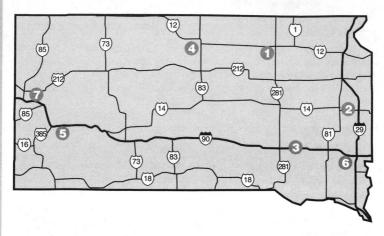

1. ABERDEEN
2. BROOKINGS
3. MITCHELL
4. MOBRIDGE
5. RAPID CITY
6. SIOUX FALLS
7. SPEARFISH

ABERDEEN

NATURAL ABUNDANCE FOOD CO-OP
125 South Main Street, 57401 • (605)229-4947
M-F 9-6, Sat. 9-5

From Hwy. 281 take Main St. exit. Go north on Main and Co-op is
on right, at corner of 2nd and Main.

BROOKINGS

NATURE'S PARADISE
1455 6th Street, 57006 • (605)697-7404
Some organic produce. Herbalist on staff in the afternoons.
M-Sat. 10-5:30

From I-29, take exit 132 to Hwy. 14 west and drive through
3 lights. Store's across from the swimming pool.

MITCHELL

WAYNE & MARY'S
1313 West Havens, 57301 • (605)996-9868
M-F 9-7, Sat. 9-5

From I-90, take Mitchell exit. Drive one mile north and take a
right onto West Havens. Store's 1/4 mile east on the right.

MOBRIDGE

GOOD NEIGHBOR STORE
308 Main Street, 57601 • (605)845-2097
20+ years old, locally owned store.
M-Sat. 9:30-5:30 (Th. 'til 8)

 Rte. 12 becomes Grand Crossing in Mobridge. Go south on Main St. and store's on left.

RAPID CITY

STAPLE AND SPICE MARKET
601 Mt. Rushmore Road, 57701 • (605)343-3900
M-F 9-6, Sat. 9-5

 From I-90, take exit 57 and go left onto Saint Joseph. Store's 2 blocks down, on corner of St. Joseph and Mount Rushmore Rd.

SIOUX FALLS

EAST DAKOTAH FOOD CO-OP
420 1st Avenue South, 57104 • (605)339-9506
A true co-op that's been around for 25 years. "We're small but we have a lot of stuff!"
M-F 9-7, Sat. 9-6, Sun. 12-5

 From I-29, take 12th St. exit east about three miles. Turn right on 1st Ave. Store's on left.

SPEARFISH

GOOD EARTH NATURAL FOODS
138 East Hudson, 57783 • (605)642-7639
M-Sat. 9-5:30

 From I-90, take exit 12 and continue on Jackson Blvd. to 7th St. Turn south and drive 2 blocks to Hudson St., then turn west. Store's on right.

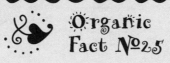

Organic Fact №25

IMPORTED PRODUCE TESTING

According to the U.S. General Accounting Office, only one percent of all imported fruits and vegetables are tested by the Food and Drug Administration for illegal pesticide residues.

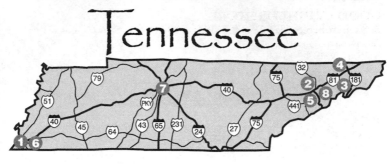

Tennessee

1. EAST MEMPHIS
2. JEFFERSON CITY
3. JOHNSON CITY
4. KINGSPORT

5. KNOXVILLE
6. MEMPHIS
7. NASHVILLE
8. NEWPORT

EAST MEMPHIS

 See Memphis for area info.

WILD OATS MARKET
5101 Sanderlin Avenue, 38117 • (901)685-2293
M-Sat. 8-9, Sun. 11-6

From I-240, take Walnut Grove exit west into town. Turn left on White Station Rd. and right on Sanderlin. Store's on left in Sanderlin Shopping Center.

JEFFERSON CITY

HILL'S HEALTH HUT
107 East Old Ajay Highway, 37760 • (423)475-2993
Grapefruit & oranges only. Snack bar coming soon.
M-F 9:30-5:30 (F 'til 6), Sat. 10-5

 From I-40, take exit for Rte. 417 (Dandridge) and after exit, go left, then drive under bridge. (McDonald's will be on the right). At 2nd light from the I-40 exit, make a right and drive 5 miles. Make a right at light onto Old Ajay Highway. Store's on right in a 2 story gray building.

JOHNSON CITY

NATURAL FOOD MARKET
3211 People's Street - Suite 74, 37604 • (423)610-1000
Store has a juice bar, a rarity for this region.
M-Sat. 10-8

 From I-181, take exit 31 - State of Franklin St. If driving from north, turn left onto State of Franklin St. Turn left 1/2 mile up on Knob Creek Rd. People's St. is first left and store's on corner. If driving from south, turn right onto State of Franklin St. then same as above.

KINGSPORT

GOOD FOOD GROCERY
138 Cherokee Street, 37660 • (423)246-3663
No produce.
M-Sat. 10-6

 From I-181, take Kingsport/Wilcox Dr. east. Take Wilcox Dr. 2 miles east toward Kingsport center. After intersection with underpass, take a left onto Sullivan St. Take the left fork onto Main, then right on Cherokee St. Store's on left in brick building.

KNOXVILLE

Recommendations by Jennifer, a Knoxville Food Co-op staffer: Check out The Tomato Head in downtown Knoxville (Jennifer says they serve fresh, high quality food at a great price), and the Southern Brewing Company on Gay St. brews great beer!

The Smoky mountains are a 30 minute drive from Knoxville. Go there for hiking, guided river tours, camping and general scenic outdoor fun.

KNOXVILLE FOOD CO-OP
937 North Broadway, 37917 • (615)525-2069
M-Sat. 9-8, Sun. 12-6

 From I-40, take Broadway exit (Rte. 441) south for less than 1 mile. Store's on right.

NATURAL & ORGANIC FOODS
7025 Kingston Pike, 37917 • (423)584-8422
Organic carrots only.
M-Sat. 10-6

 From I-75/40, take exit 380. Go 1 mile on Kingston Pike. Store's on left in West Hill Shopping Center

NATURE'S PANTRY GOURMET & WHOLE FOOD MARKET
6600 Kingston Pike, 37919 • (423)584-4714
M-Sat. 9-9, Sun. 10-6

From I-40, take exit 380 (West Hills exit). Make a left onto Kingston Pike (going east). Store's two miles up at top of hill on right.

MEMPHIS

Elvis, Elvis and more Elvis. Memphis recommendations: The Pink Palace (museum, planetarium and IMAX Theater), The Children's Museum and of course, there's always the Graceland tour.

La Montagne on Park Avenue is recommended (ethnic and vegetarian selections) and The Golden Garden on Stage Road in E. Memphis reproduces a plethora of Chinese dishes using seitan (separate vegetarian menu).

WILD OATS MARKET
1801 Union, 38104 • (901)725-4823
M-F 8-10, Sat. & Sun. 8-10

 From west side of I-240 loop, take Union Ave. exit east. Store's 5 lights down on right.

NASHVILLE

Donnie at Sunshine Grocery Natural Foods has great Nashville recommendations. Go hiking at Radnor Lake, check out Peaceful Planet, a vegetarian lunch buffet on Division St., and don't miss Nashville's music scene! Donnie suggests Cafe Milano, a jazz club downtown on 3rd Avenue, and for Bluegrass, check out the Station Inn. The legendary Bluebird Cafe is famous for great folk and country music.

SUNSHINE GROCERY NATURAL FOODS

3201 Belmont Boulevard, 37212 • (615)297-5100

Carry out deli is delicious! Original, vegetarian recipes made from scratch.
M-Sat. 8-8

From I-440, take 21st Ave. exit into the city. Take first right on Sweetbriar and turn right on Belmont at second stop sign. Store's on right in a large purple building.

NEWPORT

Located in the beautiful Smoky Mountains, there's lots of hiking and camping available close to the store.

THE MUSTARD SEED

331 Cosby Highway, 37821 • (423)623-4091

Seasonal produce and carrots.
M-Th. 10-6, F 10-4, Sun. 12-4

From I-40, take Newport/Gatlinburg exit. Drive on Hwy. 321 toward Newport. Go through three lights. Store's on left in The Village Shopping Center.

EatRite Health Promotion Center, Amarillo, Texas

Texas

FTD
FORT WORTH/
DALLAS AREA
3, 6, 8, 10, 15, 16

1. ABILENE
2. AMARILLO
3. ARLINGTON
4. AUSTIN
5. BRYAN
6. COLLEYVILLE
7. CORPUS CHRISTI

8. DALLAS
9. EL PASO
10. FORT WORTH
11. HOUSTON
12. KERRVILLE

13. LONGVIEW
14. LUBBOCK
15. PLANO
16. RICHARDSON
17. SAN ANTONIO
18. WACO
19. WICHITA FALLS

ABILENE

NATURAL FOOD CENTER
2534 South 7th Street, 79605 • (915)673-2726
Limited organic produce.
M-F 9:30-5:30, Sat. 10-5, Restaurant: M-F 11-2

 From I-20, take Downtown exit and head for south side of Abilene.
Turn left on South 7th. Store's on left.

AMARILLO

EATRITE HEALTH PROMOTION CENTER, RESTAURANT & DELI
2425 I-40 West, 79109 • (806)353-7476
Easy to get to, nice, friendly folks and great smoothies. A natural food oasis in the middle of the barren Texas panhandle.
M-Sat. 9-6

From I-40, take Georgia
exit and drive 2 blocks south of highway. Store's immediately on left - parking lot is
next to highway. (Store has a huge mural with fruit and veggies. You can't miss it.)

211

ARLINGTON

GOOD HEALTH PLACE
860 Secretary Drive, 76015 • (817)265-5261
M-Sat. 9:30-6:30 (Th. 'til 8)

From I-30, take Cooper exit south. Store's on left in Pecan Plaza.

AUSTIN

Wheatsville Co-op workers succinctly sum up Austin's music scene: "It's rockin' here!" To experience this city's live sounds, check out Emo's, Electric Lounge, Hole in the Wall, and La Zona Rosa.

Visit all-vegetarian restaurant, Mother's Cafe & Garden on Duvall St. (excellent!) and MoJo's Daily Grind serves coffee and beer. Folks at Whole Foods love the West Lynn Cafe and Little City on Congress is a fun (and hip) coffee house. Also visit the Waterloo Brewing Company on Guadalupe, and Whole Foods staffers report The Dog and Duck (also on Guadalupe) is a fun little place. Don't miss a hike on the Greenbelt along the Colorado River!

WHEATSVILLE FOOD CO-OP
3101 Guadalupe, 78705 • (512)478-2667
If Austin is the San Francisco of Texas, then Wheatsville is the Haight-Ashbury of Austin. Store features multi-recycling areas as well as composting.
Sun.-Sun. 9-11

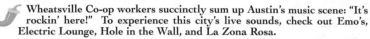

From I-35, take 38th St. exit west and turn left on Guadalupe. Store's on left.

WHOLE FOODS MARKET
914 North Lamar, 78703 • (512)476-1206
Check out the drop in Yoga classes upstairs and Waterloo across the street. They are the Indie record store that pioneered the "listening station."
Sun.-Sun. 8-11

From I-35, take MLK exit west. Turn left on Lamar. Store's on right.

WHOLE FOODS MARKET
9607 Research Boulevard, Suite 300, 78759 • (512)345-5003
Sun.-Sun. 8:30-10:30

From I-35, go north on Hwy. 183 (turns into Research Blvd.). Store's in a shopping plaza on right.

BRYAN

SMETANA GROCERY
West Highway 21, 77803 • (409)775-9337
M-Th. 6am-11pm, F & Sat. 6am-midnite, Sun. 7-11

Store's west of Rte. 6 on Hwy. 21 toward Caldwell.

COLLEYVILLE

THE HEALTHY APPROACH MARKET

4902 Colleyville Boulevard, 76034 • (817)428-4120
M-Sat. 9:30-7, Sun. 12-7

 From the 820 loop, take Hwy. 26 (exit sign will say Grapevine Hwy.). Turn north onto Hwy. 26 and drive about 3 miles into Colleyville (will become Colleyville Blvd.). Store's in Kroger Shopping Center on left.

CORPUS CHRISTI

SUN HARVEST FARMS

1440 Airline, 78412 • (512)993-2850
Limited seasonal organic produce.
Sun.-Sun. 9-9

 From I-37, take Padre Island Dr. east. Store's on right, at corner of Padre and Airline.

DALLAS

 Recommendations: Thai Soon, Mother Mesquites on Skillman and The Dream Cafe (in the Quadrangle) is a fun, kid-friendly spot. Kalachandji's Hare Krishna vegetarian restaurant serves a well attended buffet, twice daily.

WHOLE FOODS MARKET

2218 Lower Greenville Avenue, 75206 • (214)824-1744
Sun.-Sun. 8-10

From I-75, take Mockingbird Lane exit east. Turn right on Greenville. Store's on left.

WHOLE FOODS MARKET

2201 Preston, Suite C, 75206 • (972)612-6729
Sun.-Sun. 8-10

From I-635, take Preston exit north and drive about eight miles. Store's on left.

WHOLE FOODS MARKET

7205 Skillman Street, 75231 • (214)341-5445
Sun.-Sun. 8-10

From I-635, take Skillman exit south. Store's three miles down on right.

EL PASO

SUN HARVEST FARMS

6100 North Masa, 79912 • (915)833-3380
Sun.-Sun. 8-9

 From I-10, take Sumland Park exit north and turn left onto North Masa. At next light, turn right on Balboa. Store's on left in the plaza.

FORT WORTH

 The Back Porch (on Camp Bowie) serves salads and sandwiches, then check out the Museums and Theater across the street.

COW TOWN NATURAL FOOD CO-OP
3539 East Lancaster, 76103 • (817)531-1233
M-Sat. 9:30-6

 From I-30, take Oakland Blvd. exit south and turn right on East Lancaster. Store's on right.

SUNFLOWER SHOPPE
5817 Curzon at Camp Bowie, 76108 • (817)738-9051
M-Sat 9:30-7, Sun. 12-7

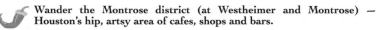 From I-30 west, take Camp Bowie exit and go left on Curzon. Store's on right corner. From I-30 west, take Bryant Irving exit. Go right on Bryant Irving, left on Camp Bowie, then right on Curzon. Store's on right.

HOUSTON

 Wander the Montrose district (at Westheimer and Montrose) — Houston's hip, artsy area of cafes, shops and bars.

Visit The Wonderful Vegetarian (vegetarian Chinese buffet) and Green Planet, both are on Westheimer. For all vegetarian Chinese, check out Quan Yin on E. Bellaire Blvd., and A Moveable Feast, a natural-vegetarian cafe on West Alabama (also a small natural food store, no produce though). The Ale House is a recommended pub.

WHOLE FOODS MARKET
2900 South Shepherd, 77098 • (713)520-1937
First class salad bar and deli section. Store is near McGonigle's Mucky Duck, a great acoustic music club.
Sun.-Sun. 9-10

From Hwy. 59, take Shepherd/Greenbriar exit and head north on Shepherd. Store's on left in Alabama Shopping Center.

WHOLE FOODS MARKET
11145 Westheimer, 77042 • (713)784-7776
Sun.-Sun. 9-10

From I-10, take Wilcrest exit south. Store's on right, corner of Wilcrest and Westheimer in The Market at Westchase.

WHOLE FOODS MARKET
6401 Woodway # 149, 77057 • (713)789-4477
M-Sat. 8-10, Sun. 9-10

From I-10, exit at South Ross. Make a left onto Woodway and store's on left.

KERRVILLE

RIVER VALLEY HEALTH FOODS
130-B West Main Street, 78028 • (830)896-7383
No produce. Go to HEB supermarket for organic produce!
M-F 10-6, Sat. 10-5

 From I-10, take either Kerrville exit to Main St. (easy to find). Store's two blocks down from HEB supermarket.

LONGVIEW

 Visit Bless Your Heart and Brothers coffee shops.

JACK'S NATURAL FOOD STORE
1614 Judson Road, 75601 • (903)753-4800
No produce.
M-F 9-6, Sat. 9-5

 From I-20, take Estes Parkway exit north. Estes becomes High St., then Judson. Store's 7 miles up on right.

JACK'S NATURAL FOOD STORE
2199 Gilmer Road, 75604 • (903)759-4262
Store has a drive-thru window. Carrots only.
M-Sat. 9-6

 From I-20, take Hwy. 259 north, turn left on 281 Loop and left at Gilmer Rd./Hwy. 300 exit. Store's on left.

LUBBOCK

THE ALTERNATIVE FOOD COMPANY
2611 Boston Avenue, 79410 • (806)747-8740
M-Sat. 9:30-6

 From I-27, take 34th St. exit west. Turn right on Boston. Store's on right.

PLANO

WHOLE FOODS MARKET
2201 Preston Road, Suite C, 75093 • (972)612-6729
Sun.-Sun. 8-10

Take I-75 to Park exit, then head west on Park. Store's at intersection of Preston & Park, on northwest side of street across from Walmart.

RICHARDSON

 Macro Broccoli on West Arapaho serves macrobiotic, vegan fare.

WHOLE FOODS MARKET
Coit & Beltline/60 Dal-Rich Village, 75080 • (972)699-8075
Sun.-Sun. 8-10

From I-75, take Beltline exit and head west. Store's on left, about 2.5 miles out on Coit Rd.

SAN ANTONIO

Whole Foods Market staffer, Annele, has San Antonio recommendations. Check out the natural Mexican restaurant, La Fiesta Patio Cafe, Adelante's (also Mexican) and chain store Cafe Lite & Bakery features vegetarian fare. Som Pong's serves Thai food and the Mad Hatter's Tea (behind the Witte Museum) is also recommended. Visit The McNay Art Museum (close to Whole Foods) and the San Antonio Museum of Art.

Visit the nifty coffee shop Espuma, just past downtown (in the historic King William's district) and Bombay's Bicycle Club, a recommend bar. For live tunes, go to The White Rabbit, an alternative rock club outside San Antonio limits.

Outdoor recommendations: Take a map to explore Enchanted Rock, a hiker's paradise with caves (1 hour west of I-10). There's also Canyon Lake, Lost Maples and Guadalupe State Park has hiking, swimming and camping.

WHOLE FOODS MARKET
255 E. Basse Suite 130, 78209 • (210)826-4676
Sun.-Sun. 8-10

From Hwy. 281 take Jones Maltsburger exit. Store's in the Quarry Market right after exit.

WACO

WACO HEALTH FOODS
1424 Lake Air Drive, 76710 • (817)772-5743
M-Sat. 9-6

 From I-35, take Valley Mills Dr. exit west. Turn right on Lake Air Dr. Store's on left.

WICHITA FALLS

SUNSHINE NATURAL FOODS
2907 Bob Street, 76308 • (940)767-2093
M-F 9-6, Sat. 10-5:30

 From Hwy. 287, drive south on Kell Blvd. Take Camp St. exit and turn left on Bob St. Store's on left in Parker Square Shopping Center.

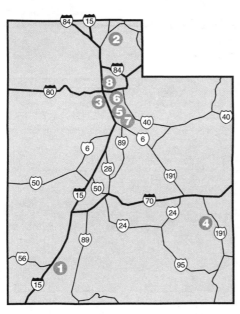

Utah

1. CEDAR CITY
2. LOGAN
3. MIDVALE
4. MOAB
5. OREM
6. PARK CITY
7. PROVO
8. SALT LAKE CITY

CEDAR CITY

SUNSHINE HEALTH
576 South Main Street, 84720 • (801)586-4889
No produce.
M-Sat. 10-6

 From I-15, take Rte. 14 exit east. Turn south on Main St. Store's on right in the Renaissance Square.

LOGAN

 This small valley town has plenty of hiking and biking nearby in the mountains. Check out the Grapevine on First E. St.

SHANGRI-LA HEALTH FOODS
438 1/2 N. Main Street, 84321 • (801)752-1315
M-Sat. 9-6

 From 89/91 turns into Main St. in Logan. Store's at corner of 4th North and Main St. in the Albertson's shopping plaza.

STRAW IBIS MARKET & CAFE
52 Federal Avenue, 84321 • (801)753-4777
Store sells homebrewing supplies.
M-F 6-6, Sat. & Sun. 8-6

 Store's 1/2 block east of Main St. (Rte. 89) and 1/2 block north of scenic Tabernacle Park on Federal Ave.

MIDVALE

 Check out the all-vegetarian Park Ivy Cafe.

GOOD EARTH NATURAL FOODS
7206 South 900 East, 84047 • (801)562-2209
M-Sat. 9-8

 Take I-15, to 7200 south, then east to 900 east. Store's on west side of street.

MOAB

 Honest Ozzie's on N. 100 West serves fun, diverse cuisine.

MOAB COMMUNITY CO-OP
111 North 100 (1st) West, 84532 • (801)259-5712
Also a bookstore, book-lending space, and gateway to national parks (4 miles away). It's "totally awesome in Moab" say staffers.
Sun.-Sun. 9-6 (Sat. closed 11am - 1pm)

 Off I-70, drive south on Rte. 191. Turn right at first traffic light in Moab (North 1st). Store's there on left.

OREM

GOOD EARTH NATURAL FOODS
500 South State Street, 84057 • (801)765-1616
M-Sat. 9-8

 From I-15, take UVSC exit and drive straight. From north, turn left at first light off exit. Go over bridge, through a few lights and at State St., turn left. Continue north to 500 South and store's on left. From south, turn right at light off exit. Drive to State St. and turn left. Continue north to 500 south and store's on left.

PARK CITY

 Bangkok Thai features tofu dishes. Check out Morning Ray Cafe & Bakery for breakfast and lunch.

FAIRWEATHER NATURAL FOODS
1270 Iron Horse Drive, 84068 • (801)649-4561
Store sells prepared soup. Organic produce only.
M-F 9-7, Sat. 10-7, Sun. 11-6

From I-80, exit onto Hwy. 224 toward Park City Ski Area. Go 5 miles "through suburbia" and turn left on Iron Horse Drive. Store's last driveway on left.

PROVO

GOOD EARTH NATURAL FOODS
384 West Center Street, 84601 • (801)375-7444
M-Sat. 9-8

From I-15, take Center St. Provo exit east (toward mountains). Store's on left.

SALT LAKE CITY

Excellent food in these parts.... Check out the all-vegetarian Park Ivy Cafe, Long Life Vegi House (vegetarian Chinese), Cafe Mediterranean, Wasatch Pizza (over 25 vegetarian toppings) and Santa Fe on Emigration Canyon is so good! The Desert Edge Pub features vegetarian burgers, sandwiches and great homebrews.

WILD OATS MARKET
2nd South and 812 East, 84102 • (801)355-7401
Salt Lake City Wild Oats' are easy to find, thanks to Salt Lake's numbered streets.
M-Sat. 8-9, Sun. 10-7

 Off I-15, take 600S (6th S) exit and head east (toward mountains). Turn left on 800E. Store's at corner of 800E and 200E.

WILD OATS MARKET
2454 S 700 East, 84103 • (801)359-7913
M-Sat. 8-9, Sun. 10-7

 From I-80, take 700 (7th) E exit. Drive east and store's right there. Heading west, go left under overpass. Store's on right.

WILD OATS MARKET
4695 South Holladay Boulevard, 84117 • (801)278-8242
M-Sat. 8-9, Sun. 10-7

 From I-15, take 4500 south exit to 23rd. Go north on 23rd East until it intersects 4700 south. Store's at intersection on west side of street.

Robert, produce manager, Hunger Mountain Food Co-op, Montpelier, Vermont

Vermont

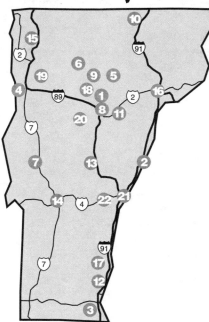

1. ADAMANT
2. BRADFORD
3. BRATTLEBORO
4. BURLINGTON
5. HARDWICK
6. JOHNSON
7. MIDDLEBURY
8. MONTPELIER
9. MORRISVILLE
10. NEWPORT
11. PLAINFIELD
12. PUTNEY
13. RANDOLPH
14. RUTLAND
15. SAINT ALBANS
16. ST. JOHNSBURY
17. SPRINGFIELD
18. STOWE
19. UNDERHILL
20. WAITSFIELD
21. WHITE RIVER JCT.
22. WOODSTOCK

ADAMANT

ADAMANT CO-OP, INC.
P.O. Box 1, Center Road, 05640 • (802)223-5760
M-F 9:30-6, Sat. 9:30-3, Sun. 10-3

 From I-89, take Montpelier exit onto Memorial. Turn left about 1 mile down at light (Business District sign) onto Main St. Drive straight through town and through traffic circle. Take first right in the circle (still Main St.) and Main will become County Road. Turn right at fork onto Center Rd., then drive 5 miles to crossroad in Adamant. Store's right there.

BRADFORD

SOUTH END MARKET
South Main Street, 05033 • (802)222-5701
M-F 9-5, Sat. 9-12

 From I-91, take Bradford exit. Head east to Rte. 25 and go north on Rte. 5 to Bradford Village. Take a hard left on 25B. Store's on left.

BRATTLEBORO

Brattleboro has a great vibe, especially in its great little downtown area. Our spies recommended The Backside Cafe (good breakfasts), the Indian Palace and Shin-La. Check out independent movie house the, Latchis Theater, any night of the week for great movies.

BRATTLEBORO FOOD CO-OP
2 Main Street, 05301 • (802)257-1841
A large store with a great deli-cafe.
M-Sat. 9-9, Sun. 9-8

From I-91, take exit 1 into Brattleboro and drive to end of Canal St. Store's in Brookside Shopping Plaza at the junction of Main St. and Rte. 142.

LLAMA, TOUCAN AND CROW
130 Main Street, 05301 • (802)254-5376
Limited organic produce.
M-Sat. 9-6 (F 'til 7), Sun. 10-5

 From I-91, take second Brattleboro exit. Drive Western Ave. east for one mile to downtown. Store's on Main St. on right.

BRISTOL

A beautiful town on the edge of the Green Mountain National Forest. Check out renowned wilderness area, Bristol Cliffs. In the winter, ask a local to direct you to the ice cliffs. They're quite spectacular!

BRISTOL MARKET
28 North Street, 05443 • (802)453-2448
A small store packed with good stuff. Their deli rocks!
Sun.-Sun. 9-7

 One block from main intersection of town on North St.

BURLINGTON

Northern Vermont's activity hub. Pick up a copy of arts & entertainment paper *Seven Days* to get acquainted with area happenings. Good food abounds here, but we especially love Stone Soup (inexpensive, buffet style vegetarian fare), Five Spice Cafe, and for coffee, Muddy Waters. Venues like Club Toast, Metronome and the celebrated stage of Nectar's offers live sounds most nights.

Grab a brew at the Vermont Pub and Brewery, and on the Church Street walking mall, check out the Peace and Justice Center (great books, library and excellent lecture series).

HEALTHY LIVING
4 Market Street, 05403 • (802)863-2569
"We will do whatever it takes to make sure customers leave with a smile on their face! We know you can buy these products anywhere, so our goal is to make our service really stand out in our customers' minds."
M-Sat. 8-8, Sun. 12-6

 From I-89, exit 14E (to S. Burlington). Bear right onto Dorset St. (directly after the exit). Market is first street on left past Barnes & Noble.

ONION RIVER CO-OP

274 North Winooski Avenue, 05401 • (802)863-3659

Up to date on local and global community info. Fantastic organic produce!

M-Sat. 9:30-8, Sun. 11-7

  From I-89, take exit 14W and head west on Main St. toward downtown Burlington (past UVM campus). Turn right on South Union St., go up to Winooski Ave. and make a right. The co-op is two blocks up on right.

HARDWICK

BUFFALO MOUNTAIN CO-OP

Main Street, 05843 • (802)472-6020

Has a sister co-op project in Northern Nicaragua.

M-Sat. 9-6 (F 10-7), Sun. 10-3

 Main St. is Rte. 15. Store's in downtown Hardwick on east side of road.

JOHNSON

 The Pie Safe, (4 doors down from Roo's), has good sandwiches.

ROO'S NATURAL FOODS

Main Street (Rte. 15), 05656 • (802)635-1788

A small and rustic country natural food store housed in the same building as The French Press Café. Café owners (and Tollbooth friends, Mara and Peter) serve up a mean iced mocha. The Café also features yummy biscotti prepared by regional twice baked expert, Ethan.

M-F 10-5, Sat. 11-4

  Store shares space with the French Press Café. Look for it in a large yellow house on Rte. 15 in the center of scenic Johnson (down the block from Grand Union).

MIDDLEBURY

MIDDLEBURY NATURAL FOODS CO-OP

1 Washington Square, 05753 • (802)388-7276

M-Sat. 8-7, Sun. 9-5

From Rte. 7, at traffic circle head east on Washington. Store's on left.

MONTPELIER

Hooray... Montpelier is the only state capital without a McDonald's! We highly recommend the legendary Horn of the Moon (downtown) for great vegetarian fare, The Single Pebble on the Barre-Montpelier Rd. is delicious and The Savoy Theater on Main Street shows independent and foreign films (and serves up excellent nutritional yeast popcorn).

HUNGER MOUNTAIN CO-OP

623 Stone Cutters Way, 05602 • (802)223-6910

Roomy and bright, this is one of our favorites. Store has a great little cafe that overlooks the Winooski River.

Sun.-Sun. 8-8

From I-89, take Montpelier exit onto Memorial. Turn left about 1 mile down at light (Business District sign) onto Main St. Take first right onto Stonecutter's Way and Hunger Mountain is at end on right.

222

STATE STREET MARKET
20 State Street, 05602 • (802)229-9353
Store has a great new deli/sushi bar in back called, The Wrap.
M-F 10-6:30 (F 'til 7), Sat. 10-6, Sun. 11-5, The Wrap: M-F 11:30-2

 From I-89, take Montpelier exit onto Memorial. Turn left about 1 mile down at light (Business District sign) onto Main St. Turn left at next light onto State St. Store's on left.

MORRISVILLE

Don't miss Tomatillo's, Vermont's best Mexican fare found in this out-of-the-way crossroads town (lovingly referred to as 'MoVegas'). Tomatillo's serves authentic Chile Rellenos, salsa and margaritas that are out of this world.

APPLETREE NATURAL FOODS
Munson Avenue, 05661 • (802)888-8481
Limited organic produce.
M-F 9-6, Sat. 9:30-6

 From Rte. 15, turn at Morrisville's blinking light (left from west, right from east), then make the next left into the Pricechopper/McDonald's parking lot. Go right onto Munson (road begins between Pricechopper & McDonald's) and turn left into strip mall to find Appletree. Sign in front says Natural Foods.

NEWPORT

NEWPORT NATURAL FOODS
66 Main Street, 05855 • (802)334-2626
M-Th. 9-5:30, F 9-7, Sat. 9-5, Sun. 11-4

 From I-91, take Downtown Newport exit, #27. At end of access road, turn left on Main St. Store's on right.

PLAINFIELD

Plainfield is home to the eclectic Goddard College, and also the River Run (fantastic breakfasts, great condiments and other dishes too numerous to list). Grab a pizza at Maple Valley general store - good stuff!

WINOOSKI VALLEY FOOD CO-OP
Main Street, 05667 • (802)454-8579
A co-op like it used to be. "We're not just fruits and nuts!" Rustic children's play area is perfect for both parents and kids.
M-Sat. 10-7 (Tu. and Th. open at 9), Sun. 10-2

 From Rte. 2 in Plainfield, bear right at blinking light and go down into village. Bear left at fork and store's a few hundred yards down on left, behind fire station.

PUTNEY

PUTNEY FOOD CO-OP
P.O. Box 730, 05346 • (802)387-5866
Lots of Vermont made stuff. We love the pesto filled pretzels.
M-Sat. 7:30-8, Sun. 8-8

 From I-91, follow signs to 5 north. The Co-op is on west side of Rte. 5, soon after exit 4.

RANDOLPH

WHITE RIVER CO-OP
3 Weston Street, 05060 • (802)728-9554
Small and friendly. Hello to friends at the Mud Season Concert Series.
M-Sat. 9-6, Sun. 10-4

From I-89, take exit 4, then Rte. 66 to Rte. 12S. Weston St. is first right after train tracks. Store's on right.

RUTLAND

RUTLAND AREA FOOD CO-OP
77 Wales Street, 05738 • (802)773-0737
M-Sat. 9-7

From Burlington take Rte. 7 south into Rutland. Come to Rte. 4 business sign (West. St.) and go right. Drive 2 blocks to Court St. and turn left. Go 2 more blocks to Washington. Take a right onto Washington and drive to Wales. Turn right and store's first building is on left. First parking lot has co-op parking.

SAINT ALBANS

RAIL CITY MARKET
8 South Main Street, 05478 • (802)524-3769
Limited organic produce.
M-Sat. 9-6

From I-89, take exit 19. Follow access road to Main St. (a.k.a Rte. 7). Head north on Rte. 7 toward St. Albans City Business District. Store's on left across from south end of park.

ST. JOHNSBURY

NATURAL PROVISIONS
130 Railroad Street, 05819 • (802)748-3587
Store's in an old church (complete with stained glass windows and hardwood floors... very pretty!) Only source for natural food in the area.
M-F 8:30-6, Sat. 9-5, Sun. 11-4

From I-91, take exit #20 (St. Johnsbury) and take Rte. 5 north. Turn right on Rte. 2. Store's on corner of Maple and Railroad.

SPRINGFIELD

SPRINGFIELD FOOD CO-OP
76 Chester Road, 05156 • (802)885-3363
M-Sat. 9-6, Sun. 11-4

From I-91, get off at exit 7 (Springfield). Take Rte. 11 into Springfield, go through town and bear left (stay on Rte. 11). Store's on left in front of Tire Warehouse.

STOWE

 The Shed on the Mountain Road brews excellent beer. Check 'em out.

FOOD FOR THOUGHT

Moody Farm Estates, 05672 • (802)253-4733
Store has an array of wonderful, fresh baked breads.

Store's on east side of Rt. 100 between Stowe's Lower Village and Waterbury Center
(set back on a hill side). Get there by traveling north on Rte. 100 from I-89.

UNDERHILL

MOUNTAINVIEW ORGANICS

14 Park Street, 05489 • (802)899-1890
M-Sat. 10-6

 From Rte. 15 going east, turn right onto Park St. in Underhill. Store's on
right corner.

WAITSFIELD

On weekend nights, don't miss American Flatbread, a restaurant with
lots of ambiance. They serve beautiful (and delicious) wood fired pizzas
in their funky restored barn space.

SWEET PEA NATURAL FOODS

Village Square, Route 100, 05673 • (802)496-7763
Prepared daily specials. Small seating area.
M-Sat. 8:30-6, Sun. 11:30-5

 From I-89, take Middlesex/Moretown exit and follow
Rte. 100 south to Waitsfield (about 20 minutes). Store's
in center of town on left.

WHITE RIVER JUNCTION

UPPER VALLEY FOOD CO-OP

49 North Main Street, 05001 • (802)295-5804
Specializing in local organic produce.
M-Sat. 9-7, Sun. 11-5

From I-91, take exit 11 (White River Junction/Rte. 5).
Head north on 5 (right from south, left from north).
Just past 3rd set of lights, go down a little hill. Store's
2nd driveway on left, in a big yellow post and beam building complex.

WOODSTOCK

EIGHTEEN CARROT NATURAL FOODS

47 Pleasant Street, 05091 • (802)457-2050
M-Sat. 8-6

 Pleasant St. is Rte. 4. Store's on
the east end of Woodstock on
north side of street.

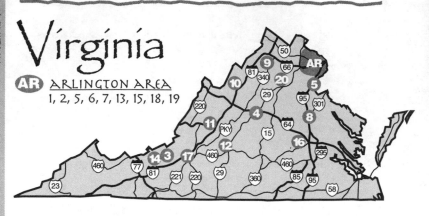

Virginia

AR <u>ARLINGTON AREA</u>
1, 2, 5, 6, 7, 13, 15, 18, 19

1. ALEXANDRIA	11. LEXINGTON
2. ARLINGTON	12. LYNCHBURG
3. BLACKSBURG	13. MANASSAS
4. CHARLOTTESVILLE	14. RADFORD
5. DALE CITY	15. RESTON
6. FAIRFAX	16. RICHMOND
7. FALLS CHURCH	17. ROANOKE
8. FREDERICKSBURG	18. SPRINGFIELD
9. FRONT ROYAL	19. VIENNA
10. HARRISONBURG	20. WARRENTON

ALEXANDRIA

 Check out Mediterranean Bakery on South Pickett Street.

FRESH FIELDS WHOLE FOODS MARKET
6548 Little River Turnpike, 22313 • (703)914-0040
M-Sat. 8-9, Sun. 8-8

From I-395, take Duke St. (# 236) exit west. Duke becomes Little River Turnpike. Store's on right in Pinecrest Plaza, two miles out.

ARLINGTON

 Visit Madhu Ban (Indian), Lebanese Taverna on Washington Blvd. and Abbi's for great burritos (right up the road from the Uncommon Market). Fresh Fields' staffer Mark says Whitlew's, a block and a half from the store, is a groovy place to hang out.

FRESH FIELDS WHOLE FOODS MARKET
2700 Wilson Boulevard, 22201 • (703)527-6596
M-Sat. 8-10, Sun. 9-9

From Rte. 1, take Rosslyn exit and drive 5 miles east on Wilson Blvd. Store's on left.

THE UNCOMMON MARKET
1041 South Edgewood Street, 22204 • (703)521-2667
The only co-op in northern Virginia; they've been around for over 20 years!
M-Sat. 9-9, Sun. 10-8

 From I-66 heading toward D.C., take the Fairfax Dr. exit (71). Turn right on Glebe and drive to south 12th. (Cross Arlington Blvd./Rte. 50 and Columbia Pike). Go left on 12th, then drive to Edgewood St. and make a left. Store's on right. Store parking lot is on left, just before the building.

BLACKSBURG

This college town on the New River features lots of live music. Check out Gillie's (mostly vegetarian) on College Ave.

ANNIE KAY'S WHOLE FOODS
301 South Main Street, 24060 • (540)552-6870
M-F 9-8, Sat. 9-6, Sun. 12-6

 From I-81, take Virginia Tech. exit. Follow signs for Virginia Tech. Turn north on Hwy. 460 to Blacksburg. Take Business District exit onto South Main. Store's on right.

EATS NATURAL FOODS
1200 North Main Street, 24060 • (540)552-2279
M-F 10-8, Sat. 9-8, Sun. 12-6

 From I-81, take southern Christiansburg exit to Blacksburg on 460. Take bypass and exit on Prices Fork Rd. toward downtown. Follow to end. Turn left on Main St. Store's on right.

CHARLOTTESVILLE

Ming Dynasty on Emmet Street prepares vegetarian versions of Chinese classics.

INTEGRAL YOGA NATURAL FOODS
923 Preston, 22903 • (804)293-4111
Veggie Heaven (deli) is part of the store, but next door.
M-Sat. 9:30-8, Sun. 11-6

 From Rte. 29 (Emmet St.), head east on Barracks Rd. and turn left into Preston Plaza. Plaza is between Barracks Rd. Shopping Center and Historic District.

WHOLE FOODS MARKET
1416 Seminole Trail, 22901 • (804)973-4900
M-Sat. 9-9, Sun. 9-8

 From I-64, take 250 east exit and turn north on Rte. 29 (becomes Seminole Tr.). Store's on left in small shopping center, across from Fashion Square Mall.

DALE CITY

THE NATURAL GROCER
14453 Potomac Mills Road, 22192 • (703)494-7287
No produce.
M-F 10-8, Sat. 10-6

 From I-95, take exit 156 and follow signs for Potomac Mills. Store's behind Day's Inn Hotel in Potomac Festival Shopping Center.

FAIRFAX

HEALTHWAY NATURAL FOODS
10360 Lee Highway, 22030 • (703)591-1121
M-F 10-7 (Th. 10-8), Sat. 10-6, Sun. 12-5

 From Rte. 66, take Rte. 123 toward Fairfax. After intersection of 123 and Lee Hwy., store's on left, one block from intersection.

FALLS CHURCH

FRESH FIELDS WHOLE FOODS MARKET
7511 Leesburg Pike, 22043 • (703)448-1600
M-Sat. 8-10, Sun. 8-8

 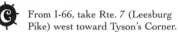 From I-66, take Rte. 7 (Leesburg Pike) west toward Tyson's Corner.
Store's on left, corner of Pimmet Dr. and Leesburg Pike.

KENNEDY'S NATURAL FOODS
1051 West Broad Street, 22046 • (703)533-8484
M-F 10-7, Sat. 10-6

 From I-66, head east on Rte. 7. Store's on right in West End Shopping Center.

FREDERICKSBURG

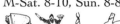 **Sammy T's on Caroline Street has a great vegetarian menu.**

HEALTHWAY NATURAL FOODS
4211 Plank Road, 22407 • (540)786-4844
M-Th. 10-7, F 10-8, Sat. 10-6, Sun. 12-5

 From I-95, get onto Rte. 3 west. Drive about 5 miles and store's on right.

PANTRY SHELF NATURAL FOODS & GOURMET
811 Sophia Street, 22401 • (540)373-2253
Set up like a natural food grocery store. Store has 1,000 books.
M-Sat. 10-6 (F 10-7)

 From I-95, take first Fredericksburg exit (Rte. 1 Bypass). At Lafayette, go right and drive to end. At end, make a left and go up 4 blocks. Store's on left.

FRONT ROYAL

BETTER THYMES
411-C South Street, 22630 • (540)636-9209
Organic carrots only.
M-W 9-6, Th. & F 9-8, Sat. 9-5, Sun. 12-5

 From I-66, take Front Royal exit. Take 340 south to 55 east. Store's in first shopping center on right.

HARRISONBURG

KATE'S NATURAL PRODUCTS
451 University Boulevard, 22801 • (540)433-2359
M-Sat. 9-6

 From I-81, take exit 247A. Make a right at second light and store's 1/2 mile up on right.

LEXINGTON

ROCKBRIDGE FOOD CO-OP'S HEALTHY FOODS MARKET
110 West Washington Street, 24450 • (540)463-6954
Store has a hot soup bar.
M-Th. 9-6, F 9-8, Sat. 9-5, Deli: M-F 11-4

 From I-81, take Lexington exit and follow signs to Lexington Visitor Center. Store's just past Visitor's Center on left.

LYNCHBURG

 "The city of Seven Hills" on the foothills of the Blueridge Mountains... this sure is a pretty spot!

FRESH AIR NATURAL FOODS
3225 Old Forest Road, 24501 • (703)385-9252
No organic produce.
M-F 10-8, Sat. 10-5

 Take Rte. 29 to 501 north. At second light, road becomes Old Forest Rd. Stay straight through 3 lights, then make a right into Forest Plaza Shopping Center. Store's straight ahead.

MANASSAS

HEALTHWAY NATURAL FOODS
10778 Sudley Manor Drive, 20109 • (703)361-1883
M-Th. 10-7, F 10-8, Sat. 10-6, Sun. 12-5

 From Rte. 66, take Rte. 234 south one mile. Store's on right in Bull Run Plaza Shopping Center.

RADFORD

ANNIE KAY'S WHOLE FOODS
601 3rd. Street, 24141 • (540)731-9498
M-F 9-8, Sat. 9-6, Sun. 12-6

 From I-81, take Radford exit. Head toward town on Tyler. Turn left on Norwood (becomes 1st St.) and left on Wadsworth. Store's on right, corner of 3rd and Wadsworth.

RESTON

FRESH FIELDS WHOLE FOODS MARKET
11660 Plaza America Drive, 22091 • (703)736-0600
M-Sat. 8-9, Sun. 9-8

    From Dulles Tollroad (237), take exit 12 (Reston Parkway). Make a right at next street onto Sunset Hill. Make a right 3 stoplights down onto Plaza Dr. Store's in shopping center.

RICHMOND

 Main Street Grill (downtown) has great vegetarian fare.

ELLWOOD THOMPSON'S NATURAL MARKET
4 North Thompson Street, 23221 • (804)359-7525
M-Sat. 9-9, Sun. 10-8

 From I-95, take I-195 (Powhite Parkway) east. Take Cary St. exit. From north, turn left on Cary and left on Thompson. Store's on left in a shopping center next to Blockbuster Video. From south, go straight on Thompson.

GOOD FOODS GROCERY
1312 Gaskins Road, 23233 • (804)740-3518
M-Sat. 9-9

 From I-64, take Gaskins Rd. south exit about 2.5 miles. Store's on right.

GOOD FOODS GROCERY
3062 Stony Point Road, 23235 • (804)320-6767
M-Sat. 9-9

 From I-195 south, take Powhite Parkway exit, then take the south Forest Hill Ave. exit. Turn right on Forest Hill Ave. and cross Hugenot Rd. into Stony Point Shopping Center.

ROANOKE

 Easily accessible to the Appalachian Trail. Visit the Science and Art Center and the downtown farmer's market runs year round. Check 'em out.

ROANOKE NATURAL FOODS CO-OP
1330 Grandin Road SW, 24015 • (540)343-5652
M-F 9-7, Sat. 9-6, Sun. 1-6

 From I-581, take Colonial Ave. exit and bear right onto Colonial. Take a left onto Brandon St. Go right on Grandin. Store's on right.

SPRINGFIELD

FRESH FIELDS WHOLE FOODS MARKET
8402 Old Keene Mill Road, 22152 • (703)644-2500
M-F 9-9, Sat. 8-9, Sun. 9-8

 From I-395, take Springfield exit onto Old Keene Mill Rd. south. Store's approximately 8 miles south.

HEALTHWAY NATURAL FOODS
6402-4 Springfield Plaza, 22150 • (703)569-3533
No produce.
M-F 10-7 (Th. 'til 8), Sat. 10-6, Sun. 12-5

 From I-95, exit at Old Kilmer Rd. Store's on right in Springfield Plaza.

VIENNA

 Tara Thai on Maple Ave. West is good!

FRESH FIELDS WHOLE FOODS MARKET
143 Maple Avenue East, 22180 • (703)319-2000
Sun.-Sun. 8-9

From I-66, take Vienna/Natalie St. exit east. Drive to Maple and take a right, going east. Store's 4-5 blocks down on right.

WARRENTON

 30 minutes from Shenandoah National Park.

THE NATURAL MARKETPLACE
5 Diagonal Street, 20186 • (540)349-4111
M-F 9-6 (Th. 9-7), Sat. 9:30-5

 From I-66, take Gainesville/Rte. 29 exit south about 12 miles. Go right onto 29/211 Business Route. At Bob's Big Boy, go left. Drive 1/4 mile on Waterloo. Store's on left corner of Waterloo and Diagonal in a light yellow house.

Organic Fact № 26

BUY WITHOUT WORRY

Organic certification standards are the public's assurance that their food and products have been grown and handled according to strict sustainable procedures without persistent toxic chemical inputs. Until the federal guidelines for regulating the use of the term "organic" are in place "certified organic" is the only guarantee consumers have to ensure products are genuinely organic.

Washington

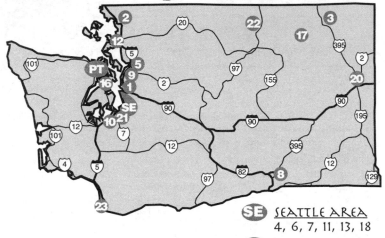

 SEATTLE AREA
4, 6, 7, 11, 13, 18

PT PORT TOWNSEND
14, 15, 19

1. BELLEVUE
2. BELLINGHAM
3. COLVILLE
4. EASTSOUND
5. EVERETT
6. FEDERAL WAY
7. GIG HARBOR
8. KENNEWICK
9. KIRKLAND
10. LAKEWOOD
11. MERCER ISLAND
12. MT. VERNON

13. OLYMPIA
14. PORT HADLOCK
15. PORT TOWNSEND
16. POULSBO
17. REPUBLIC
18. SEATTLE
19. SEQUIM
20. SPOKANE
21. TACOMA
22. TONASKET
23. VANCOUVER

BELLEVUE

Check out Moghul Palace on NE 10th Street, one of Bellevue's many Indian restaurants.

NATURE'S PANTRY
10200 NE 10th, 98004 • (425)454-0170
Organic salads and fruit & vegetable juices!
M-F 9-7, Sat. 9:30-6, Sun. 11-5

Located in downtown Bellevue. From the 405 Freeway, take the West NE 8th St. exit. Drive to 102nd, then make a right. Store's at 10th and 102nd.

NATURE'S PANTRY
156 NE 8th Street #K15, 98008 • (425)957-0090
Organic produce only.
M-Th. 9-8, F & Sat. 9-9, Sun. 11-6

 From I-520 E, take Rte. 148 exit south and bear to right when exiting. Head straight and turn left on NE 8th a few minutes down. Follow through intersection at 156th, then make a left at next light. Go through to parking lot. Store's across parking lot on left.

BELLINGHAM

Set on a hill, Bellingham overlooks the beautiful Bellingham Bay and its rocky shoreline. Head east to Mt. Baker for skiing, hiking and camping in a very beautiful alpine environment, or visit the Bay and purchase a ticket on the ferry to Alaska!

Check out the Cookie Cafe, the Cosmos Cafe for live music and Casa Que Pasa for amazing burritos. The Community Co-op deli is delicious!

COMMUNITY FOOD CO-OP
1220 North Forest, 98225 • (360)734-8158
Big as a supermarket with a lovely sit-down deli-cafe.
Sun.-Sun. 8-9

 From I-5, take Lakeway exit. Road turns into Holly. Turn left on State St., left on Chestnut and left on Forest. Store's on right.

TERRA ORGANICA
929-A North State Street, 98225 • (360)715-8020
99% of store's food and herbs are organic or wild-crafted. They research products to ensure they are the purest available and ethically produced.
Sun.-Sun. 9-8

 Three blocks south of the Bellingham Herald building on North State St.

COLVILLE

Lots of mountains, backpacking and skiing. It's beautiful around here!

NORTH COUNTRY CO-OP
282 West Astor, 99114 • (509)684-6132
M-F 9-6 (Summer 'til 7), Sat. 10-5

 Rte. 395 becomes Main St. Turn west on 2nd, left on Wynn and right on Astor. Store's on right.

EASTSOUND

In Eastsound, check out the Garden Cafe (summer only), Bilbo's (Mexican) and La Familia serves great Italian fare.

ORCAS HOME GROWN MARKET
North Beach Road, 98245 • (360)376-2009
The largest natural food store in the San Juans.
Sun.-Sun. 8-9

 Take ferry from Anacortes. Land at Orcas, take Horseshoe Highway into Eastsound. Store's right in "downtown."

EVERETT

Check out Pride of India on Hewitt Ave.

SNO-ISLE NATURAL FOODS CO-OP
2804 Grand Avenue, 98201 • (425)259-3798
M-Sat. 8-8, Sun. 12-6

 From I-5, take downtown Everett exit. Follow Pacific Ave. west approximately 1 mile to Grand Ave. Make a right and store's 3 blocks up on left.

FEDERAL WAY

MARLENE'S MARKET & DELI
31839 Gateway Center Boulevard South, 98003 • (253)839-0933
M-Th. 9-9, F 9-10, Sat. 9-8, Sun. 10:30-6

 From I-5, take middle Federal Way exit, Store's right off west side of I-5 in Gateway Center (look for blue tile roofs).

GIG HARBOR

WHOLE FOODS MARKET
3122 Harborview Drive, 98335 • (253)851-8120
An independent store, not part of the chain.
M-Sat. 9:30-6

 In center of downtown Gig Harbor.

KENNEWICK

HIGHLAND HEALTHFOOD SUPERSTORE
101 Vista Way, 99336 • (509)783-7147
Fruit only.
M-Th 9:30-8, F 9:30-5, Sun. 12-5

From I-82, take Hwy. 395 north and turn right on Vista Way. Store's on right.

KIRKLAND

KIRKLAND PCC
10718 NE 68th Street, 98033 • (425)828-4622
See Seattle PCC listings for more info on Puget Consumer Co-ops.
Sun.-Sun. 8-10

 From I-405 north: Take NE 70th Place exit (#17). Turn left at stop sign, then make another left onto NE 70th Place (turns into NE 68th St.). Store's on right in Houghton Village Shopping Center. From I-405 south: Take NE 70th Place exit (#17). Turn left onto NE 70th Place, then same as above.

LAKEWOOD

LAKEWOOD NATURAL FOODS
8111 Steiacoom Boulevard SW, 98498 • (253)584-3929
M-Sat. 9-9

 From I-5 south: Take exit 129.
From I-5 north: Take exit 119.
From either direction, follow signs to Steiacoom Blvd. Store's right down block.

MERCER ISLAND

NATURE'S PANTRY
7611 SE 27th Street, 98040 • (206)232-7900
As of 10/98, store will be changing from a retail food market to an organic juice bar and deli. They will no longer carry organic produce, but the other two Nature's Pantrys will.
M-F 9-7, Sat. 9:30-6, Sun. 11-5

 From I-90 east: Take the 77th St. exit, go right, make another right at stop sign and store's one half block up on left. From I-90 west: Get off at Island Crest Way and make a left. Go right on 27th, drive 3.5 blocks and store's on left.

MT. VERNON

 Home to the yearly tulip festival, Mt. Vernon is close to the mountains and the Sound. We recommend dining at Pacioni's on 1st St.; a small Italian restaurant with delicious pizza and a friendly staff.

SKAGIT VALLEY FOOD CO-OP
202 S. First Street, 98273 • (360)336-9777
M-Sat. 9-7, Sun. 9-6

 From I-5, take
Kincaid exit west. Turn right on 3rd St. (3rd meets 1st. St.). Store's on left.

OLYMPIA

Olympia is beautiful! Visit Olympic Hot Springs in Olympic National Park or head over to the Evergreen College campus for various happenings. Check out the Capital Theater, an alternative movie theater open Sun-Wed.

OLYMPIA FOOD CO-OP (EASTSIDE)
3111 Pacific Avenue, 98501 • (360)956-3870
Sun.-Sun. 9-9

 From I-5 north, take exit 107 (Pacific). Go west and take first left on Lansdale. Store's at corner of Lansdale & Pacific.

OLYMPIA FOOD CO-OP (WESTSIDE)
921 North Rogers, 98502 • (360)754-7666
Sun.-Sun. 9-8

 From I-5, take exit 104 to Hwy. 101. Take 101 west (only goes one way) and take Black Lake Blvd. exit. Turn right on Black Lake (changes name along the way). Turn right on Bowman. Store's on corner of Bowman & Rogers.

PORT HADLOCK

SWAN FARMS
10632 Rhody Drive, 98339 • (360)385-6365
M-Sat. 10-6, Sun. 11-5

7 miles south of Port Townsend on Hwy. 20.

PORT TOWNSEND

On the Puget Sound and the Olympic Peninsula, Port Townsend is absolutely lovely. Once resident Jen says, "It's very walkable and the bus system is great. There are many used bookstores, a Seed Saver's exchange and a Hostel right in the Park. The people are wonderfully friendly and practically everywhere you go you can see The Sound. This town is great!"

Check out the summer Farmer's Market (near the Co-op), the Silver Water Cafe features vegetarian fare, Ft. Warden has great camping and hiking and the Rose Theater downtown is a refurbished alternative movie house.

COLINWOOD FARMS FRUIT STAND
1210 F Street, 98368 • (360)379-9610
Open May through October in a converted two-car garage. All vegetables and fruit are organic and almost all locally grown. They don't have much grocery, but they do sell locally produced cheese, milk, and eggs, as well as naturally grown beef.
Wed.-Sat. 10-6

 From the Food Co-op, go north on Lawrence 1 block. Take a left at stoplight (F St.). Go through 4-way stop sign, down a hill and store's at bottom on right.

THE FOOD CO-OP
1033 Lawrence Street, 98368 • (206)385-2883
A gem! Beautiful, light and fun community co-op. One traveler says, "Quaint and hidden from the more bustling part of the town, the co-op seems to be a mainstay for most locals. I enjoyed going there just to experience the energy!"
M-Sat. 9-8, Sun. 12-6

 From Rte. 20, head into Port Townsend. Road becomes Sims. Turn left on Kearney and right on Lawrence. Store's on right at corner of Pope and Lawrence.

POULSBO

CENTRAL MARKET
20148 10th Avenue NE, 98370 • (360)779-1881
Grocery store with organic produce and natural food sections.
Sun.-Sun. 24 hours a day

 Take Bainbridge Island/Seattle ferry. Take Hwy. 305 right off ferry, go about 8-10 miles, store is right off Hwy. on the right.

REPUBLIC

Surrounded by National Forest and the Okanogan & Colville (many hiking and skiing opportunities). Check out Mexican restaurant, Esther's.

FERRY COUNTY CO-OP
34 North Clark Street, 99166 • (509)775-3754
M-F 7:45-5:30 (open 'til 6 in the spring), Sat. 10-4

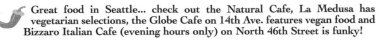 From Rte. 20, turn north on Clark. Store's one block up on right.

SEATTLE

 Great food in Seattle... check out the Natural Cafe, La Medusa has vegetarian selections, the Globe Cafe on 14th Ave. features vegan food and Bizzaro Italian Cafe (evening hours only) on North 46th Street is funky!

"Seattle is home to a large and well-known open farmers market (Pike Place Market)," says Nancy Gagnat at PCC member services. "Seattle also has great retail stores like REI, and an abundance of ethnic and culturally-diverse restaurants, both vegetarian and non-vegetarian."

CENTRAL CO-OP
1835 12th Avenue, 98122 • (206)329-1545
Sun.- Sun. 9-10

 From I-5, take Madison St. exit east. After about 8 blocks, take a left on 12th. Store's 3 blocks down on left at corner of Denny and 12th.

FREMONT PCC
716 North 34th Street, 98103 • (206) 632-6811
PCC (Puget Consumers Co-op) began in 1961 and now has over 40,000 active members. Membership is not required to shop at PCC stores, but there are lots of benefits to being a member. PCC Mission Statement: "PCC provides the highest-quality natural food and products. We create and cultivate the marketplace for locally-grown and organic products and are a vital community resource on food, nutrition and environmental issues." All PCC's have espresso bars. Full-time nutritionist available by phone.
Sun.-Sun. 8-11

 From I-5, take NE 45th St. exit. Head west on 45th, turn left at Stone Way, right on N. 34th St. Store's on right just before Fremont Ave. North.

GREENLAKE PCC
7504 Aurora Avenue North, 98103 • (206)525-3586
Sun.-Sun. 8-11

From I-5, north or south, take 50th St. exit and go west to Aurora Ave. N. (To get on Aurora Ave. N, get on overpass. Just before overpass, at the "Y," go up the incline to left leading to Aurora Ave. N). Turn right onto Aurora Ave. N (Hwy. 99). Store's on right, just north of Winona Ave. N and Aurora Ave. N intersection, across from Aurora Cycle. (To park, turn right on Winona. Store parking lot is on left).

RAINBOW GROCERY
417 15th Avenue East, 98112 • (206)329-8440
Sun.-Sun. 9-9

From I-5 south: Take Olive Way exit east (which becomes John). Turn right as John turns. Turn left on 15th. Store's on left. From north: Take Denny Way exit east, turn left on John, then left again on 15th. Store's on left between Republican and Harrison Streets.

RAVENNA PCC
6504 20th NE, 98115 • (206)525-1450
Sun.-Sun. 9-9

From I-5 south: Take NE 71st St./NE 65th St. exit (171). Turn left at stop sign, right at Roosevelt Ave. Then go left at NE 65th St. and left again at 20th Ave. NE. Store's on right.

SEWARD PARK PCC
5041 Wilson Avenue South, 98118 • (206)723-2720
Sun.-Sun. 7-10

From I-90 west: Take Rainier Ave. South exit. Turn left at Genesee (about two miles). Turn right at 50th Ave. South (Street turns into Wilson Ave. South). Store's 3 blocks past Angeline St. on right. From I-5: Take Columbia/Spokane St. exit. At second light (Y intersection), go to the left onto Alaska. Take a left (north) on Rainier Ave., turn right onto Genesee, another right onto 50th (turns into Wilson Ave. South). Store's 3 blocks past Angeline St. on right.

VIEW RIDGE PCC
6514 40th Street NE, 98115 • (206)526-7661
Sun.-Sun. 8-10

From I-5 south: Take NE 65th St./Ravenna exit. Drive to NE 65th St. and turn right. Store's on left at corner of 65th and 40th. From I-5 north: Take NE 71st St./NE 65th St. exit (exit 171). Turn left at stop sign, right on Roosevelt Ave., and left on NE 65th. Store's on left.

WEST SEATTLE PCC
2749 California Avenue SW, 98116 • (206)937-8481
Sun.-Sun. 8-10

From I-5, take West Seattle Freeway exit (exit 163A going south, exit 163 going north). Take Admiral Way exit. Turn left on California Ave. SW. Store's on right.

SEQUIM

SUNNY FARMS COUNTRY STORE
261461 Highway 101, 98382 • (360)683-8003
Sunny Farms grows much of their own organic produce. These folks are very nice. Stop on out and see them!
Sun.-Sun. 8-8

Approximately 1 mile west of Sequim on Hwy. 101.

SPOKANE

 Check out Eat-Rite on W. Montgomery.

BOUNTIFUL FRESH FOODS
North 204 Division, 99202 • (509)456-2552
M-F 10-6, Sat. 10-4

From I-90, exit at Division St. and head north for seven blocks. Store's at corner of Division and Main on right.

LORIEN HERBS & NATURAL FOODS
East 414 Trent, 99202 • (509)456-0702
M-F 10-6, Sat. 10-5

 From I-90, take exit 281 (Division) north. Turn right on Trent. Store's on right.

TACOMA

 Visit the Antique Sandwich Shop (vegetarian), natural Chinese restaurant May's, on N. Proctor St. and the East-West Cafe on Tacoma Mall Blvd.

MARLENE'S MARKET & DELI
2951 South 38th Street, 98409 • (253)472-4080
M-F 9-8, Sat. 9-7, Sun. 11-6 (deli closes 1 hour earlier)

 From I-5 take 38th St. W. exit, follow 38th St. down a slight hill. Store's on right in Best Plaza.

WESTGATE NUTRITION CENTER
5738 North 26th Street, 98407 • (253)759-1990
M-F 9-7, Sat. 10-5, Sun. 12-5

 Just off Pearl St. and N. 26th. Near Point Defiance Park.

WHOLE FOODS MARKET INC
6810 27th Street West, 98466 • (253)565-0188
An independent store, not part of the chain.
M-F 10-6, Sat. 10-5:30

 From I-5, take Bremerton/Gig Harbor exit (Hwy. 16). On Hwy. 16, take 19th West (TCC) exit. Follow 19th west, then turn left on Mildred. As Mildred curves, it becomes 27th. Store's in the curve on left with a blue awning (part of building is behind Paragon Plaza).

TONASKET

 Check out the barter fair in October (around the full moon). Ossitta says it's not to be missed!!

OKANOGAN RIVER NATURAL FOODS CO-OP
21 West 4th Street, 98855 • (509)486-4188
M-F 9-7, Sat. 10-5, Sun. 12-4, Winter: M-F 9-6, Sat. 10-5, Sun. 12-4

    From Rte. 97 (becomes Main St.), turn west on 4th St. Store's one block down on left.

VANCOUVER

 Try Cactus Ya Ya on SE Mill Plain Blvd.

NATURE'S MARKETPLACE
8024 East Mill Plain Boulevard, 98664 • (360)695-8878
This is your one-stop shopping kind of natural food supermarket. They have a pizza bar, sushi bar, potato bar, a floral department, a full service salon that uses non-toxic products... and they offer massage.
Sun.-Sun. 9-9

   From 205 north, take Mill Plain exit and head west. Store's at corner of Mill Plain Blvd. and Garrison at Garrison Square Mall.

West Virginia

1. BUCKHANNON
2. CHARLESTON
3. ELKINS
4. FAYETTEVILLE
5. GLENVILLE

* Note: Not much organic produce to be found in West Virginia natural food stores, but we've heard Kroger supermarkets sells it.

6. MORGANTOWN
7. PARKERSBURG
8. SPENCER
9. WHEELING

BUCKHANNON

MOLLY'S PANTRY INC.
39 College Avenue, 26201 • (304)472-5283
Seasonal produce.
M-Sat. 10-5

  From I-79, take Rte. 33 east (exit 99 to Buckhannon). Take Main St. exit. Go south on Main to Florida St., take a right on Florida. Store's at intersection of Florida and College.

CHARLESTON

Check out **Common Grounds Coffee Bar and Restaurant** on Summers Street. They serve vegetarian food and feature live music.

HEALTH FOODS ETC. OUTLET
408 Virginia Street West, 25302 • (304)343-0323
M-F 9-6, Sat. 10-5

 From I-64/77 heading north/west, take Virginia St. exit. Heading south/east, take Washington St./Civic Center exit. Head west on Randolph to Delaware Ave. Take a left and go to Virginia St. Store's on left.

ELKINS

GOOD ENERGY FOODS
100 3rd Street, 26241 • (304)636-5169
No produce. Store's located in a historic building.
M-Sat. 9-5:30

 Hwy. 33 turns into Randolph Ave. in Elkins. Store's in historic downtown area (it's the biggest store downtown!).

FAYETTEVILLE

Rich at Healthy Harvest recommends the Sedona Grill, Bazil, and Cathedral Cafe (not vegetarian, but they do feature veggie options). Located by the rim of the New River Gorge (the bridge is the longest arch span bridge in the world), this area is known for its abundant white water rafting, climbing and biking.

HEALTHY HARVEST
309 North Court Street, 25840 • (304)574-1788
Sun.-Sun. 10-7

From Rte. 19, turn south at traffic light onto Court St. Store is 100 yards down on right.

GLENVILLE

COUNTRY LIFE
211 North Lewis Street, 26351 • (304)462-8157
Citrus in Winter.
M-Th. 10-6, F 10-3

From I-79, take Burnsville exit. Take Rte. 5 west 15 miles. In Glenville, take a left at the "T". Store's 3/4 mile up on right.

MORGANTOWN

Check out the Blue Moose Cafe, Maxwell's and West Virgina Brewing Company features good food and beer (not all-vegetarian). Mountain People's Co-op folks recommend Cooper's Rock State Forest, 10 miles out of town.

MOUNTAIN PEOPLE'S CO-OP
1400 University Avenue, 26505 • (304)291-6131
One of Dar's favorite stores.
M-F 9-8, Sat. & Sun. 10-6

From I-79, take West Virginia University exit toward Morgantown. Street becomes Beechurst. Store's on left, at University and Fayette St.

PARKERSBURG

MOTHER EARTH
1638 19th Street, 26101 • (304)428-1024
M-Sat. 9-7

From I-77, go west on Rte. 50 into town. Take a right onto Plum and drive to 19th St. Store's on corner of 19th and Plum.

SPENCER

GROWING TREE
142 Main Street, 25276 • (304)927-3619
No produce.
M-F 9-5 (closed W), Sat. 10-1

From I-77, take Rte. 33 east and drive about 25 miles into Spencer. Turn right on Church. Store's on left.

WHEELING

Check out Wheeling Park.

HEALTH NUTS
1908 Market Street, 26003 • (304)232-0105
No produce.
M-Sat. 10-5:30

ℹ️ Store's at north end of Center Market (on Market St., a block from Ohio Valley Hospital).

Organic Fact №27

SWISSAIR GOES ORGANIC

In a 1997 press release, Swissair announced that "the trend towards organically grown foods is increasing across the globe," and by the year 2000 Swissair will ensure that 90% of the products they use to prepare meals are organically grown. Even their coffee will be fair trade coffee.

Wisconsin

* Hooray... mostly
Cooperatives in
this state!

1. ASHLAND
2. CUMBERLAND
3. EAU CLAIRE
4. GAYS MILLS
5. LA CROSSE
6. LUCK
7. MADISON
8. MANITOWOC
9. MENOMONIE
10. MILWAUKEE
11. MOUNT HOREB
12. NEW RICHMOND
13. OSHKOSH
14. RICE LAKE
15. RICHLAND CENTER
16. RIVER FALLS
17. STEVEN'S POINT
18. VIOLA
19. VIROQUA

ASHLAND

CHEQUAMEGON FOOD CO-OP
215 Chapple Avenue, 54806 • (715)682-8251
M-Sat. 9-8

From US Hwy. 2, turn south on Chapple. Store's on right
between Main and 3rd.

CUMBERLAND

ISLAND CITY FOOD CO-OP
1155 6th Avenue, 54829 • (715)822-8233
Co-op folks say Cumberland is, "the rutabaga capital of the world!"
M-F 10-5:30, Sat. 10-3

Store's half a mile southwest of Hwy. 63. There's a sign for it
on the highway!

EAU CLAIRE

SUNYATA FOOD CO-OP & BAKERY
409 Galloway Street, 54703 • (715)832-7675
Store carries winemaking & homebrew supplies.
M-F 10-6 (Th. 10-7), Sat. 10-4

From Hwy. 53, turn west on Main
St., right on Farwell St. and left
into parking lot, just over bridge.

GAYS MILLS

KICKAPOO EXCHANGE FOOD CO-OP
P.O. Box 117 / Main Street, 54631 • (608)735-4544
"The very best food co-op in the smallest town," says a Kickapoo Exchange staffer. "You would never expect to find a great co-op here!"
M-Sat. 10-6

 Rte. 171 is Main St. in Gays Mills. Store's on south side of street.

LA CROSSE

 The Mississippi River and the bluff give this old and diverse town a beautiful landscape. "La Crosse has a caring, committed community... it's a wonderful place to live!" say People's Co-op staffers.

PEOPLE'S FOOD CO-OP
315 5th Avenue South, 54601 • (608)784-5798
M-F 7-8, Sat. 7-7, Sun. 8-6

 From I-90, take Hwy. 16 exit south (becomes Losey Blvd.). Turn right on Main St. and left on 5th Ave. Store's on left.

LUCK

 In Luck, check out the Wild Goose restaurant!

NATURAL ALTERNATIVES FOOD CO-OP
241 Main Street, 54853 • (715)472-8084
M-F 9-5, Sat. 9-3

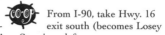 From Rte. 48, head south on Main St. Store's on right.

MADISON

 The capital of Wisconsin and home of the U of W., this politically conscious town has a lot going on. "And there's always a debate over how PC Madison really is," comments Jess at Whole Foods Market, "Madison is a laid back community with cool people."

Jess recommends LuLu's, a vegetarian restaurant on University (close to Whole Foods), Red Pepper (Chinese) and Genna's (a great bar). Memorial Union Terrace has a huge seating area by the lake where music, food and drink is always plentiful. James Madison park is a beautiful downtown spot on the lake. Visit Four Star Heaven, a neat video store and for the price of a movie, check out Comedy Sportz, a comedy club. Higher Ground has great muffins!

Martin at Magic Hill Market East suggests the legendary State Street area for great book stores, coffee shops and restaurants. "State Street has been the center of activity since the 60's and 70's," he explains. "There are all kinds of wonderful vegetarian restaurants... everything from Afghanistan to Ethiopian to Indian, Mexican and Chinese food."

MAGIC HILL NATURAL FOOD MARKET - EAST
1757 Thierer Road, 53704 • (608)242-8666
Store offers free coffee.
M-F 8-8, Sat. & Sun. 9-7

From I-90 north, take exit 135B - Madison. From I-90 south, take exit 135A - Madison. Once off exit, drive straight down E. Washington Ave. toward capital. Keep an eye out on left for Thierer and make a left onto it. Take next immediate left into Princeton Place shopping center and store's there.

MAGIC HILL NATURAL FOOD MARKET - WEST
2862 University Avenue, 53705 • (608)238-2630
They pride themselves as an independent, customer oriented store.
M-F 8-9, Sat. & Sun. 9-8

From Hwy. 12/18, take Midvale Blvd. exit north to end. Turn right on University. Store's on left in University Station.

MIFFLIN STREET COMMUNITY CO-OP
32 North Bassett Street, 53703 • (608)251-5899
Sun.-Sun. 9-9

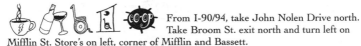

From I-90/94, take John Nolen Drive north. Take Broom St. exit north and turn left on Mifflin St. Store's on left, corner of Mifflin and Bassett.

NORTH FARM COOPERATIVE STORE
204 Regas Road, 53714 • (608)241-2667
Everything but produce.
M-F 9-6, Sat. 10-5

From Hwy. 51, exit at Milwaukee St. Exit on ramp to right and at end of ramp, go left. Continue under overpass. Just beyond the main Madison Post Office building on right is Regas Rd. Turn right, go through a stop sign and bear to right. Store's on left with a green awning.

WHOLE FOODS MARKET
3313 University Avenue, 53705 • (608)233-9566
"People who work here make it a fun place and the customers really feel that," says one staffer. (Store workers have been known to test movie trivia over the intercom).
Sun.-Sun. 8-9

Traveling west on I-90, take exit for Hwys. 12/18 in Madison. Then take Midvale Blvd. exit and turn right off exit. Follow Midvale all the way to University. Turn right on University and store's 3 blocks down on right.

WILLIAMSON STREET FOOD CO-OP
1202 Williamson Street, 53703 • (608)251-6776
The famous Willy Street Co-op has been in business for over 20 years! This is a little neighborhood store that most customers walk to.
Sun.-Sun. 8-9

From I-90/94, take Hwy. 12/18 west, then John Nolen Drive north. Turn right onto Williamson. Store's on left.

MANITOWOC

MANITOWOC FOOD COOP
713 Buffalo Street, 54220 • (920)684-3000
M, Th. & F. 9-7, Tu. & W 9-5, Sat. 9-3

From I-43, take Waldo Blvd. exit east four miles. Turn right on Maritime Dr. and right on Buffalo. Store's 2 miles down on right.

MENOMONIE

MENOMONIE MARKET FOOD COOP
1309 N. Broadway, 54751 • (715)235-6533
M-F 9-8, Sat. 9-5, Sun. 12-4

Take I-94 to exit 41 (Hwy. 25) south (turns into Broadway). Store's 1 mile from I-94, on right.

MILWAUKEE

Brewed Awakenings on East Brady St. serves coffee, sandwiches and baked stuff. Check out Vietnamese restaurant, West Bank Cafe (evenings only) on E. Burleigh.

BEANS & BARLEY
1901 East North Avenue, 53202 • (414)278-0234
M-Sat. 9-9, Sun. 9-8

From Hwy. 43, take North Ave. exit east all the way to Oakland Ave. Store's on right at corner of Oakland and North.

MILK-N-HONEY NATURAL FOODS
10948 West Capitol Drive, 53222 • (414)535-0203
M-F 10-7, Sun. 10-5

From Hwy. 45, take Capitol Dr. exit (Hwy. 190) east three blocks. Store's on left on north side of street.

OUTPOST NATURAL FOODS
100 E Capitol Drive, 53212 • (414)961-2597
Sun.-Sun. 8-9

From I-43, take Capitol Dr. east exit. Store's on left about 7 blocks down (or 3 stoplights down).

MOUNT HOREB

GENERAL STORE FOOD CO-OP
517 Springdale Street, 53572 • (608)437-5288
This member owned and operated cooperative dedicates an area of the store for local artisans to showcase their pottery, jewelry and sewn crafts.
M-F 10-6, Sat. 10-4

From Hwy. 18/151, take Business 18/151 (becomes Springdale St.) where you'll find the store.

NEW RICHMOND

NATURE'S PANTRY CO-OP
258 South Knowles Street, 54017 • (715)246-6105
M-F 9-5, Sat. 9-1

 From I-94, take 65 north. Go through the town of Roberts to Hwy. 12. Go right on Hwy. 12 (east) for 1-2 miles. Then pick up 65 north again. Drive into New Richmond and at 2nd intersection, find store on right at corner of South Knowles and 3rd.

OSHKOSH

KITCHEN KORNER HEALTH FOOD
507 North Main Street, 54901 • (920)426-1280
Limited organic produce.
M-F 9:30-5, Sat. 9:30-3:30

 From Hwy. 41, take Hwy. 45 exit north and turn left on New York. Turn right on North Main. Store's on right.

RICE LAKE

ALL SEASONS FOOD CO-OP
1 South Main Street, 54868 • (715)234-7045
This co-op is the only store in town that sells organic produce. They also offer cooking classes.
M-Sat. 9-5:30

 From Hwy. 53, take north exit (Hwy. 48) and drive to Rice Lake (make a right at exit ramp). Drive about 1 mile to Main St. Take a right on Main and drive about 10 blocks to Messenger. Store's at second stop light on corner of Main and Messenger.

RICHLAND CENTER

PINE RIVER FOOD CO-OP
134 West Court Street, 53581 • (608)647-7299
Occasional organic produce, though deli uses local and organic produce.
M-F 9-6, Sat. 10-4

 Turn east off Hwy. 14 onto Court St. Store's 1 block over on left.

RIVER FALLS

WHOLE EARTH FOOD CO-OP
126 South Main Street, 54022 • (715)425-7971
The only vegetarian spot in town. Great veggie deli.
M-F 9-7, Sat. 9-6, Sun. 12-4

 From I-94, get off at Hwy. 35 heading south (brings you into Downtown River Falls). Store's in town on right.

STEVEN'S POINT

STEVEN'S POINT AREA FOOD CO-OP
633 Second Street, 54481 • (715)341-1555
Store is 25 years old. They carry homebrew supplies.
M-F 9-8 (Tu. closes at 7), Sat. 9-5, Sun. 10-4

 Hwy. 51 (business 51) goes through town. Turn west at third stoplight onto Fourth Ave. Store's on right in a big brick building.

VIOLA

VIOLA NATURAL FOODS CO-OP
P.O. Box 243/Commercial Street, 54664 • (608)627-1476
M-F 10-6, Sat. 12-4

 From 131 north, come into Viola. Take a right onto Commercial Dr. Store's three buildings down on right.

VIROQUA

VIROQUA FOOD COOP
303 N. Center Street, 54665 • (608)637-7511
M-F 9-7, Sat. 9-7 (9-5 Winter)

 Store's one block north of Hwy. 56 behind Nelson's Agri-Center.

"Support Mother Earth and all that lives with her. Choose organic."

— Matt Koch, Road's End Organics
Producer of Dairy Free Macaroni & ChReese

Wyoming

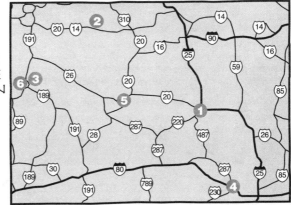

1. CASPER
2. CODY
3. JACKSON
4. LARAMIE
5. RIVERTON
6. WILSON

CASPER

ALPINGLOW NATURAL FOODS
242 South Wolcott, 82601 • (307)234-4196
Deli and juice bar open for lunch.
M-F 9:30-6, Sat. 9-5

From I-25, take Center St. exit south. Turn left on Midwest. Store's on left corner of Midwest and South Wolcott.

CODY

 Cody is 50 miles east of Yellowstone National Park on Highways 20-14/16. Check out Maxwell's, a local Italian restaurant.

WHOLE FOODS TRADING CO.
1239 Rumsey Avenue, 82414 • (307)587-3213
No produce.
M-Sat. 9:30-5:30

From Rte. 14 (Sheridan), turn north onto Rumsey. Store's on right.

JACKSON

HARVEST
130 West Broadway, 83001 • (307)733-5418
Bakery uses organic flour for their European style breads and pastries (among other treats).
M-Sat. 7-6, Sun. 8-2, Summer: M-Sat. 7-8

Rte. 89 is Broadway. Store's on west side of street, 2 blocks from town square.

LARAMIE

WHOLE EARTH GRAINERY
111 Ivinson Avenue, 82070 • (307)747-4268
A small, friendly store. Good restaurants nearby.
Sun.-Sun. 10-6

 From I-80, take 3rd St. exit north and turn left on Ivinson. Store's on right.

RIVERTON

WIND RIVER MERCANTILE
221 East Main Street, 82501 • (307)856-0862
Soon expanding to include a bakery, deli and espresso bar!
M-Sat. 10-5:30

 From I-80, take 287 north. Turn right onto Rte. 135 (goes straight into Riverton). Turn left onto East Main and store's on right across from Ace Hardware.

WILSON

HERE AND NOW NATURAL FOODS
1925 North Moose Wilson Road, 83014 • (307)733-2742
No produce. In business since 1970! They deliver.
M-Sat. 12-6 (June-Sept. 10-6)

 From Hwy. 22, turn right on Teton Village Rd. (also North Moose Wilson Rd.) Store's 1/2 mile down on left (Teton Village ski area is further down this road).

> *"We have not inherited the Earth from our fathers, we are borrowing it from our children."*
>
> — Lester Brown